Resisting Writings
(and the Boundaries of Composition)

SMU Studies in Composition and Rhetoric
General Editor: Gary Tate, Texas Christian University

Resisting Writings

(and the Boundaries
of Composition)

Derek Owens

Southern Methodist University Press
Dallas

First edition, 1994

Requests for permission to reproduce material from this work
should be sent to:
    Permissions
    Southern Methodist University Press
    Box 415
    Dallas, Texas 75275

Library of Congress Cataloging-in-Publication Data

Owens, Derek, 1963—
    Resisting writings (and the boundaries of composition) / Derek
Owens. — 1st ed.
        p.   cm. — (SMU studies in composition and rhetoric)
    Includes bibliographical references and index.
    ISBN 0-87074-343-0
    1. English language—Composition and exercises—Study and
teaching.   2. English language—Rhetoric—Study and teaching.
I. Title.   II. Series.
PE1404.O94   1994
808'.042'07—dc20   93-18752

For Teresa, and my parents

Contents

Preface

SOME will find my path into this field we call
Composition Studies nothing if not unusual. So a few words on
how I got here, why this book was written, and who helped me
get it out might prove useful.

When I went directly from undergraduate to graduate school
my intentions were to pick up a master's in poetry writing, then
move on to art school where I could paint, sculpt, and make
prints. But long before I completed that master's it finally sank in
that poets and artists, no matter how fulfilling their work, had
lousy luck using their craft to draw salaries, get health benefits,
and support families. I needed a vocation, something to do,
preferably a job where my interests in poetry (linguistic and otherwise) could factor into my career, not as unrelated fetishes but
as vital components of my work at hand. I'd been toying with the
idea of teaching at the college level for some time, and since the
graduate program at the State University of New York at Albany
included pedagogy among its professed strong points (rhetoric,
creative writing, and theory being the others), it seemed an
opportune place to experiment with poetry, teaching, and composition in general, seeking potential linkages among these different areas in a spirit of critical, inquisitive play. The result: as I
was being introduced to a wide body of radically innovative,
cross-cultural poets and compositionists, while at the same time
wondering about the nature(s) of composition theory, I saw that

these seemingly alien realms could indeed be considered deeply related—despite the fact that traditional and contemporary pursuits in composition have, in my eyes, generally failed to encourage intense discursive experimentation. And so I began reading the work of composition studies through the eyes of a poet, and twentieth-century poetries from the vantage point of a writing teacher.

I discovered that despite my deep interest in poetics, and despite having been lucky enough to be taught by some wonderful writers, I didn't much like creative writing workshops. The assumption that these were isolated theaters where students were permitted to flex their imaginations using rhetorics unthinkable in the larger curriculum lent an artificiality to the writing enterprise that just didn't gel with who I was or how I wanted to write. On the other hand I grew to enjoy the potential of the composition classroom, its central emphasis on writing and conversation, but had little interest in current-traditional or liberal expressionist approaches to writing—not because of what they could help students create but for all the viable means of expression they could deny. The current work is the result of my attempt to overlap the worlds of composition and poetics, marrying impulses I don't think should have been estranged in the first place.

Though like many graduate students I did my share of complaining about the assorted politics of my department, looking back I see how fortunate I was to stumble on SUNY Albany's English program. Much of the argument in the following pages aims at convincing teachers how important it is to give students ample opportunity to fashion creative texts that resist conventional academic discourse. A number of my professors allowed me the flexibility to do just this: Judith Barlow, Don Byrd, Gene Garber, Judith Johnson, Rudy Nelson, Steve North, Harry Staley. By observing the range of creative teaching styles represented in these people, plus those of Jeffrey Berman, Lil Brannon, Helen Elam, Cy Knoblauch, Jerome Rothenberg, and Charles Stein, I gathered ideas and insights that helped make my first few years of teaching a lot more constructive than they might otherwise have been. Though I made and continue to make mistakes in the classroom, at least I've learned to try to make them *adventuresome* mistakes. Exciting pedagogies always involve some element of risk taking; it's nice to remember how much of this I witnessed in my graduate program.

More specifically, I owe much thanks to Lil Brannon, who urged me to try to publish this manuscript and without whose support it probably never would have appeared; Gary Tate and Keith Gregory, for publishing a rather idiosyncratic book by a relatively young member of the profession; Cy Knoblauch, for giving me powerful, unflinching, and exhaustive criticism on the dissertation where some of these ideas struggled to make themselves understood, thereby saving me from a certain amount of future embarrassment; Steve North, whose constant support, sense of humor, and down-to-earth understanding of this field have helped me keep things in their proper perspective; and Judith Johnson, and especially Don Byrd, who introduced me to many of the alternative, "resisting" poetrics and philosophies that influenced this entire manuscript—from these two exciting people I learned enough about innovative composition to more than make up for the dozen or so years of academic drudgery incurred at the hands of repressively unimaginative "educational" institutions. Past conversations with Joe Amato, Michael Blitz, Greg Hewett, Mark Hurlbert, Danny Mahala, Jody Swilky, and John Winner have been important in helping me crystallize ideas that eventually found their way into this book. I'm grateful to have had so many friends who are also my teachers, and vice versa.

To be honest, I teach writing primarily because I like the company. My main goal isn't to make students more functionally or culturally literate, or help them improve their understanding of standard English, or even teach them how to play the academic game more productively, although every one of these concerns does play a role in my teaching, at times intensely so (it's hard to have the company of students if they're flunking out). Nor do I envision myself as someone who teaches students ways of "empowering" themselves through their writing; these days, given the horrific ecological and sociopolitical habitats we've made for ourselves, I'm not feeling all that empowered myself, and so I'm dubious of whether I've any transferable "power" worth talking about. My main reason for teaching writing has to do with the constant curiosity I have for the medium: the mystification and simple amazement I find in the fact that words and grammar, with their infinite malleability and unexpected contortions, have the capacity to evoke amazing emotions and actions. Language is utterly mysterious, a biological architecture humming with potential energies. But unless it's recognized as a communal catalyst, a social, transformative medium, that energy remains dormant, untapped. Though many still consider writing a private activity, others have realized that if it's not intentionally construed as part of some larger social communion, whether among a select gathering of readers and listeners or as a meditative dialogue with one's various internal personas, the act becomes embarrassingly, boringly solipsistic. It's the teaching—that is, the collective exploring—of writing, of discourse and dialects, that keeps me from falling into that kind of quicksand.

The motivation behind the following work is essentially the same: I took the time to assemble this book because, after investigating a selection of intriguing, colorful, and unusual approaches to written, oral, and performative communication, I wanted to share my excitement with others. I hope this material will strike chords in the minds of a few readers, who might then steal or modify any ideas striking their fancy and apply them toward more interesting results. On the other hand, a lot of the composing strategies I discuss will undoubtedly annoy, perhaps even repulse others. In such cases my only hope is that I might at least provoke some conversations (attacks?) as lively and inventive as the work of the compositionists addressed in the following pages.

Resisting Writings
(and the Boundaries of Composition)

Inflexible standardization is the
arteriosclerosis of language.
—CHARLES BERNSTEIN

Introduction
Surveying the Landscape

THIS is one way I view it (bear with me here, it's a rather extended metaphor, about eight paragraphs):

A great many islands, some in chains, some scattered in isolation. Each island representing a particular *discourse focus*. On one prominent chain of islands, for example, the natives speak what we might call "academic discourse," which is not so much a shared language as an array of conflicting communicative habits that generally tolerate each other's existence. Although numerous dialects thrive on these plots of ground—many of them wholly incompatible with one another—there seems to be a shared consensus among most of the different users; as if some implicit albeit abstract institutional rubric ideologically joins the different islands, thereby metaphorically linking them into a solid "chain."

On one of these islands the locals speak various "scientific" dialects, indicated by the production of lab reports, algorithms, abstracts conforming to fairly regimented principles of design, equations, computer printouts in numerous sublanguages, and journal articles marked, among other things, by highly specialized vocabularies and linear argumentation. But even the inhabitants of Scientific Discourse Island, though loosely identified by some of these basic stylistic uniformities, don't necessarily talk to each other: nanotechnologists, marine biologists,

3

gynecologists, and Introductory Physics instructors hardly speak the same tongue, no matter how allied their rhetoric might appear to the outsider. (The situation is comparable to someone identifying Chinese ideograms as representative of all of China, though the wealth of spoken dialects in that country is numbingly diverse.)

Now, in this same chain but on another nearby island there live tribes of a very different breed. We might call this Composition Island, home to people interested in the business of teaching and writing about "rhetoric," "composition," and "literacy." Just like their neighbors the scientists, the composition theorists are also fragmented into motley bands with ill-matched if not irreconcilable argots. Formalists and current-traditionalists inspired by new criticism and classical rhetoric set up camps often removed from those who describe themselves as "process oriented" and favor "expressive" discourse (which might mean adopting styles of personal narrative typified by a desire to locate "natural writerly voice," whatever that is). Still other clans choose to dissociate themselves from either of these opposing "voices," adopting instead "social constructivist" or "transactive" perspectives, socioepistemic critiques directed through lenses of Marxist, poststructuralist, feminist, and other ideological hues (which, of course, allude to yet another string of islands occupied by the literary theorists). And many of these natives can be further classified according to terms that continue to complicate the demarcations of their discourse: some are primarily "practitioners," others "scholars," still others "researchers." Even these groupings have subgroupings like "historian," "ethnographer," "philosopher," "clinician," and so forth.[1] All of these bands generate an overwhelming stream of written and discursive products, but relatively little of it is intended for audiences beyond the sort who produce it to begin with, thereby making extratribal communication difficult at best. (Remember, these are big islands; their size alone generally inhibits any but the most local of conversations.)

Of course there are other islands, too. One is where "creative writing" happens—where poetry, fiction, plays, and screenplays are the privileged discourses, the bulk of which don't get published but rather are passed around in tribal rituals called "workshops." Nor are the discursive bands living on this island immune from the clashing of unlike dialects—the fiction writers might have little understanding of the poets, and vice versa. Even the poets don't communicate en masse with their compatriots but rather separate into tiny, insular, often temporary families. Then there's the island of Business and Legal Discourse, a body of land as splintered as any of the above, though certainly more powerful and influential than that where the poets live. Elsewhere there are those busy islands where one is apt to find any number of students manufacturing history research projects, lit-crit papers, philosophy term papers, article reviews and so forth with intense productivity.

If this entire chain of islands, this Galápagos of academic discourses, is bound by any glue, it would be the powerful armada constantly traveling to and from the different isles, disseminating and ordering the perpetual production of all manner of institutional memoranda, mission statements, committee reports, budget requests, faculty letters, etc.[2] This navy—the stewards of the academy—is run by the rhetoric of administrators, deans, presidents, provosts, and professors who sustain models of authoritarian grammars that thereby set a national tone. This fleet of institutional rhetoric doesn't just maintain the government, it *is* the government. Each discourse island in the chain, no matter what its native dialects, pays dues to this colonizing, enforcing language system. No matter how many incompatible voices live on the same island, everyone is familiar with and helps perpetuate the dominant and surveillant lingua franca. In this sense the Academic Discourse Islands aren't all that different from the IBM Islands, or any other corporate discourse conglomerate.

But even this armada has its boundaries. Remember, so far I've been talking about just one string of islands—the academic archipelago, so to speak. But if we distance ourselves and take an aerial view of this setting, the immensity of this conglomerate really stands out. From the atmosphere the academic islands appear as little more than a splotch of closely knit freckles, surrounded by a myriad of other dots and specks, each of them sites of equally fascinating, equally serious tribal dialects.[3] For beyond the islands of academic language lie other communities where nonacademic, non-Western customs hold sway. If we travel not too far we find islands where various African American rhetorics govern language usage. Elsewhere bodies of land pop up marked by feminist principles of composition, which try their best to dissociate themselves from the typically masculine grammars of academic power. Some islets are noticeable by their modernist, "postmodern," and avant-garde workings. The further we look, the more we become aware of the alternative spread of writing and communication strategies alive and well outside the academy. Viewed from this distance, it's an amazing constellation.

This isn't to say these islands exist in isolation. Plenty of travelers migrate back and forth between different countries. Many students well versed in the tropes of African American discourse are equally proficient in various academic rhetorics. A great many of the experimental compositionists, though they may feel most at home among the "postmodern" tribal communities, earn their paychecks while teaching college courses, continually ferrying to and fro between workplace and studio. It's a safe bet that writers who advocate so-called feminine writing practices, whether they like it or not, know full well how to get their point across using decidedly Euro-patriarchal modes of discourse. There's constant roving taking place between these bodies of land. To make things even more interesting, circulating among these islands is a babble of multiple voices and conversations operating nonstop, twenty-four hours a day, on electronic mail and discussion lists, a shifting collective of thousands of writers who, though affiliated with their own localized zones of discourse, hyperactively dive into a web of networks originating from remote sites and disciplines. And all of this is of course complicated by the multiple dialects of polyphonic student bodies on campus and in the classroom, which resist and mimic one another in continual flux.

The problem is that the academic discourse islands, held together by a fleet of institutionally imposed rhetorical habits, operate according to a fundamentally ethnocentric philosophy: too often the residents live and teach as if their discourse collective is the only one that really matters. It's okay if once in a while whiffs of discourses happening on all those other islands in the bay are carried into the waters of the academic territories. But for the most part, these other countries are best kept outside; their respective literacies, though perhaps interesting enough (in small doses), aren't really what higher education is about. The point of education is to teach discourse from an *academic* framework. Functional, formalist, institutional literacy is important, not call and response or African American "signifying." Students write according to current-traditional formulas, not projective verse. Though we might encourage personal narratives in student journals, less attention is paid to constructing oral performative texts, say those representative of much Amerindian discourse. Making well-honed, finely polished linear arguments in response to assigned readings is valuable; experimenting with fragmentation, mixing of genre, or multiple personas isn't. In other words, learning how to make written language look, sound, and read so that professors will validate the results—not discourse that would succeed by a host of alternative, nonacademic standards.

My goal is to provide this armada with some much-needed competition. Not to destroy or dismantle the accepted collective of academic discourse (I'm not that naive), but to make it more receptive to all those other ways of writing and talking "on the outside." I want to call into question the entire notion of an "outside" by making bridges between unlike islands: navigating waterways between unique worlds of writing and talking to one another. For these "marginal" discourses already exist inside the academy, but under erasure—lurking in the corners, fearful of speaking too loudly lest the institutional enforcers of appropriate language habits actively squelch (i.e., fire or fail) those whose discourses would resist academic norms. Norms, we have to remember, that weren't chosen by the users but are preordained and perpetuated by omnipresent, abstract forces of institutional power. It's the opinion throughout this book that the discourse of the academy is in serious need of some powerful ventilation. One of the best places we can begin is with the study of composition and rhetoric—the writing classroom.

The notion that we are scholars and teachers of "writing" in any global, pluralistic, or multicultural sense is simply false. We don't teach writing or rhetoric per se, we teach *our* kinds of writing, enforce the rhetorics we like to see. I include myself in this characterization, for I'm hardly without my own ideological biases; it's just that I'm fond of open-ended variety, I prefer the motley rather than the purebred. And since I feel some repugnance at deciding for my students what languages, vocabularies, and rhetorics they *must* adopt, I'm interested in contemplating how classroom environments and English curricula might be structured so as to emphasize a more heterogeneous embrace of multiple discourse strategies. This is the attitude that shapes this book.

One reason composition studies intrigues us is its enormous breadth. It covers so much terrain I find it nearly impossible to outline with any precision the boundaries that separate the different theories of composition. This is why my metaphor of discourse islands must eventually be laid to rest. These "islands" are fictions, of course; discourse simply doesn't separate itself into neat little bundles for easy viewing and packaging. (And I haven't even begun to make allowances for other societal discourses—what Carlos E. Cortés calls the "immediate curriculum" of friends, family, church, and community, as well as the "serendipitous curriculum" of television, popular film, magazines, tabloids, billboards, and other advertisements for consumption that influence students infinitely more than those conveyed in the "institutional curricula" of our schools.) A better way of envisioning the multitude of discourses might be to picture them as so many musical tonalities, each with its own shape and color that can blend together harmoniously or clash in raucous confrontation, while the academy works as a monotonal composer trying very hard to keep what he (the gender is intentional) believes to be the discordant combinations from infecting his preferred arrangements, which are then passed off as the only legitimate music.

Difficult as it might be to outline "boundaries" for a field so multifocused, however, it is possible to get a sense of how those in composition define our professional goals by identifying the rhetorics that are *not* discussed within this field. One of the most effective ways of assessing any discipline is to pinpoint what it doesn't let its members do; discover the taboos of any community and you have found its foundations.

One might think that the term *composition theory* signifies an investigation of nothing less than how human perception is communicated through the composing of language, both oral and scribal, performative and textual. Despite its attractiveness—its invitation for us to launch into multiple avenues of inquiry about how and why different people communicate in different ways— one of the drawbacks of this immense field is that its subject, composition, is too easily simplified when addressed in the limited space of the one-semester writing course. When we recognize that composition involves a great deal more than just the creation of student essays in the ENG 101 classroom—that composition is also the study of how writers of cross-cultural, feminist, and experimentalist outlooks make and share texts—the discrepancy between the study of composition theory in its global sense and the more confined understanding of composition as practiced in most colleges is too glaring to go unnoticed.[4]

In my experience, discourse as perceived by teachers of writing commonly centers around expository prose, whether adhering to fundamentals of classical rhetoric, more recent philosophies accentuating process and personal voice, or some idiosyncratic ideal of academic discourse informed by essayists the teacher simply happens to admire. And though fiction and poetry might be covered to a lesser extent in some writing classes, these forms too are interpreted from viewpoints unaware of or unwilling to acknowledge the many ways "creative writing" can be made. Oral discourses among African American, Native American, Asian American, and Latino communities, for example, are completely foreign to those taught in an average English classroom. Recent feminist explorations into alternative forms of composition that resist *phallocentric* discourse defy many standards assumed as givens in the comp and lit class. Throughout the twentieth century, modernist and contemporary writers have created texts that contradict many assumptions made by writing instructors, their works arguing that grammar and syntax can and should be rendered malleable like so much raw material; that the composer can be answerable to other than the linguistic formulas of traditional systems.

In essence, I believe the English department—and the college curriculum in general—has an obligation to expose students to more than traditional variations of academic discourse. By academic discourse I mean not only the most classical and formalist of rhetorics but also the personal narratives encouraged by liberal

expressivists, as well as whatever textual forms social constructivists favor. As I hope to make clear in the ensuing chapters,
these opposing views represent an irritatingly foreshortened field
of possibilities, comprising just a tiny fraction of the ways people
write, critically and imaginatively. This manuscript is the record
of my struggle to familiarize myself with ways of writing and
modes of discourse that were never taught to me, but which, had
I learned of them in school, could have offered me valuable ideas
for new ways of making knowledge, while at the same time helping me develop an intellectual respect for cultures and dialects
unlike my own.

Providing students with a polyfocal vocabulary of discourse
forms gives them greater material with which to compare their
own generally unexamined habits of writing and speaking. They
might also get better at critiquing the ideologies embedded within traditional academic rhetorics. To teach students only what
David Bartholomae and Anthony Petrosky call "the language of
the academy" is simply to perpetuate our own status quo. And it's
a status quo fundamentally flawed in design since the criteria it
assumes and the texts it praises are the products of institutional
environments founded primarily by Caucasian males schooled
according to Euro-American traditions that historically have had
little or no interest in viable alternative rhetorics. Obviously
there's nothing inherently evil or even inappropriate with the
rhetorics used by white guys in powerful positions; I'm always
annoyed when white males jump at the chance to denounce
other white men and leave themselves out of the equation in the
process, a slippery tactic whereby one attains power by positioning himself outside the category under attack. My target isn't
Eurocentric rhetorics perpetuated by white male educators and
the institutions they run, but rather the glaring, discriminatory
lack of balance that accompanies this kind of teaching.

Rather than labeling conventional academic discourses as
either "good" or "bad," it makes more sense to view such language as simply particular versions of social realities, methods of
communication that have the potential to offer considerable
leverage to those who know how to enter into and assimilate
them. To criticize conventional academic discourse in and of
itself, as a literary artifact failing by the terms of some personal or

arbitrary aesthetic, would be hypocritical. After all, I happen to be an academic, I rather like being one (nobody pushed me into this profession), and I'm writing this book for other academics. Besides, what we teach in the academy will always somehow remain inherently "academic"—you can't enroll in a class and get a grade without interacting within an academic system, no matter how subversive or "nonacademic" the course material might be. This book is an argument that seeks to praise, even promote the notion of academic discourse—but an idea of what academic discourse might some day entail, not its current state. Basically this means a call for pedagogies of composition privileging supreme variety rather than an aesthetics of exclusion.

Certainly this argument is in direct opposition to theories offered by writers like E. D. Hirsch, who've tried to develop ways of scientifically measuring the value of languages according to (Western) psycholinguistic processing models (*The Philosophy of Composition*). For we have come to realize that the quality of language is not measured solely at the level of the phoneme, or in accordance with some universal standard for appropriate handling of grammar and syntax. Value is measured by social, cultural, sexual, political, and economic stimuli that, filtered through tangled ideologies, influence local communities with a complexity that is mind-boggling. Power lies not just in the actual verbal artifact, but in the institutional structures that determine how one's privileged discourse will look and sound.[5] Too many academics have been dishonest; they've failed to present their discourse as simply one privileged mode of communication among many, selling it as *the* primary way of transmitting knowledge. By perpetuating this viewpoint they transmit a silent but effective message to students: learning how to make arguments, talk to others, and write down words in ways that defy the academic tone aren't worth our time. And so the student is prevented from expanding and thereby transforming the lexicon of philosophies with which she composes her vision of the world.

Nor is my argument concerned only with providing additional coverage. If we're serious about acknowledging the richness of additional composing philosophies, then we will seek to give students ample opportunity to try their hands at making these texts. This means not just gaining a better understanding and respect

for the complexities of African American discourse, but providing atmospheres where students can orchestrate and construct
their own performances, utilizing some of the same characteristics. Not just introducing students to some contemporary
thoughts on "feminine composition," but actively helping them
construct their own resisting discourses. Not just showing students a more representative range of twentieth-century innovative writing styles, but making the creation of like-minded texts a
vital part of the classroom experience. Basically I'm urging teachers to undermine our self-constructed positions of authority by
admitting additional composing philosophies into our classrooms.

In addition I'm arguing that scholars and teachers ought to be
receptive to colleagues eager to engage in a variety of discourses
not traditionally expected or encouraged in academia. The composition theorist, though obviously interested in writing, will
probably spend more time writing *about* writing and pedagogical
concerns than experimenting with various discursive forms. The
composition teacher is judged by her ability to guide students
into the world of academic prose, or academically sanctioned
forms of "personal narrative," not her ingenuity in introducing
them to the conflicting forms of poetry, fiction, literary nonfiction, belles-lettres, eclogues, dramas, screenplays, manifestos, or
any number of other legitimate compositional forms. (Indeed, the
composition theorist who does spend time working in literary
genres outside the academic essay can easily find her professional
career in jeopardy. As a graduate student I remember advisors
telling us to downplay our creative writing publications if we
wanted a job—either leave out these additional interests altogether, or embed them surreptitiously near the back of our vitae.)
If teachers, scholars, and particularly our professional journals
don't further this kind of multirhetorical intermixing on their
own ground, any pedagogy claiming to foster a pluralistic stance
toward discourse has little chance of appearing genuine.

In this respect my book might be seen as my own worst enemy,
for if I were truly serious about demonstrating my commitment to
cross-rhetorical play, the best way to do so would be through
example. In fact, my original intention was to do precisely that,
write this book in a hodgepodge of styles mirroring the rhetorical
alternatives raised in each chapter: the chapter on African Amer-

ican discourse using elements reminiscent of signifying, call and response, and "the dozens"; the section on feminist alternatives open to collaboration, silence, and the possibility of contradiction; the discussion on contemporary innovative writings done in multiple genres, promoting nonlinearity, fragmentation, and so on. If I'd taken this tack surely the book would have been more fun to write, certainly more interesting to read. But two things stopped me. For one, I didn't want to make it seem as if one *must* deviate from convention—my point, as I'll reiterate throughout, is not to give undue attention to any one rhetoric, but instead promote greater balance among disparate forms within the academy. Whether people wish to write in accordance with convention or prefer to turn traditional forms inside out, either way it's their business; my point isn't to tell anyone how they should or shouldn't go about composing (although I am dogmatic enough to say that English departments and writing programs should teach a constellation of conflicting forms). The second and more influential reason I didn't construct this manuscript according to a more experimental plan was because I wanted it published. Which helps illustrate my point: that many in the field of composition studies—indeed, in all of English studies—despite their love for writing and desire to help students experience new ways of using language, tend to be more than a little adverse to resisting discourses.

Another weak spot with this book is its concentrated emphasis on new curricula and directions of study, while only the final chapter focuses on the grimmer realities of everyday teaching. As I urge those in our profession to investigate, respect, teach, and try on a slew of writing styles almost never discussed in most composition classes, my argument would be easier to swallow if we had an overabundance of writing classes and an excess of professors skilled in teaching the details of these different rhetorics. Realistically, of course, students take, on the average, very few writing-intensive courses, and writing instructors (often already burdened by heavy teaching loads, not to mention the abuse and neglect associated with being part-time adjunct faculty) feel intense pressure to initiate their students into the academic conversation.

And so one might well ask how teachers are supposed to: (a) help students gain proficiency in academic discourse so they can interact on the academic and professional level with some degree of success; (b) introduce them to the philosophies that inform various multicultural, feminist, and contemporary composing practices; (c) convey the message that writing and speaking are not just tools to be mastered but sites of intense artistic possibility—and do all this in just one or two semesters. Also, what's to prevent this eclectic approach from backfiring? If only a few teachers acknowledge the importance of addressing conflicting writing methodologies, students eager to pursue alternative forms in other classes might become disillusioned and embittered once they realize that straying from the path of academic conformity can result in failing grades. If we stress too many cross-cultural, feminist, and exploratory modes of discourse too quickly, we might be setting students up for future failure in the eyes of colleagues with little patience for these resisting writings. But censor those forms, and therefore the communities that create them, and we definitely set students up for another type of failure as they walk away without having had the opportunity to develop any awareness or appreciation of excitingly nonconventional language forms. And since many of our students already belong to these various unacknowledged communities, we silence not only opposing ways of communicating but the legitimate voices of our students too—an act of cultural and linguistic intolerance in the name of academic success.

To all of this I'd respond, sure, it's a difficult tightrope to walk, but one more problematic to ignore. We need to find ways of helping our students become critically aware of the political realities that shape their learning, and the language of that learning, within the academy. They need to decide when these political realities silence additional ways of thinking, learn how to move beyond these barriers (as well as recognize when such crossing might be inadvisable), and through it all avoid estrangement from the university and the benefits it can offer. Through trial and error and sincere commitment, I believe we can get closer to accomplishing these goals by introducing a healthy eclecticism to our students, without their losing sight of the "language of the academy" that other professionals will expect them to have mastered. In time, the nature of the academic dialect might metamorphose in exciting ways as the range of institutionally legitimate discourses expands.

Let me pause for a moment and try to anticipate some of the more popular criticisms the ensuing argument might expect to face: (1) I problematically confuse poetry, literature, and "creative writing" with composition, thereby conflating styles and genres that ought to remain separate for the sake of effective writing instruction. (2) I haven't necessarily succeeded in convincing skeptics that all these alternative composing philosophies are really as exciting and worthwhile as they apparently are to me. (3) The new rhetorics referred to here are relatively small in comparison to the predominating influence of standard English and the linearity of conventional expository prose, and as such fail to warrant the same degree of attention. (4) All of this preoccupation with style, rhetoric, and genre is really secondary to what the students write about—the content of their ideas is what we should be concerning ourselves with most, not so much the variety of grammatical vehicles within which those ideas are delivered.

To which are offered the following quick responses. First, in this book I do define composition in a global sense as roughly synonymous with "writing," a term that certainly can and does include all forms of what's pejoratively referred to as "creative writing." If this problematizes the inherent nature of our entire discipline, it is because composition studies has refused to acknowledge what for so many twentieth-century writers and critics has long been obvious: that clinging steadfastly to traditional distinctions of genre—fiction as separate from nonfiction, poetry from prose, the lyrical from the scholastic—betrays a stubborn refusal to recognize the changing forms of written discourse that have actually emerged in the past century. (Particularly ironic are those compositionists and literary theorists enthralled with various poststructuralist theories who choose in practice not to acknowledge the imaginative, multigenre texts that inspired so much of the poststructuralist turn. Derrida might be an icon for hundreds of theorists, but most are too timid to follow in his footsteps, opting merely to analyze and comment on his innovations rather than create their own *Glas*[ses].) Composition, then, as I see it, is absolutely germane to poetics; creative writing is composition, and vice versa.

Second, I realize many readers simply won't like the kinds of texts discussed in these pages, and so will find it difficult to buy any argument proposing that we examine such writing styles more closely. I have no desire to present myself as apologist for either the traditional or the unconventional. Instead my argument is that, because we are teachers who intercept and interact with large numbers of students whose cultures, backgrounds, desires, and intellectual motives are unknown to us, it's best to present at least some semblance of a heterogeneous curriculum, where students will have the chance to explore a gamut of ideas and philosophies and do so within an equally variegated range of discourses. The goal is for all of us, students and faculty alike, to continually investigate what we don't know, not simply to make students look, write, and talk like us.

As for the criticism that the popularity of a discourse should determine whether or not it receives coverage, my reply is that the types of writing we already teach in the classroom have never been reflective of the most widespread or predominating rhetorics. Writing a research paper with proper methods of citation and a Works Cited page is an activity existing almost solely within the academic realm; this isn't something most people do once they leave college, unless of course they enter other academically related fields. The same could be said for the personal journal, the comparison-contrast paper, the short story, the lab report, etc. If our goal were to work within the most prevalent modes of discourse, then we would be analyzing and teaching the rhetoric of the magazine ad, the junk mail letter, the bumper sticker, MTV, and the Home Shopping Network. Statistics aside, action and change are local; for the classroom to be effective it is necessary to work immediately and pragmatically with the diverse individuals who show up and talk to one another on a regular basis. This doesn't mean we can naively disregard the larger ideological frameworks that shape the overall structure of our respective academies, of which any classroom always remains a fundamental component. But neither can we allow abstract conceptions of discursive or philosophical realities to take precedence over the immediacy of the students. We can have students write and talk in all manner of forms and styles, but unless the content of the course material is frequently related to the student's local environment, the enterprise risks pedantry. And since the composition classroom has the potential to respond to such a wide collection of different social realities, highlighting that variety of expression via the inclusion of multiple rhetorics can be one way of anticipating the cultural, sexual, and creative multiformity of student, faculty, and neighborhood populations.

Finally, some might argue that so much attention to form and additional composing styles misses the point—that our primary task is to make environments where students can explore their ideas, values, and opinions more fully; can come into closer contact with what they think, and start understanding how such thinking is modified as it rubs against other ideas. But as a host of twentieth-century writers have shown, conventional forms of expository prose just don't suffice. The mechanics of standard grammar and syntax, as demonstrated by recent theorists and poets, are never isolated from the textual content; style and form are as influential as the subject of any thesis statement, though their effect upon a reader may be far more subliminal. The chosen rhetoric, the discursive medium, the rhythm of the prose, and its acceptance or rejection of standard grammar are always intrinsically extensions of any writer's political and aesthetic motives. Many ideas simply cannot make themselves heard within the conventions of the tradition; for many, resisting forms are the *only* way for certain thoughts to evolve and take shape. Ideas, after all, never exist "outside" of forms, but are themselves forms. Perhaps worse, if we assume that any and all important ideas must surface from within standard English and academic discourse, we display a depressing absence of imagination. If anything, it's this sense of the imaginative I want to foreground in the writing classroom. I want writing to be exciting, risky, strange; dull, safe, conventional texts put me and my students to sleep. I suppose I see my job as keeping myself and my students from automatically succumbing to the hypnotic rhythms of the obligatory, the required, and the institutionally sanctioned talk of the academy. If, after tasting an array of oppositional forms—those "resisting" writings—they choose to remain with the conventional (as have I, on many occasions), fine. But at least the decision will be theirs, not mine.

Before entering any discussion about teaching writing in the college classroom, it's important to understand how that word is generally defined within the context of the English department.

Basically when the profession of composition theory discusses, teaches, and writes about *writing*, what's usually being referred to is the writing of expository prose, the production of essays conforming to certain stylistic expectations housed within the mind of the instructor (or, in a more abstract way, within the "mind" of the department itself). Whether we are quite conscious of the rhetorics we want to see our students take up or have little more than vague impressions of what constitutes "good prose," our criteria tend to be typified more by restrictive constraints than by elaborate variance. Most of us, after all, don't ask our students to write short stories, prose poetry, or dramatic monologues on their midterm exams, but require them to write about these genres in an expository form with some degree of proficiency. At semester's end we collect final research papers on Shakespeare's sonnets, not final sonnets on Shakespeare's ideas; in seminars on nineteenth-century literature it's expected that students write essays about poetry and novels, but never poems and fiction about nineteenth-century lit.

These distinctions are obvious enough, but bringing them to the surface is crucial because they allow us to nail down what exactly we mean by the teaching of writing. And usually what this turns out to be is forcing students to make essayist prose conforming to some pretty narrow guidelines—guidelines that, when presented without the balance of viable alternatives, lend students a distorted view of what composition can mean (not to mention making our task of getting students excited about writing all the more difficult, as we severely limit their options for expression).

Let's take a step back and look at some of the differences between our concepts of "literature" and "nonliterature," and at how this dichotomy can cripple our creative thinking.

Literatures and Pseudo-Literatures

In order to get a handle on the various, often conflicting methods of making writings, we have to examine the differences between texts created inside the classroom and some of those from outside. While essays are the primary source of textual exploration permitted students in most English classrooms, the texts students are expected to read and respect are generally not essays at all but "literature"—short stories, plays, poems, and nov-els by established writers. And when the students do read pub-lished essays, even those are something more than expository prose; for these selections must have first metamorphosed into belletristic nonfiction, or literary prose. Indeed, one of the high-est marks of praise an anthologist can give one of these essays is to describe it as "poetic," underscoring the common urge to praise really exceptional prose by moving it into that magical realm of literature.

Robert Scholes, distinguishing between literature and nonliter-ature, has described this split as one "between the production and the *consumption* of texts, and, as might be expected in a society like ours, we privilege consumption over *production*" (5). It's a world where consumption of styles decreed as "acceptable" by the institution will be rewarded, whereas creation of new alternatives is curbed. In addition, a permanent chasm is created: the pub-lished, literary prose on one side of the canyon, separated from student imitations on the other. The field is intensely hierarchi-cal: writings brought to the students' attention from outside class-room walls are already imbued with a certain aura of power and success that student texts never attain. Actually, viewed from this angle, writing classrooms might be described as miniature facto-ries where ream after ream of academic writing accumulates in a constant flow but never leaves the confines of the factory, forever separated from the worlds of "real" (published) texts that articu-late the landscape outside those factory walls. These academic texts hammered out by students are what Scholes refers to as either "pseudo-literature," creations of the creative writing work-shop, or "pseudo-nonliterature," products of the composition course. What's interesting about Scholes's terminology is that this division can be applied to the bulk of professional texts written by composition and literature specialists. As academicians our own writings fall primarily into areas that might be viewed as "professional nonliterature"—articles about teaching, historical analyses of some author or period, theoretical critiques of various texts, and so forth—as opposed to the creative writing professors, who are expected to balance the flow of production by churning out poems and fiction. The balance, of course, is asymmetrical at best, the academic scholarly prose always gaining most of the attention whereas the primary vehicles for creative deviations are "small" presses and "little" magazines. "Creative" writers clearly occupy the margins of the English department, as is apparent in how many of them often hail from outside the academy ("*Writer in Residence*"; "*Visiting* Poet"). The balance of power clearly lies with those who choose (or are forced to choose) to write scholarly, academic prose.

This separation between writers of literature and writers of non-literature has nothing to do with one side being more valuable than the other; labels like "good" and "bad," after all, when applied to texts, depend on numerous social and political, not ontological parameters. The problem is that the academic discourse that compositionists tend to be most familiar with—the prose and speech of our colleagues and our professional journals, all of which inform and surround our profession—molds our expectations of what student prose ought to look like. Poetic forms, techniques used in fiction, and other interdisciplinary, cross-genre stylistics are seldom introduced to students as rhetorical tools worthy of consideration. Since our professional writings are typically required to conform to certain laws—embrace an academic tone marked by linear clarity; use a professional "voice" characterized by authoritative scholasticism wary of sounding overly emotional, or use a consciously anecdotal, personal rendering that nevertheless has its own guidelines of propriety; quickly and effectively summarize a thesis, then expound upon that thesis toward a logical conclusion, etc.—we consequently expect similar things from our students. As teachers of writing we need only look as far as our own discourse to gauge what it is we're trying to teach: the kind of prose found in *College English*, *College Composition and Communication*, and *JAC* might be said to be the embodiments of what successful writing is all about, at least in the eyes of the composition theorist.[6] In a sense, we are more than just the referees of a particular type of discourse: we are the players, the creators of that discourse, and as such our enterprise might be seen as sustaining our own authority, enforcing a position patterned after our own creations, in our own image.

Confusingly, we also teach our students a limited variety of other rhetorics. By expecting students to read and respect poetry, fiction, and drama, while requiring them to create written texts of a fundamentally different nature, we send mixed signals. Though we situate literature, capital L, and poetry, capital P, at the summit of the linguistic evolutionary ladder, seldom if ever do we encourage our students and colleagues to produce so-called poetic discourse. And by poetic discourse I don't mean just the creation of sonnets and sestinas, but any written discourse less concerned with potentially restrictive conventions than with the exploration and invention of language, even if such creative manipulation pushes the resultant product beyond professionally recognized barriers of genre. In essence, students read *literature* in the classroom; afterward, they write *texts*. Teachers and scholars write *about* poetry, but that writing, if it is to be taken seriously, cannot *be* poetry.

The sad result of all this is that we enforce genres so dogmatically that the spontaneity and excitement that can come from mixing, blurring, overlapping, and dissolving boundaries is lost on the student (not to mention most teachers). In the 1770s the infamous Johann Friedrich Blumenbach forever altered the course of historical and anthropological study when he came up with the idea of studying not individuals but *races* (see Bernal 28). In a similar way our professional habit of compartmentalizing—and thus privileging and condemning—unlike genres of discourse has had the same ugly consequences. Jed Rasula describes it this way:

> Now we see genre distinctions practised as a kind of racism. The "characteristics" are learned (& what is worse, taught), strict demarcations are observed to a crippling extent [readers of novels can't read poetry, readers of poetry can't read philosophy, readers of discursive workaday prose can't read anything for very long, etc.] All of this snaps back from the praxis into the shadow of an attitude: "poet" "novelist" "dramatist" "painter" "sculptor" "critic", i.e., submission to the sociological demand that everyone identify themself in the form of a racial obsession. (Rasula, "Notes on Genre" 103; his brackets)

The danger in being a rhetorician is the compulsion to weed out various discourse styles and isolate them from one another, fencing them off into segregated corrals where they may remain "pure" and untainted. Rather than cultivating hybrids of new design, we too easily codify genre distinctions, often to preposterous degrees, as our students are quick to remind us. For not only is poetry made separate from expository prose, but the essay is further distilled to amazingly reductive formulas passed down to students who unquestioningly perpetuate them ("never use the first person"; "never begin sentences with 'and' or 'but'"; "keep paragraphs between three and five sentences in length"; "refrain from introducing excessive humor or vernacular into the prose," and so on). We need to keep in mind that precepts like these are not the product of student imaginations but the residue of their educational experience. Teachers promote these restrictions; students merely echo what has been pounded into their heads.

Sometimes, of course, teachers do break away from the confines of scholarly, academic prose as they compose "creative" texts— poetry, fiction, diaries, and the like. But unless the teacher is a poet or novelist of some renown, these brief ventures are really little more than our own professional versions of the creative writing class, the only difference being that we expose our creative work on a more public (and therefore perhaps more anonymous) level than the small environments students encounter within the creative writing workshop. For example, at conferences such as the Modern Language Association and the Conference on College Composition and Communication, several hours are usually set aside one evening during the conference in which participants can read their poetry and listen to the work of others in an informal setting. Compared to the hundreds of sessions featuring literally thousands of presenters reading their essays, however, these brief poetry readings serve as a kind of professional lip service to a genre obsolete in comparison with our production of essays, but of too much symbolic importance for us to ignore entirely. We keep the notion of "the poetic" alive because it signifies extreme literary achievement, which is, after all, what English professors profess to know something about; but within our own professional texts the poetic, the artistic, and the rhetorically innovative remain hollow concepts of little professional relevance.[7]

Or consider the poetry published in our professional journals. *College English*, for example, prints a small handful of poems in each issue; and yet this practice is less a sign of the role of poetic

discourse in a professional context than it is a sort of public service announcement reminding us of a genre we are supposed to
honor. In fact, one of the quickest ways to grasp the limits of what
the editors of *College English* will and won't permit in their journal
is to take a look at the poetry in every issue, usually sandwiched in
a tiny cluster midway between the featured essays. It's obvious that
the poems are included simply for show, a halfhearted literary
tokenism intended to indicate support for that loftiest of rhetorical arts; no one is expected to read these tiny interludes, at least
not with the same critical attention that the essays warrant (were
it otherwise, the editors would devote more space to the poems,
providing forums for critical interchange about the poetry, and
would actively solicit more diverse work from a greater range of
writers).[8] More telling, though, are the kinds of poetry published
in *College English* through the years: the bulk of it bemused and
romantic, often affecting quiet intellectual distance while some
"socially relevant" issue is neatly and aesthetically framed for the
reader from the clichéd landscape of white middle-class America.
Most of the work is of a standard length (rarely exceeding one
page), almost always left justified, avoiding classical forms but
adopting the contemplative free verse available in any issue of the
New Yorker or *American Poetry Review*. More than anything else,
the poetry found in *College English* reveals a fundamental
hypocrisy: the journal will accept essays that cry out for revision of
canons, tolerance for multicultural literatures, and pedagogies of
diversity, yet its editorial policy prohibits the inclusion of poetry
mirroring the same cultural expansiveness. Reading *College
English*, one might infer that innovative contemporary, feminist,
and non-Western poetries—African praise poetries, Language
poetry, futurist visual texts, surrealist prose poetry, sound poetry—
aren't worthy of publication. Besides serving as attractive filler,
the poems in *College English* are fundamentally iconic in nature:
worship of a genre not for its content but for its symbolic aura.

Actually, studying literature is very much like attending a
church or museum. Our icons of written language are housed in
galleries we call anthologies, the classroom environment serving
as a walking tour past priceless relics created by writers granted
immortal status. These works are taught as the creations of masters, people who earned the right to make texts according to their

own personal design, even if this meant resisting conventional avenues. But these walking tours do less to foster the generation of new ideas or inspire admiration for other writings than they underscore the silent message found in every museum: the "Don't Touch" signs warning the public to keep its distance. As an undergraduate I remember asking questions like why, in his tale *The Bear*, William Faulkner was permitted to write run-ons of interminable length (some even containing their own paragraphs!), while we would receive failing grades if any of us attempted similar experiments. The answer was always the same: the author in question had already learned the rules of conventional writing and could thus direct his energies into new venues, whereas we had first to prove ourselves worthy of such liberties by excelling in standard, conventional English through years of study: "before you can break the rules, you have to have already mastered them," went the credo.[9] As a student, though, all this logic did for me was confirm my inferior status. Such institutional censorship, reluctant to entertain serious play as a valid means of critical written expression, permitted creative experimentation to advance in only the most limited of directions, and sometimes extinguished it completely. After years of workbook drills, spelling tests, sentence combining, mandatory outlines, and thesis statements—and through it all, every attempt measured by a hateful numerical grading procedure—it's no wonder students often view writing as a chore conceived by teachers to produce anxiety, and not as an aesthetic medium capable of being orchestrated (literally, *composed*) into a pastiche of exciting, critical forms. Although there's a logic to steering the disadvantaged writer away from Faulknerian prose and the like in order that she gain much-needed insight into the workings of standard English, eliminating the chance for the student to engage in experimental, alternative, or nonacademic discourse can be equally incapacitating.

The Compartmentalization of Discourse

Writing, interpreted through the eyes of the academy, is strictly compartmentalized. We have neighborhoods of discourse, and they are not all created equal: some are ghettos, some middle-class suburbs, while a few belong to the upper crust. Strat-ification like this is rendered particularly difficult because it does little to encourage leaping of boundaries and the pursuit of cross-disciplinary aims.

At the bottom level are the slums, where we find the writings of students. These ghettos are littered with the wrappings of a depressingly infinite body of research papers, term papers, work-book exercises, midterms and final exams, quizzes, journals, in-class responses, exercises in sentence combining, and so forth. This is the garbage that never gets picked up. (Literally; think how often a teacher comments extensively on final portfolios and papers, only to watch them sit in the office long after the semes-ter has ended. Students often don't retrieve their writing because it has no value to them; it is, pure and simple, rubbish.) To be sure, there must be students and teachers who find writing assign-ments like these valuable, maybe even enjoyable (some might even say "empowering"). But it seems that a great deal of this produce is seen by many more students as so much busywork. For several years I served in a dual capacity not only as a faculty member in an English department, but also as an Educational Opportunity Program counselor for undergraduates in that same institution. After several semesters of having daily conversations with students I counseled, I was discouraged by the number of them who never bothered to read any of the comments made on their papers, or who disposed of their writings immediately after they were returned. What depressed me the most was when I would ask students, upon their completing some English or writ-ing course, if they enjoyed writing any more than when they had begun the class. Rare was the student who had learned to view the act of composition as a potentially creative enterprise. Though these reflections are hardly the result of any empirical study, I'm confident that a considerable amount of the writing students do in higher education is regarded not so much with enthusiasm as with dread. Writing, for too many students, is not critical exploration but a hollow, pointless chore, and much of this has to do with our ghettoization of discourse. To explore and discover new perspectives one has to be mobile; but that mobility is severely hampered by the constraints we place on students, the linguistic corrals we confine them to.

The majority of our professional writings (dissertations, papers presented at professional conferences, journal publications, scholarly texts) are situated in the middle-class suburbs. Here our writings, although successful in that they've been recognized or published, run the risk of blending into a landscape of sterile cleanliness: the manicured lawns of the literati. Some of the nicer homes stand out from the crowd: dwellings, for example, with names of more popular and established (usually tenured) theorists and pedagogues on the mailboxes. These nicer homes cast shadows over the working-class and middle-class blocks where thousands of writers—many of them graduate students and junior faculty—churn out dissertations, professional notes, reviews, and essays that for the most part go unread by almost everybody. These homes all have names on their mailboxes too, but most of them blur together—just skim through the names attached to the plethora of dissertations completed each year, or the host of people found in the index of any Conference on College Composition and Communication catalog. The ironic part of this is that those who produce these works by and large know that only a tiny, tiny few will ever read their words. If nothing else academics might be seen as "abstract lumberjacks," as my friend John Winner once pointed out, the one undeniable consequence of this annual deluge of academic texts measured in the number of trees and environmental resources destroyed to create it.[10]

And then at the top of the chain are those few wealthy neighborhoods, populated mostly by dead literary giants or oft-cited theorists who have achieved mythic or cult status: the iconoclasts, the stars of our discourse, whose texts (or names) at one point became classics. Whether these works are deemed inspiring or incomprehensible, they are often the most sterile of all, precisely because none can afford to live in these neighborhoods, let alone wander across their lawns. The auras that many teachers feel compelled to wrap around totems like "Shakespeare" and "Derrida" can have the same effect as the iron gates and guard dogs protecting celebrity mansions: admirers must keep their distance. Even if we take tours through these castles, many of us forget, as we ogle the architecture, that these artifacts were produced by folk who enjoyed getting their hands dirty with language, writers who wrote, we can assume, because they enjoyed the play of the medium.

The problem with this metaphorical neighborhood is that the implicit hierarchy contained in such a model offers the student writer little elbow room to imagine new possibilities for composition. Obviously there's no getting around the enshrinement of some authors, and the ghettoization of much student writing—audiences have a need to canonize select individuals. But we can open up new possibilities for writing by subverting—that is, integrating—this neighborhood of discourse in our own idiosyncratic ways. This means looking at the role of the teacher and the student as something like that of a rover, a migratory inquisitor. We might draw energy from Gilles Deleuze and Félix Guattari's notion of "nomadic thought," or Hakim Bey's insistence on "psychic nomadism" and "rootless cosmopolitanism," picturing ourselves as transients roaming among any number of philosophical, rhetorical lenses: vagrants traversing new neighborhoods of discourse, urging students and colleagues to walk on the less understood side of the rhetorical tracks.

 *Essaying Alternatives*

Iτ has been argued that if we could peel away the many layers of discourse manufactured in the academy, we would discover almost all of it to have in common a shared structural foundation: the form of the essay (Marius 28). Nonfiction prose is clearly the communicative medium of choice for those connected with academe. And elements of the essay form influence not only our written texts but our verbal texts as well. It is assumed that when our conversations and monologues are transcribed into written interviews and lectures, our words will be transformed into sentences and paragraphs. "'Educated' speech imitates writing: the more 'refined' the individual, the more likely their utterances will possess the characteristics of expository prose. The sentence, hypotactic and complete, was and still is an index of class in society" (Silliman, *The New Sentence* 79). Consequently, many academics feel that the more our everyday speech imitates some model of concise, efficient prose, the more intellectual and persuasive we sound. I know this has been the case with me: after presenting a paper at a conference, I strain to make any impromptu comments I might offer sound as "polished" as the sentences I've just read. My attempt often fails, though, given that my natural speech is distinguished by occasional stuttering, a wandering propensity to think in tangential asides, lapses in short-term memory, and a struggle to find the elusive word.

The reason behind this insecurity—and I doubt I'm much different from many in this respect—is that I am surrounded, almost daily, with the sounds of the academic essay: textbooks, lecturing professors, debates, editorials, books, journals, and conference presentations, the bulk of which use tropes associated with the essay form. The patterns aren't necessarily pleasing, certainly— plenty of professors ramble, just as many published essays are sloppy or affectedly dense. Mutated or pure, though, the discursive DNA binding all this talk and all these words together is traceable to the essay and its most obvious components. Introductions and conclusions, primary theses, repeated premises, linear progression, obligatory citation, orderly and incremental dialectic, supportive anecdotes, professional vocabulary, "standard" usage, footnotes and endnotes, bibliographies and appendices: these are the capital ingredients of our academic language, all spun together with the interrelated rhythms of the sentence and the paragraph. Alliteration, grammatical experimentation, lively dialogue, metrical stress, plot, pacing, attention to silence, vocal technique and body language—all important elements in "creative" written and performative discourse—are hardly primary concerns for the academician.

What I'd like to do here is pull a handful of overlooked rhetorical alternatives into the boundaries of our pedagogical conversation, so we can confront unexamined biases that determine what we do and don't permit our students (and ourselves) to do when it comes to writing. Given that the essay is built into the genetic code of our professional dialect, it seems appropriate to begin by taking a look at some intriguing and to my mind powerful essays that resist (if not obliterate) academic convention in exciting ways. By holding such works up to the light, we might come closer to delineating—or dissolving—the lines that separate the academically appropriate from the intellectually explorative.

First, though, let's move a bit closer to identifying the qualities of "good academic discourse," at least how it has been defined from within several self-consciously academic perspectives. During the past few years I've been impressed by the popularity of a certain anthology used in composition classes, Donald Hall's *The Contemporary Essay*. I used to see this influential volume turn up repeatedly as a required text for introductory writing courses at various colleges, and would hear some discuss it enthusiastically at conferences and in department hallways. *The Contemporary Essay* is a good example of how one person's predilections can be packaged in such a way as to infer a more totalizing, rather than culturally and socially specific, body of shared suppositions influencing the ways writers compose.

The Myth of "The Best"

It helps to become conscious of how we read.
—DONALD HALL

For me any attempt to assign measures of value to artistic constructs, including the linguistic artifact, has significance only when those in the conversation keep in mind the local dimensions of their dialogue. I would have reservations claiming that Shakespeare, for instance, is great and brilliant and awe-inspiring in any *universal* sense, for this is true only for those who know his work and are so affected by his language. Shakespeare may be a source of immutable awe for scholars, students, actors, and poets (myself included); in the minds of others he might be something entirely different. Indeed, for the vast majority that have never read his writing, "Shakespeare" is nothing more than a symbol, like "Einstein," a label signifying little more than an aura of lofty accomplishment. We can insist until blue in the face about some particular author's intrinsic greatness, the obvious worth of some literary form over another, but there will always be those who remain to be convinced, not to mention those who are indifferent.

Despite this, a great many people have a need to pass off their private tastes and convictions as the stuff of metaphysical truth—a condition from which writing instructors are hardly immune. Even composition teachers who on the surface advocate multiplicity can be unaware of the biases that govern their preferences. Arguments that seemingly promote diversity can be undermined by an educator's need to enforce a private aesthetics, and it doesn't take too much effort to locate the strictures loosely governing which literary and discursive formulas are being privileged and which silenced.

In his influential anthology *The Contemporary Essay* (second edition, 1989), Donald Hall brings together over fifty writers who for him clearly represent "the best work of our own literary moment" (vi). Although Hall claims that an exceptionally eclectic blend of styles circulates within this collection, the texts are actually more complementary than conflicting in their rhetorical decisions. In his table of contents the editor accompanies each author's name with a brief excerpt from his or her work, a quote generally two or three sentences long. Not only do these passages offer a glimpse into the content of the selection, presumably in hope of piquing a reader's interest, but they also characterize some of the flavor, the rhetorical signature of each essayist. These previews are supposed to give us a quick taste of each writer's prowess and originality; they could even be taken as "proof" of each author's worthiness to be selected for this collection. These are some of the best snippets from some of the best essays; as such, we should be able to learn from them. We might even infer that what they do, we should do; what they avoid, so too should we.

At the risk of reading too much into these excerpts, it's worth noting their similarities in design. I see a number of these essayists working within one of two stylistic orientations. Many of these excerpts, for example, are marked by a sense of contemplative concern, a pensive musing articulated with quiet intensity—a calm and orderly syntax, carrying forth messages of some depth or humor, made all the more effective because of their matter-of-factness and subtlety. Drama, in other words, minus the vociferation: "Nobody, man or woman, knows the country until he has lived in it and has taken out his citizenship papers" (Malcolm Cowley); "The apparent ease of California life is an illusion, and those who believe the illusion real live here in only the most temporary way" (Joan Didion); "What [my dog] Belle has is an ability to act with moral clarity, and this is a result of having qualities that have to do with real love, love with teeth" (Vicki Hearne); "The mare in labor can exert 170 pounds per square inch of pressure, so rotate a wrongly placed foal between contractions, otherwise you may get your arm broken" (Maxine Kumin). There are no exclamation points to be found in these passages, no words in boldface or capitals. If impact is made, it's done within the voice of rational control, no shouting necessary. Already, we can guess what might constitute a lousy essay—perhaps something like Michael McClure's "Phi Upsilon Kappa," for instance, a daring work unabashedly packed with exclamatory remarks and a graphic (some would say obscene and blasphemous) vocabulary practically bursting off the page with unbridled energy.

Those essayists in this anthology who choose not to make their point with understatement seem instead to resort to "rich" metaphor, simile, and analogy, attempts to make the writing as "poetic" as possible within the constraints of expository prose: "Canyons curved down like galaxies to meet the oncoming rush of flat land" (Gretel Ehrlich); "Swept off my feet, I floated from one side to the other, swiveling my brain, staring astounded at the beavers, then at the otters" (Lewis Thomas); "She waits and blinks, pumping her throat, turning her head, then sets off like a loping tiger in slow motion, hurdling the jungly lumber, the pea vine and twigs" (Edward Hoagland); "The wolf's body, from neck to hips, appears to float over the long, almost spindly legs and the flicker of wrists, a bicycling drift through the trees, reminiscent of the movement of water or of shadows" (Barry Lopez). Notice how an increase in poetic modifiers is accompanied with an excess of commas, almost as if each pause is an attempt to quietly embed the feeling of a line break within the prose—a way of incorporating turns within sentences, so that hints of verse might echo within paragraphs.

A lot of the essays in this collection vacillate between these two extremes—streamlined directness mixed with quiet drama, versus self-conscious lyricism and a density of images calling attention to themselves as they build on one another in layers of metaphors. There are exceptions, certainly; James Baldwin's razor-sharp anger, and the minimalist staccato of Raymond Carver, for example, lend alternative strains to the collection's rhetorical chorus. But in general the pieces are more coagulated than eclectic, in both style and theme. Common subjects are the contemplation of animals, the mourning of vanishing landscapes, recollections of mothers, fathers, and their deaths, and issues of social, economic, and political concern (U.S. nationalism, rape, education, government tyranny, torture, drug abuse), viewed for the most part from behind what might be considered a liberal (but not radical or anarchistic) lens.

The fact that these pieces share similar stylistic patterns hardly lessens their impact. For the most part I find them to be well-crafted essays (some are really quite splendid), probably for some of the same reasons Hall finds them worthy of inclusion in his anthology. I've used a number of these authors in my classes. Their material is often insightful, provoking, skillfully argued, concise, and frequently infused with what appears to be a sincere tone of urgency, a desire to inform a readership of values thought to be worth discussing. But the issue I want to draw attention to is that this collection is held together by a predominating common glue: the personal tastes and aesthetic preferences of Donald Hall.

And what's wrong with that? In and of itself, nothing; all anthologies are inevitably reflections of those who assemble them. No editor, curator, or teacher can remove herself entirely from the decision-making process that informs her work. That *The Contemporary Essay* offers us an unconscious portrait of its editor may even be its most interesting feature. There is nothing inappropriate with the fact that Hall's editorial shadow is what brings these pieces together; the problem, rather, is that the editor assumes his selected essays are unquestionably "the best," rather than merely his version of expository greatness. A student could easily get the impression that these essays exist in a state of rhetorical purity, a literary vacuum—as if any measure of their worth could be isolated from the corporate and capitalist agendas of the magazines and papers in which they first appeared, or the socioeconomic conditions that shaped the experiences of the individual authors. As if Hall's decision to exclude countless other essayists published in small presses ignored by the *New York Times Book Review* does not shape the aesthetics of the anthology (the vast majority of the selections were first printed by giant publishing companies like Harper and Row, Simon and Schuster, Straus and Giroux, Macmillan, Knopf, and Oxford University Press; thus, one can be left to assume that the most exciting essay writing of our time is unlikely to be represented by anything other than the most wealthy and prestigious publishing houses). Consequently, from a pedagogical perspective, the three most interesting essays in this collection might be Hall's own: his preface for instructors, his introduction written for students, and his notes on the proper way to read expository texts. If we examine the assumptions and techniques inlaid in Hall's own prose, we can identify the authority he claims as he defines for his readership, in both subtle and blatant terms, the essence of good expository writing.

Like all good academic rhetors, Hall doesn't make his argument unaccompanied; he surrounds himself with quotes from literary giants that fit well with his premises, making it seem as if his opinions are those of many. He accomplishes this most effectively when he writes in the third person singular—the objectification introduces a sense of greater distance, helping the argument to sound less subjective (and thus suspect). The sense of confidence rises significantly when Hall switches to the first person plural, the kingly "we" (the other members of which are never identified): *"The editor's* burden in making this anthology has been to choose wisely and representatively among a dazzling variety of the best. *We* have tried for diversity of author, style, and subject" (3, my emphasis). (It's interesting to note that although Hall prefers this intentional avoidance of the first person singular, it's precisely the unembarrassed embrace of the subjective "I" by some of the literary journalists represented in his anthology that has in part made them attractive to readers like him.)

But when the editor begins to dole out maxims and rules, his authoritarian intent has the most obvious impact, for it is here that the boundaries of his aesthetics emerge into sharper focus. "These writers agree [notice how Hall has taken to speaking for his contributors], by and large, to use the concrete detail in place of the abstraction; to employ the active, not the passive, mood; to withhold the adjective and search for the verb. They agree to pursue clarity and vigor" (4). In other words, bad writers will probably prefer abstraction, the passive voice, and lots of adjectives—but does this mean, then, that the paratactic webwork and suspensive patterning of a Henry James, or the baroque density of a Henry Miller, are no longer options? Hall goes so far as to proclaim that good nonfiction is above everything else efficient, like a well-balanced machine: "A sentence is good the way an ax handle is good" (4). Leaving aside the obvious masculinist implications of this metaphor (good sentences equal good tools? weapons?), this analogy is laden with complexities. Why has Hall, in introducing the symbol of a machine, chosen a primitive instrument wielded by "savages" and pioneers and not, say, the machines that really help us write our sentences, i.e., computers, software, and printers? The choice is not insignificantly a romantic metaphor. Smooth, strong, and rugged, the ax handle is a *simple* machine, harking back to a time prior to the abstractions and complexities of our contemporary world. The symbol is overly simplistic, and ill-chosen considering the tangled business of sentence construction acknowledged by many composition theorists, but it is telling in that it points to Hall's predisposition for a return to a state of simplicity and efficiency—hence his interest in present-day writers who describe their contemporary world with (in his eyes) precision, vigor, and clarity.

Other incongruities in Hall's introductory essays warrant attention. "We live in a time," he writes, "that allows writers freedom to choose what they investigate, to follow their thoughts wherever they lead, and to use a variety of styles and strategies" (1). But we know this isn't entirely true; at best we have degrees of flexibility within undeniable constraints. Though we might be somewhat free to choose topics for inquiry, the data at our disposal is always shaped by various influences outside our control—the publishers that print the material we read, the subtle ideologies present in the authors we come into contact with, the capitalist agendas that motivate our media. Though we might follow our thoughts wherever they lead (then again, it's probably impossible not to do this), chances are the results will only be published or validated if they conform in some degree with the leanings of one's publisher, editor, or teacher. And the fact is, most of us don't have much stylistic variety available to us because alternative rhetorics are rarely taught, discussed, and published within our profession—they're kept at bay by editors who fail to take seriously any challenges to their own aesthetic leanings. For example, though Hall pads his argument by quoting a few words of Ezra Pound ("good writers are those who keep the language efficient . . . accurate . . . clear"), his notion of fine expository prose is fundamentally opposed to the type of excitingly polemical text Pound was prone to make, which could include abbreviations, capitalization, ideograms, anecdotes, blunt sarcasm, widely varied citation, musical scores, unexpected transitions, multiple languages, and a winding organizational flow packed with twists and turns, all of it forcing the reader to remain constantly alert— a prose as unrelentingly energetic as any found in the twentieth century. But this is not necessarily what Hall wants us to read; at least, its like is nowhere to be found in his anthology.[1]

But what is most intriguing, and perhaps a bit disconcerting, is that Hall's examination of the expository essay is ultimately not about rhetoric at all, or current trends in expository writing, or an examination of contemporary concerns and avenues of expression. It turns out his project is a *moral* undertaking, his concern nothing less than *ethics*, specifically "the ethics of clarity in sentence structure and transition." This is where things get rather vague, as Hall equates good writing with good politics and sensible morals. "For good prose to aid us," he writes, "both socially and psychologically, it need not speak of society or psyche; for good style, all by itself, is good politics and mental hygiene. Thus John McPhee [one of Hall's "best"], who writes without revealing his values, contributes to ethics by the lucidity, clarity, and vigor of his exposition" (4). First of all, no matter how successfully he paints an objective narrative, even John McPhee can't eliminate all traces of his values when he writes—after all, what to write about, where to get it published, and what investigative strategies to use all hinge upon decisions formed from definite social and political convictions. That McPhee chooses to publish much of what he writes in the *New Yorker* makes him an accomplice of sorts in the magazine's highly selective editorial policy (that is, advertisements, essayists, and editorial policy are all accomplices in the same endeavor).

Second, and more importantly, Hall is saying that good prose—which it should be clear by now means basically *his* taste in prose—is in itself "good politics and mental hygiene." But how can George F. Will *and* James Baldwin, both of whom are represented in this anthology, both represent "good" politics, when their beliefs are so fundamentally opposed to one another? Is it good politics when Richard Rodriguez's moving autobiographical accounts are used by proponents for the English Only movement and others who would like to see bilingual education dissolved? If George Bush had George Will as a speech writer, would that enhance the "mental hygiene" of his television audience?

When Hall agrees with Orwell that lousy prose is marked by vagueness, triteness, jargon, and pomposity, this might sound like common sense; I certainly spend more time than I'd like to admit struggling to make sure my prose won't be thought of in such terms. But Hall's own term "mental hygiene" is arguably more vague than specific, and his argument that good writing equals good politics problematic. Ultimately, it comes down to this: some will agree with much of what Hall says and love the essays he has chosen; others will hate his selection and have serious problems with his assumptions. Many more will have mixed feelings or will be entirely indifferent—Hall cares about what he is saying, I care about what he is saying, but I'll bet a number of the students who read this won't be deeply stirred one way or the other.

All of these observations are unfair to Donald Hall. Unfair because none of these problems are unique to him; this is not some shifty pedagogue whose overriding goal is to forcefully convert the masses. He's a teacher who gets excited when he reads prose he likes, and wants to convey that excitement to students and colleagues. If his approach is to propose his personal tastes as if they were objective truths, it is nothing more than what many of us have done in the classroom ourselves. By dissecting for a few moments the words of one particular editor, it's my hope that we might see how similarly disguised assumptions lurk within our own favorite claims to truth. For it's not really Hall I'm criticizing, but the exceedingly pervasive assumption within our discipline that it's our job to teach students how to differentiate between "good" and "bad" writing so they can create the former, as if such an act were even possible without first examining a range of differing rhetorical philosophies within varying contexts. The issue isn't whether or not the writers in Hall's anthology are really good or bad—they are all both and neither, depending upon who reads them. But what kinds of rhetorical styles and tastes have we ignored in our attempt to define good composition? Why have we ignored these alternative modes of discourse? And how might such disregard prove more successful at measuring our prejudices than at proving the inherent worth of our favored discourse?

One of our most vocal advocates for the prescriptive approach to the "best essays" and the best way to write, not to mention the best bits of general information worth knowing, is E. D. Hirsch. The political ramifications of Hirsch's national agenda have been documented widely; indeed, *Cultural Literacy*, years after its first appearance, continues either to win over devotees with its straightforward master plan or to rile the emotions of those who find it deceptive and discriminatory. I share Hirsch's frustration at the ineffectiveness of so many American schools (I still cringe when I hear students freely admit they know little about, say, this country's geography, foreign cultures, or current events). But I am made uneasy by Hirsch's reductive logic which, if not bordering on the fascistic, is certainly wedded to the notion of a "state" education. *Cultural Literacy* isn't concerned with education so much as how to access power. That it confuses issues of disenfranchisement and enlightenment with professional advance, but does so within a naively apolitical context, makes it a scary book, particularly considering its popularity.

What interests me more at the moment is Hirsch's earlier work, *The Philosophy of Composition*, and more specifically a technique George L. Dillon used to attack it, quite solidly. Hirsch's book is an unapologetic attempt to lay forth the difference between good and not-so-good writing, as well as good and bad writing instruction. At the core of this Hirschean aesthetic are two primary factors: speed and efficiency. The Hirschean reader is in a hurry, basically, and wants to avoid mental perspiration as much as possible; the more effectively a passage cuts down the reader's processing time, the better it will be. Hence, English is supposedly far superior to the dinosaur of German because it's less bulky, more streamlined. However, since Hirsch knows that texts as divergent as a *New York Times* editorial and *Finnegans Wake* can both be regarded as "successful" by readers, despite the fact one can be read in 15 minutes while 50 years may not be enough to digest the other, he tosses in a concept of "relative readability," which makes the "readability" of a piece dependent upon its stylistic goals. In other words, a work like *Finnegans Wake* takes so long to digest because it's *supposed* to, because its stylistic aims are consonant with its semantic purposes (151). This is Hirsch's attempt to make his formulas appear less mathematical than they really are, but the attempt to infuse relativity into his prescriptive collection of maxims and "universal principles" is all too transparent.

Linearity, for example, becomes an unquestioned component of all good writing: the linear text "is writing that has not crossed over the boundary line into unreadability. Linearity determines that boundary line, and only rarely does a writer have a communicative justification for stepping over it" (136). Hirsch even itemizes for us the three major components of the "principle of linearity":

> (1) Closure must occur frequently enough to accommodate short-term memory and not interrupt the forward movement of the mind. (2) Expectation must be sufficiently fulfilled to achieve semantic integration without interrupting this forward movement. (3) Contextualization must be sufficiently explicit to indicate the contours of implication without interrupting the forward movement. Adequate closure, adequate constraint, and adequate integration: these ingredients of linearity should be balanced against each other so that none is altogether neglected. Linear prose is not always easy prose, but linearity is a minimal requirement of communicative prose. (137)

Hirsch's book is full of discourse commandments like these. He assumes such dictates are grounded in common sense, unspoiled by any private ideologies or personal preferences; these are universal requirements removed from the messiness of socially constructed political agendas. Class, ethnicity, gender, culture, individual artistic sensibilities—none of these have anything to do with the uncontaminated Hirschean edicts. Indeed, Hirsch tells teachers that in their responses to student writing they should "make clear from the tone of the comments that they deal with a craft to be learned and not with the teacher's personal taste" (161). One of the more intriguing qualities of *The Philoso-*

phy of Composition is that it makes Hirsch seem as if he *has* no taste; that is, he pretends to serve as a neutral vehicle through which the elements of good prose are filtered and delineated, uninfluenced by his personal desires.

But criticisms like these have been made before. George L. Dillon, in his book *Constructing Texts: Elements of a Theory of Composition and Style*, underscores the fallibility of a theory of composition founded on psycholinguistics and the logic of language processing models. He helps expose the silliness of Hirsch's assumed nonpartisanship: "[Hirschean] rules of good writing can then be viewed as grounded in nature, and any anxiety that what the composition instructor teaches may be arbitrary and picayune, not to mention classist and sexist, can be laid to rest. 'Writing' becomes a teachable skill and English composition a technology" (18). Rather than argue for any pecking order of sentence types, Dillon argues that intuition plays a far more critical role in our appreciation and dislike for various writings than any "adequate" usage of vocabulary, subordination, parallelism, connective words, and so on.

> The curious fact is that writing that exhibits care and artfulness in the details of its expression flatters the reader and evokes a willing appreciation for the writer's craft; writing that suggests a low estimation of the reader's attention and involvement projects a dull writer. All of this seems to reflect a primary social reality that other people are generally more interesting, and interested, if you assume that they are. (75)

To support his argument Dillon refers periodically to excerpts from essays by six writers who, though highly admired in academic circles, nevertheless deviate from Hirschean rules of order, and whose prose styles are syntactically more complex than the "plain style" advocated in *The Philosophy of Composition*. Passages from essays by "acclaimed masters" Samuel Johnson, Matthew Arnold, Lord Macaulay, Edith Hamilton, Rachel Carson, and George Miller are examined and compared to Hirschean paradigms of great writing. As might be expected, inconsistencies abound. According to Hirsch, these essays should be flops, but they are widely respected by plenty of educated readers. Dillon's thorough analysis lends support to the claim that notions of order, ways of expressing specificity and reference, flow of information, tactics of subordination, and word choice are marked more by flexibility and variation than by unconditional rules.

The decision to take respected, "safe" essayists and call attention to the incompatibility of their rhetorical strategies with Hirschean doctrine is a smart move on Dillon's part, especially since Hirsch would probably consider some of these writers essential (Samuel Johnson, for example, is included in Hirsch's National Vocabulary List, and is even quoted in an epigraph in *Cultural Literacy*). Plus, the themes in these samples are for the most part in tune with Hirsch's Eurocentric biases: Johnson, in the essay chosen by Dillon, argues that Shakespeare faithfully portrays *all* of human nature, unimpeded by culture, history, ethnicity, or gender. Lord Macaulay heaps considerable praise on Milton, Dante, and Dryden, while Matthew Arnold canonizes Wordsworth and Goethe. And Edith Hamilton is the romantic (and historically inaccurate) Hellenist with her glowing homage to the unsurpassed brilliance of classical Greece. Dillon's decision to select a handful of texts Hirsch would approve of and dissect them in accordance with Hirsch's very different obligatory grammar is perhaps the quickest way to undermine the Hirschean theory of composition.

But now look at Dillon's own selection of essays: what rhetorical assumptions do these texts have in common? Although they're offered as examples of rich and conflicting variation, these pieces are not by any means challenging or radical in either form or style, but firmly entrenched in formalist academic convention. It may not be Dillon's intention, but there is a clear subtext to his choice of alternative essays: by compiling a sample of such limited compositional strategies, some status quo is maintained; based on these passages one might conclude that one should embrace diverse ways of writing, but only up to a point—that there are boundaries of acceptability that one ought not to cross.

For the remainder of this chapter I'm going to address a selection of writings by authors who collectively stretch the boundaries of the essay to limits beyond those acknowledged by either traditional or liberal rhetoricians. Some of these works might clearly resemble the expository essay, others less so; still others might seem to defy any easy categorization, other than "experimental hybrid." As we read a series of passages that successively deviate from academic standards of appropriate expository prose, readers might be led to two possible conclusions: either all these forms, no matter how startlingly unique, will be valid options for the writer (depending, of course, upon her targeted audience); or else some of these techniques will be simply inappropriate, clearly examples of "bad writing." If I'm at all successful, readers will opt for the former perspective—this entire book is aimed at trying to foster precisely that kind of open-minded tolerance. But as for those who lean toward the latter, and who after considering the following essays are made more confident than ever that there exist undeniable dos and don'ts writers must adhere to no matter what, I hope such readers will be persuaded to begin defining, in exact detail, where they believe those boundaries lie—to spell out in no uncertain terms the rhetorical strategies that should not be permitted in student writing. At the very least such educators ought to commit themselves, publicly and precisely, about how they do and do not want to see their students write. If nothing else, it would be refreshing to hear a Donald Hall come right out and say, "Sentences that go like *this* are bad; prose that looks like *this* is good, and here's why I say so." We may or may not agree with the formula, but at least the ambiguity characterizing a lot of composition theory might come to be replaced with a bit more honesty and precision. There's nothing more frustrating than the liberal writing instructor who on one hand praises the "empowering" advice offered by a Peter Elbow or an Ann Berthoff, but simultaneously would never allow a student to turn in an assignment that resembled the prose of, say, a Gertrude Stein.

Prose/Poetry, Poetry/Prose

There is a continuum, rather than a barrier . . .
between poetry and prose (the language of inspiration
and the language of common and special discourse).
—JEROME ROTHENBERG

One way of easing into this discussion is to examine a style of essayist prose that, while antithetical to standard academic methods of essay construction, is already privileged due to the author's position within the canon. Consider the following passage from William Hazlitt's essay "On the Pleasure of Painting":

> The air-wove visions that hover on the verge of existence have a bodily presence given them on the canvas: the form of beauty is changed into a substance: the dream and the glory of the universe is made 'palpable to feeling as to sight.'—And see! a rainbow starts from the canvas, with all its humid train of glory, as if it were drawn from its cloudy arch in heaven. The spangled landscape glitters with drops of dew after the shower. The 'fleecy fools' show their coats in the gleams of the setting sun. The shepherds pipe their farewell notes in the fresh evening air. And is this bright vision made from a dead dull blank, like a bubble reflecting the mighty fabric of the universe? Who would think this miracle of Rubens' pencil possible to be performed? Who, having seen it, would not spend his life to do the like? See how the rich fallows, the bare stubble-field, the scanty harvest-home, drag in Rembrandt's landscapes! How often have I looked at them and nature, and tried to do the same, till the very 'light thickened,' and there was an earthiness in the feeling of the air! (169–70)

The musical, decorative tone of this passage (written around 1820) is typical of the rhetorical style of one who has been described as one of the best essayists of his age. What Hazlitt is doing here is not just writing about painting, but making every attempt to become a painter of language, using a palette of words and syntax rather than oils. There is a struggle underway to invest the language with the same tactility of imagery, color, and form Hazlitt finds so emotionally fulfilling when visually encountered. As a painter might use chiaroscuro or a repeated pattern of brushstroke, so Hazlitt tries to enhance his description through alliteration—"air-wove visions that hover on the verge," "Rubens' pencil possible to be performed." As a painter will use visual composition as a means of showing a simple narrative, leading the viewer's eye from a general overview of the horizon to closer inspection of a tiny shepherd and his flock, Hazlitt uses anticipatory colons, dashes, and brief exclamatory remarks, as well as rhythmic repetition ("The spangled landscape . . . The 'fleecy fools' . . . The shepherds . . . ") to grab our attention and pull us into the details he deems important. Hazlitt even allows himself the luxury of briefly interrupting his narrative flow by waxing philosophical as he introduces several rhetorical questions, only to abruptly end his musing by excitedly pointing again to the details of the artist's canvas.

Whether readers find Hazlitt's baroque style savory or gaudy is not really relevant (personally I find him a bit too dripping, if not unwittingly self-parodic). What is important is that Hazlitt has tried to reflect his subject matter not only in the essay's obvious thematic content but in its syntax and grammar as well. In praising the accomplishments of the painter, Hazlitt is also quietly praising the craft of the writer, who can use a simple palette of limited monochromatic words to evoke colorful vistas like those of the artist. But in order to do this Hazlitt must write his prose using many of the strategies of the romantic poets he admired: alliteration, personification, metaphor, breathless exclamations, and detailed description of nature. His chosen medium is the essay, his tools the sentence and the paragraph, but what makes Hazlitt interesting to readers is the fact that the impulse behind his work is that of a poet. Though few would categorize Hazlitt's essays as poetry *per se*—they're usually described as a "poetic essays" in anthologies—it's interesting to note that this prose draws more consciously from poetic techniques of its day than many of our contemporary works commonly referred to as prose poems. Many of the more popular prose poets (Russell Edson, Robert Bly, Maxine Chernoff) are arguably fiction writers who have chosen to frame their work in crystalline, impressionistic miniatures.[2]

Another characteristic of writers for whom poetics remains an inseparable component of the essay is a tendency to employ a tone of direct, often animated conversational appeal. Obvious mechanical differences might be present (increased capitalization, frequent exclamation points, heightened usage of first person singular, excessive dashes and run-ons), or a dramatic sense of candor in an attempt to link reader and writer in a more intense embrace (Hazlitt's "And see!" is amusing because he's calling attention not to any actual canvas, but to his own rhetorical technique). A tone of unabashed excitement and willingness to veer away from conventional syntax and grammatical propriety can easily thrust a reader into a more active participation with a text. In cases like these it becomes clear how intricately the content of a piece is fused with the syntactic architecture in which it is housed. Grammar *is* content, a point that is hammered home in the following passage from Charles Olson's famous essay "Projective Verse":

> Now (3) the process of the thing, how the principle can be made so to shape the energies that the form is accomplished. And I think it can be boiled down to one statement (first pounded into my head by Edward Dahlberg): ONE PERCEPTION MUST IMMEDIATELY AND DIRECTLY LEAD TO A FURTHER PERCEPTION. It means exactly what it says, is a matter of, at all points (even, I should say, of our management of daily reality as of the daily work) get on with it, keep moving, keep in, speed, the nerves, their speed, the perceptions, theirs, the acts, the split second acts, the whole business, keep it moving as fast as you can, citizen. And if you also set up as a poet, USE USE USE the process at all points, in any given poem always, always one perception must must must MOVE, INSTANTER, ON ANOTHER!
>
> So there we are, fast, there's the dogma. And its excuse, its usableness, in practice. Which gets us, it ought to get us, inside the machinery, now, 1950, of how projective verse is made. (*Selected Writings*, 16–17)

The spirited insistence, pounding repetition, excessive capitalization, conversational and parenthetical asides, and the marked contrast between the businesslike, no-nonsense itemization ("fact" #3) and the excited choppiness of extended phrasings (the wonderful propulsion of a clause like "get on with it, keep moving, keep in, speed, the nerves, their speed, the perceptions, theirs, the acts, the split second acts, the whole business, keep it moving as fast as you can, citizen"): these are not minor rhetorical flourishes but elements of utmost importance to Olson's goal. Standard grammatical convention simply will not do when one is called upon to "USE USE USE *the* process" (which of course becomes potentially any and all processes one can get one's hands on). If the writing act must remain true to social convention simply because of communal habit, then any text seeking a poiesis as radical as projective verse will have no choice but to fail. Some things, for example, simply need to be bellowed off the page. Imagine Olson's text rewritten to better serve the conditions warranted for an academic journal:

> Finally, the third component of what I have so far termed "projective verse" places no small emphasis on the process of the compositional operation: i.e., the merit of a rapid and unceasing incremental succession of what might be simply categorized as "perceptions" (Dahlberg 47). Note that no perception is too small to be of value in such an endeavor; indeed, the mundane percipience one might take for granted can—one might venture to say "must"—be taken into consideration. For the poet in particular, resourcefulness of this nature will prove especially beneficial.
>
> Thus, if the reader keeps in mind the three essential factors of this recent impetus in contemporary poetics, he should find it considerably less difficult to promote an understanding of the philosophy operant within the struggles of our present-day literary climate, the rhetorical nature of which, I trust, has been accurately portrayed above.

But of course this is asinine (not to mention scary, in that it comes so easily to me); one can't possibly paraphrase this passage without losing its primary essence, for Olson's discourse is the very measure of the "energy-discharge" he seeks to articulate ("its excuse, its usableness, in practice"). As form is always an extension of content, any substitution for unconventional form of one that is safer results in a partial if not total evaporation of that content. One doesn't really come close to fathoming Olson's idea of projective verse without tasting the rhythm of all those punching assertions, and that splendidly eccentric syntax.

Another prominent feature of Olson's prose is the sheer confidence of the rhetoric. Look at the opening lines of Olson's critical study of Melville, *Call Me Ishmael*:

> I take SPACE to be the central fact to man born in America, from Folsom cave to now. I spell it large because it

comes large here. Large, and without mercy.

It is geography at bottom, a hell of wide land from the beginning. That made the first American story (Parkman's): exploration.

Something else than a stretch of earth—seas on both sides, no barriers to contain as restless a thing as Western man was becoming in Columbus' day. That made Melville's story (part of it).

PLUS a harshness we still perpetuate, a sun like a toma-hawk, small earthquakes but big tornadoes and hurrikans, a river north and south in the middle of the land running out the blood.

The fulcrum of America is the Plains, half sea half land, a high sun as metal and obdurate as the iron horizon, and a man's job to square the circle. (11–12)

As with the essays of Gertrude Stein, Ezra Pound, William Carlos Williams, D. H. Lawrence, Mina Loy, H. D., Virginia Woolf, and other modernists determined to reconstruct the form of the criti-cal essay to meet their own needs, Olson's is the prose of an exceedingly confident ego. Though such raw conviction may not rest easy with readers who prefer a self-consciously nonauthoritar-ian posture, I find something exhilarating about spending time with a writer who knows his words are laden with truth (to my eyes, at least), and who presents his views with absolutely no desire to frame them in accordance with popular lexical conven-tion. It's a confidence student writers rarely, if ever, have the opportunity of tasting. There are some obvious reasons for this, not the least of which is that a great many students are defiantly antiintellectual, have absolutely no interest in writing (let alone poetry), and therefore can't begin to contemplate the untem-pered fascination Olson had with the space and mythic geogra-phy of our mental landscapes (graduate students, and creative writing professors, have trouble enough with Olson's poetics).

Nevertheless, student writers may often insert odd strains of superficial confidence into their prose as they make sweeping generalizations and unqualified assumptions in their papers. And one reason is that students are rarely introduced to creative options for rhetorical construction; in writing classes students learn to conform far more than invent. Consequently the most effortless way for them to produce what they think to be a powerful argument is to mimic the self-assured tone they hear from their teachers and their required texts; so instead of making challenging authoritative writings, their works sound like parodies of authoritarian models. In fact, students get caught in a perplexing double bind. For years they've been taught numerous stylistic constraints—"never use first first person," "state only the facts," "avoid personal opinions." Yet when asked to write expository essays the success of their work is often gauged by their ability to voice information "in their own words"—indeed, students are warned repeatedly of the punishments for plagiarism. Since their "own words," however, have rarely evolved, due to the dozens of stupid rules learned prior to their freshman year in college, students have little choice but to produce vague, bipartisan generalizations, burying any emotion beneath the passive voice and neutral stances while blurting out unsupported, unjustified, and often contradictory claims in an attempt to wear the clothes of "proper" academic discourse. They learn imposed confidence, which is always false confidence, and never the bolts of genuine perception that fill the works of thinkers like Olson. And part of that has to do with the fact that Olson and company made it their business to rewrite the grammar of their time so as to keep pace with their hunger for cognitive exploration.

These three short passages are obviously unlike almost everything student writers are exposed to in their writing classes. Does this mean we can safely say the stylistic techniques represented are unworthy of contemporary students? Are these strategies outdated? Or tendencies that simply made "bad" syntactic sense from the very beginning? If so, we should be able to isolate the rhetorical decisions represented above into a list of compositional gaffes: Don't confuse poetry with prose—for example, use alliteration only in moderation. Don't use exclamation points. Don't capitalize entire words or sentences. Don't refer to figures the reader might not be familiar with without proper citation (Olson's offhand references to Dahlberg, Parkman). Don't make your sentences too full of commas and additional modifiers—don't permit the flow to be interrupted with so much panting. Don't be so concerned with creating a prose that is rhythmic and full of dense description that you forget to develop a clear thesis statement in your introductory paragraph (vs. Olson's sharp, rapid-fire opening paragraphs in *Call Me Ishmael*, and Hazlitt's ornate detailing). Avoid unnecessary repetition (Olson's "USE USE USE" is a waste of space).

Probably few of us would come out and mandate such restrictions, at least publicly, but students still learn them through osmosis. And so a question: does it make sense to speak of encouraging students to locate their "own voices" when their constructions are inhibited in ways neither they nor many of their teachers are aware of?

Fictive Nonfiction

So, is it not the PLAY of a mind we are after, is not that that shows whether a mind is there at all?
—CHARLES OLSON

Scholars have been hopping genre boundaries for some time now. Clifford Geertz's classic cultural criticism on Balinese cockfighting, a splendid piece of prose as compelling in places as much contemporary fiction, played a significant role in making academics rethink long-unquestioned assumptions about appropriate and inappropriate professional discursive style: maybe it was okay after all for an anthropologist to write like a literary journalist, and spin a narrative as captivating in places as a good suspense story. After all, Geertz's is hardly the classical textbook approach:

They were wrong. In the midst of the third match, with hundreds of people, including, still transparent, myself and my wife, fused into a single body around the ring, a superorganism in the literal sense, a truck full of policemen armed with machine guns roared up. Amid great screeching cries of "pulisi! pulisi!" from the crowd, the policemen jumped out, and, springing into the center of the ring, began to swing their guns around like gangsters in a motion picture, though not going so far as actually to fire them. The superorganism

came instantly apart as its components scattered in all directions. People raced down the road, disappeared headfirst over
walls, scrambled under platforms, folded themselves behind
wicker screens, scuttled up coconut trees. Cocks armed with
steel spurs sharp enough to cut off a finger or run a hole
through a foot were running wildly around. Everything was
dust and panic. (*The Interpretation of Cultures* 414–15)

As Geertz was to write several years later, "the casting of social
theory in terms more familiar to gamesters and aestheticians than
to plumbers and engineers is clearly well under way" ("Blurred
Genres" 516). Since then the new historicism has appeared on
the scene as a valid hermeneutic enterprise, variations on what
Linda Hutcheon calls "historiographic metafiction" (54). We've
entered a time when thick descriptions of subjects like
Wordsworth's dental records or Lenin's taste in underwear could
be considered ripe material for extensive historical critique. All
of this underscores the fact that more and more theorists are discovering the appeal of telling stories; it turns out that constructing lengthy theoretical narratives from seemingly insignificant
historical crumbs is not all that different from the work of the
historical novelist. Not that Geertz's account of the Balinese
cockfight is fiction in any conventional sense—we are supposed
to believe that the cops raided the scene and dispersed the crowd
just as Geertz described it—but he and scholars since him have
consciously embraced rhetorical techniques generally associated
with journalism, autobiography, travelogues, manifestoes, and
even novels. Attention to plot, pacing, color, setting, montage,
and denouement have taken their place alongside the close reading as worthwhile elements of interesting expository prose, academic or otherwise. As a result, the boundaries of scholastic
discourse have become more than wobbly; in some arenas they
have all but dissolved. To quote a frequently cited line of
Geertz's, "one waits only for quantum theory in verse or biography in algebra" ("Blurred Genres" 515).

All of which begs the question: what is to prevent the essayist
from slipping all the way over into the realm of fiction? Is it even
possible any more to draw that line—are the divisions between
the two tangible, or illusory? In a piece of writing where separa-

tions between fiction and expository prose are intentionally confused, what illuminating side effects might we find that are unattainable in a more straightforward work of nonfiction?

William Carlos Williams's *In the American Grain*, though published in 1925 (long before Geertz's identification of overlapping
genres), remains an exhilaratingly intuitive mosaic of American
history. In keeping with the imagination of a man whose dual
career—poet and physician—reflected his habit of mixing unlike
elements, Williams's prose likewise straddles several fences. This
is the opening passage of the first essay in this book, a piece about
"Red Eric," pariah and father of Lief Ericsson:

> Rather the ice than their way: to take what is mine by
> single strength, theirs by the crookedness of their law. But
> they have marked me—even to myself. Because I am not
> like them, I am evil. I cannot get my hands on it: I, murder-
> er, outlaw, outcast even from Iceland. Because their way is
> the just way and my way—the way of the kings and my
> father—crosses them: weaklings holding together to appear
> strong. But I am alone, though in Greenland.
>
> The worst is that weak, still, somehow, they are strong:
> they in effect have the power, by hook or by crook. And
> because I am not like them—not that I am evil, but more in
> accord with our own blood than they, eager to lead—this
> very part of me, by their trickery must not appear, unless in
> their jacket. Eric was Greenland: I call it Greenland, that
> men will go there to colonize it.
>
> I, then, must open a way for them into the ice that they
> follow me even here—their servant, in spite of myself. Yet
> they must follow. (1)

Here we find Williams, in order to tell his historical account of
Red Eric, not just describing but actually assuming the voice, the
emotions and temperament of the ancient Norseman. Elsewhere
in the book Williams submits his impressions through other
masks: as Columbus in "The Discovery of the Indies," and even
as the American continent "herself" at the time of De Soto's con-
quest in "De Soto and the New World." When not imagining the
historical melodrama of this country's evolution through the eyes
of its key actors, Williams's prose makes his point through other

means like straightforward documentation, personal recollection, impassioned critique, imagined dialogue; and it is this consistent eclecticism that makes *In the American Grain* so brilliantly innovative. To play historian through the eyes of an actor is essential for Williams's project; in order to pull off his enterprise, the enfolding of fiction within the expository essay became a vital necessity.

What if one's expository prose is aimed not at the historical but the psychological? What if, in order to effectively convey the intuitions and impressions gleaned from contemplating something so slippery as the nature of thought itself, the thinker finds herself pursuing narrative trails that diverge blatantly from lines of conventional inquiry? Must such impressions be translated into the more appropriate forms of analysis, even if considerable material gets lost in the translation? Or can a case be made for holding onto the curious if it best portrays the self-examined state of mind? The following excerpt is from H. D.'s *Notes on Thought and Vision*:

> Our minds, all of our minds, are like dull little houses, built more or less alike—a dull little city with rows of little detached villas, and here and there a more pretentious house, set apart from the rest, but in essentials, seen at a distance, one with the rest, all drab, all grey.
>
> Each comfortable little home shelters a comfortable little soul—and a wall at the back shuts out completely any communication with the worlds beyond.
>
> Man's chief concern is keeping his little house warm and making his little wall strong.
>
> •
>
> Outside is a great vineyard and grapes and rioting and madness and dangers.
>
> It is very dangerous.
>
> An enormous moth detached himself from a bunch of yellow grapes—he seemed stupefied with the heat of the sun—heavy with the sun and his soft belly swollen with the honey of the grapes, I would have said, for there was a bead of gold—resinous—that matted the feathers at his throat.
>
> He fell rather than flew and his great feet scratched with a

faint metallic ring, the side of my golden cup.

He stumbled, awkward and righted himself, clutched the rim of my cup, waved his antennae feebly.

I would have rescued him but I myself was dizzy with the heat and the fumes of the golden wine and I heard a great shout of laughter as I tried to steady my cup and I shouted in reply, *he* is drunk—*he* is drunk.

So he was drunk.

Outside is a great vineyard and rioting and madness and dangers. (40–42)

When I read H. D.'s prose I am mystified, mystified at what this little story of the moth is supposed to represent (it's the only reference in the piece to the insect), at the logic behind the drunkenness, at the presence of danger in an otherwise languid setting—and especially at how all this factors into comprehending the essence of thought. This passage, taken from a fragmented essay that bounces among female consciousness, Greek mythology, jellyfish, and correlations between the womb and vision, body and mind, certainly raises more questions than it answers. Which, when discussing topics like thought and imagination, can actually be quite apropos. Mystery, intuition, dream imagery, these are all components of the active imagination. Certainly, formal analyses of the imagination (and we ought to keep in mind that in these cases it is always, at least indirectly, one's *own* imagination under scrutiny) that avoid such qualities can be valuable. Indeed, the inclusion of impressionistic and surrealistic asides could easily constitute obnoxious intrusions in many texts. But this is not to say that mysteriousness is altogether impermissible in all expository prose. As in this piece by H. D., conveying some sense of the writer's struggle to articulate the abstractness of her mental creations is paramount. There's not much in this passage I can paraphrase or summarize with any sense of certainty; and yet in an odd way it tells me more about thought and vision than any number of other texts that attempt to do so along more conventional avenues.

Whether H. D.'s drowsy, surreal image of a drunken moth or Williams's appropriation of Red Eric's voice, what remains striking about both these narratives is their need to forfeit a standard tone of academic professionalism in favor of maintaining a contrived fiction relevant to the essay at hand. For these two writers the pursuit of the active imagination, to wherever it might lead, becomes a primary agent in their rhetorical enterprise. While many writers, in their worry over straying "off topic," smother ideas before they've had a chance to evolve, H. D. and Williams take the opposite angle: they seek lines of thought that veer into unknown areas, even if it means speaking in the voice of a dead Viking or pursuing bizarre waking dreams. Sure, there are times when indulgence like this is ineffective, if not annoying. But there are others when fictive exploration within a nonfictional arena becomes a crucial factor of the composition. Part of the reason people like Williams and H. D. continued to write had to do with the excitement of jumping headfirst into unplotted realms of imaginative concentration. One reason why readers—both students and teachers—often have difficulty with writers like these is because so few of us are encouraged, professionally and academically, to write within similar states of mind.

The Spoken Essay

no reason why one should not write
as one speaks, familiarly, colloquially
— VIRGINIA WOOLF

As compositionists experiment with their craft, one of the more interesting side effects is that they come closer to realizing the limitations of their rhetorical vocabularies. What, exactly, do we call a text like this:

when i agreed to come here   to indiana   barry alpert didnt
have a title for what i was going to talk about   i think maybe he
  forgot to ask me   which was   i suppose   just as well
      because he had an idea   i had given it to him   of the
kind of thing i was now doing   and i had an idea too   of going
places to talk to people   i was seeking an occasion   for the
  kind of talking i want to do   which would of course modify the
  kind of talking i wanted to do   and how i was no longer   so
  clearly a poet   a linguist   an art critic   all of which i had

so clearly been   and how my work was therefore no longer so
clearly a poem a criticism an investigation but somehow   lying
  between them   or on their borders (55)

This is the transcription of one of David Antin's improvised lectures collected in *talking at the boundaries* (1976), an excerpt from
one of what he calls his "talk poems." These texts were created
in the following manner: Antin would be invited someplace to
lecture, whereupon he would show up without any prepared text
but only a head full of ideas, and would simply start speaking
until he stopped. Later on he would convert the spoken text into
the above form.[3] At first glance this prose would seem to be little
more than the simple transcription of spoken speech; on closer
consideration, though, the prose unveils a highly conscious
attention to craft. Antin is an essayist, and an astute one at that.
Keep in mind that, though originally spoken, these written texts
were created solely for the page; far more energy has gone into
getting these works published than was expended during their
initial creation.

While he has referred to them as a form of poetry, these words
do not become overtly "poetic" until they are arranged on the
page in the above fashion; actually the live version of these texts
probably sounded like the "verbal prose" common to all lecturing
professors. Had Antin adhered to conventional means while
making a written record of his talk, using justified margins and
standard syntax, these pieces would read like any other chatty
monologue. What makes their grammar worth noting is how, like
Antin's description of himself, their written form occupies an odd
position balanced "on the borders" between between poetry,
autobiography, criticism, and lecture.

Recorded in this way their visual arrangement creates effects
that would not be evident from listening to Antin speak, or from
reading his words in standard prose format. For instance, the
prose takes on a rhythmic lilt at once regular and haphazard.
While Antin riddles his text with gaps to denote the randomness
and spontaneity of the pauses that poke through his speech, they
are nonetheless highly stylized gaps: every pause is represented by
exactly the same length (approximately five spaces long, the
standard tab setting on a typewriter), a precision impossible in

spoken speech. Also unnatural is the uniformity of the essay/talks, for each is conveyed as one solid lump. Without the interruption of paragraphs the prose reads as one interminable run-on, advancing on its own momentum, resisting closure until the very end; in a manner of speaking, each of Antin's talks is a convoluted, twenty-five-page thesis statement. In addition Antin's decision to print all words in lower case, including proper names, grants his prose a semblance of unobtrusiveness. When entire words and phrases are capitalized they can seem louder, more adamant, almost as if they are yelling off the page; in contrast a text written entirely in lower case can seem noticeably unpretentious, as if going out of its way to shed any authoritarian airs. And Antin's absence of grammar (except for quotes, question marks, and exclamation points, which appear regularly) and intentional misspellings lend the prose an unsophisticated air, an affected naivete that, coupled with his friendly anecdotes and overall excessive chattiness, makes him appear all the more witty and cerebral in those places where he waxes philosophic, nonchalantly tossing out phrases in German, alluding to classical antiquity, and basically talking like a scholarly professor. The overall effect is not accidental. That Antin's prose has appealed to many post–World War II artists and poets stems in part from his conscious rhetorical calculations, the balance between the learned and the spontaneous.

Anthropologist and poet Dennis Tedlock pursues this method of "thinking aloud" (or "writing aloud") with even greater precision. When Tedlock translated the oral poetries of Zuni Indians, he realized that to convert these performances into conventional narrative prose would have grossly distorted their overall meaning, let alone shown disrespect for the art of the speaker (the difference between "primitive" poetries in their native state and their reductive conversions in the hands of an alien rhetoric might be suggested by seeing the *Odyssey* in binary code). And so to do justice to the original text, syntactic improvisation was necessary.

Where Antin's transcribed speech follows a fairly linear path, deviating basically in the elimination of punctuation and capitalization and the addition of staggered spatial breaks, Tedlock's essays are more clearly linguistic scores, scripts for an active performer, whether that performer is physically telling the tale before an audience or reading silently to herself. To more accurately capture the essence of a spoken Zuni narrative, a number of cues are incorporated into the text: dots separating lines indicate a two-second pause, words in small type are to be spoken softly, split lines are to be chanted, and italicized commentary inside parentheses denotes visual movements, coughs, laughter, expressions, and so forth. Directives like these are essential to effective translation; Tedlock points out in his introduction to *Finding the Center: Narrative Poetry of the Zuni Indian* that the tone of some repetitive passages would be lost if conveyed in standard prose:

> At that moment his mother
> embraced him
>   embraced him.
>
> His uncle got angry
>   his uncle got angry.
>
> He beat
> his kinswoman
>   he beat his kinswoman. (xxvii)

What's interesting is that many of the rhetorical cues used in his Zuni translations have carried over into some of Tedlock's own work. This is from the author's spoken essay, "Tell It Like It's Right in Front of You":

> An oral story is not an object [as if holding an object in the hand] * an object of art or any other kind of object * it is an action, it is something I *do*.
> It's an action that's *now* * and that speaks * of ancient things.
> If we get into * storing *that* in a *book* * we've begun * to forget.
> We begin to attribute the past to that book which if we please we can put up on the shelf and forget.
> A book that was published in 1789, that was published in 1801, that was published in 1902.
> Those are like *tombstones*.

The story is what I'm telling * *now* * with my own breath.

With my own body.

That means that * the work of translation isn't *done* when you've finished getting it all on the *page*.

It means you also have to figure out how * what's on that page * should be spoken * aloud by someone reading it.

The end point of the translation becomes not * *this* that I *hold* in my *hand* [as if holding a book] * but something that I might *say* sometime on a particular *occasion*. (375–76)

Though here Tedlock's concern is with ways of directing performers how to read written texts aloud, his innovative grammar offers a variety of new strategies for the essayist. For instance, though we know a particular word or phrase can be emphasized by putting it in italics, this strategy is generally used in accordance with an unspoken rule that we should use this technique sparingly, lest our texts reverberate with too much undue stress. But *why* ought writers *always* adhere to such *obligatory* moderation? Tedlock doesn't, and as a result his prose echoes with an intensity that would be lost without such frequent insistence. And by breaking up sentences with asterisks and making the paragraphs exceptionally brief Tedlock alters the pace of the reader: text like this is hard to read slowly, just as a work with no paragraphs or line breaks can be intimidating in that it offers no ledges or pauses for the reader to momentarily rest her eyes.

These are not arbitrary stylistic decisions; for Tedlock and Antin to write, as so many compositionists are fond of putting it, "in their own voice," it becomes essential to redefine grammar, *on one's own terms*. The focus on writing as performance is an important one. Envisioning texts as extensions of oral and bodily activity, and words and grammar as manipulative objects like musical notes and rests, renders our two-dimensional alphabets tactile, thereby reintroducing breath, texture, and motion into prose.

The Expository Fragment

*In a book, as in all things, there are lines of articulation
or segmentarity, strata and territories; but also lines
of flight, movements of deterritorialization and
destratification. Comparative rates of flow on these lines
produce phenomena of relative slowness and viscosity,
or, on the contrary, of acceleration and rupture.
All this, lines and measurable speeds, constitutes an
assemblage. . . . Literature is an assemblage.*
— DELEUZE AND GUATTARI

A great deal of contemporary critical prose resists the common academic assumption that worthwhile essays must by definition stay clinically objective, proceed according to linear structure, never straying from a central tone of professional decorum. Critics and poets have found it necessary to relay their ideas through what Richard Howard, in describing the prose style of Roland Barthes, calls "an evidently random succession of fragments: facets, aphorisms, touches and shoves, nudges, elbowings, bubbles, trial balloons . . . of an invisible design" (vii). Some writers—Clark Coolidge, Bernadette Mayer, Madeleine Burnside, Fanny Howe, and Lyn Hejinian, for example—with their arrangements of disjointed yet related commentaries presented in piecemeal fashion, construct texts lending themselves to ideas collected in fragmented progression, hinged to one another like a chain of islands rather than one solid, unfissured land mass. Other writers like Susan Howe, Roland Barthes, and Anne Carson have produced scholarly works that are as much poetry, biography, and autobiography as they are models of perceptive literary criticism, all of it presented in a lacework of variegated but vigorous introspection.[4]

The following is from a lecture by John Cage, whose work commonly seeks a marriage between elements of chance and highly elaborate codes (using the I Ching in conjunction with a roll of the dice, for instance). The following passage, from Cage's "Lecture on Commitment," was formed as a collage of impressions and anecdotes written separately on cards, which were then shuffled and read within arbitrary, preselected time constraints.

Let me say it schematically. This point is it. That point is you. We draw an arrow between the two points, indicating that you have dedicated yourself to it, unquestioningly. That is commitment. Where does it get you? Well, there are lines from that point that is it that are arrows to every other point in space and time. Any "it" is like a Grand Central Station, or rather a space platform in orbit. Once there, you can move out in any direction.[5] You can float through the air, as Mila Repa did, in the form of a thistle. Appear in several places at the same instant (the way the mass media do). You can even come back to yourself: toward the end of his life, Ramakrishna put a rope of flowers around his own neck and cross-legged sat in self-worship.

•

What was it actually that made me choose music rather than painting? Just because they said nicer things about my music than they did about my paintings? But I don't have absolute pitch. I can't keep a tune. In fact, I have no talent for music. The last time I saw her, Aunt Phoebe said, "You're in the wrong profession."

I'll tell you one thing: being committed as I am now to commitment is very odd. As Gertrude Stein said, "There isn't any there there." If only it were a pearl, I could reach to my forehead and find it. As Suzuki said: Living in the city I don't see how you're going to do it; living in the country you'd have a chance. And there's his article entitled Hands. (Let them get dirty. And who was it said something about roots—not just the roots but the dirt attached to them? Compare the trees sent to Nebraska which refused to grow simply because their roots had been cleaned up.)

•

Is it true that when a murder is committed, each one of us is the murderer? If so, then ought we not be more generous to one another? (Cage 117–18)

With Cage the silences between the segments are especially important, a rhetorical device permitting the "digestion" of ideas; there is a quiet tone to an essay/presentation like this, for it presents itself not as a linear construction, where each new argument builds upon the last, but instead as a smorgasbord of idea-points, which we can separate out and contemplate as isolated miniessays and crystalline abstracts. One might argue that one can do the same when listening to many otherwise conventional essays read aloud; the difference here, however, is that most conventional essays and lectures are expected to be experienced from beginning to end—the text as one hermetically sealed unit, approachable from point A and nowhere else. In a work like Cage's quoted above, the written text is perforated, allowing the reader room to enter and depart at each and any point. As with Cage's metaphor, every instant of the text becomes its own Grand Central Station, accessible from all other places. And the silences between Cage's islands of text are not vacuums, but can resonate in the same way the final note of a symphony does after the conductor has brought the piece to an end. This rhetoric of silence achieves a power unattainable in other conventional approaches to the essay that make their impact by composing one large, integrated zone.

To many, a collage of notes might indicate a writer's inability to construct a central thesis, or failure to provide a reasonably coherent argument glued together with appropriate transitions. And yet these constructions of notes (and it is important to think of this word in both its linguistic and musical context) don't necessarily indicate raw, uncooked arguments, any more than all linear-hierarchic essays guarantee logical coherence. In fact, theorists like Deleuze and Guattari argue that most and maybe all essays and expository prose are essentially a series of intellectual minutes and tones, the only difference being that it is conventionally apropos to smooth out all the edges and corners with transitional sentences rather than offering an assemblage like Cage's, or the self-consciously "nomadic" layout of Deleuze and Guattari's writing (A *Thousand Plateaus*).

Although the fragmented text can appear particularly odd to those unaccustomed to grappling with this kind of grammar, the demands it places upon readers is not really all that new to us; it's just that our innate tendency to gather information in a piece-meal fashion, a condition we tend to forget as we synthesize the data surrounding us into manageable gestalts, is here amplified.

All of us, unless we have a photographic memory, will after reading an essay probably come away with little more than an impressionistic picture of the total informative content, while a handful of vivid images and claims remain foremost in our minds—imprints that, as reader response theory has shown us, can vary widely depending upon our orientation as readers. Reading any essay or book can be like driving past several hundred miles of landscape: once at our destination we are hard put to recollect entire spans of countryside, let alone in the chronological order in which they rolled by us, whereas specific landmarks will stand out with clarity. Consequently, an argument can be made against viewing any text as a completely unified entity, for no other reason than that we read across spans of time and not within atemporal vacuums. The durational flow in which the reading process is contained makes it inconceivable for any of our perceptions to be static. Whether one stands before a miniature postimpressionist painting or a wall-sized mosaic, neither can be digested in any motionless totality; our eyes dance across the canvas in continual flux, touching on a series of points. So too with the essay. In part it's this phenomena that writers like Cage are fascinated with and highlight within their work.

Cage is also important because of his reliance upon chance operation. The composing process is now widely talked of as being a recursive rather than linear act. There might be a drawback, though, to taking this model too literally, for even a back and forth movement linking alternating stages of prewriting, drafting, and revising, no matter how staggered, remains a linear model. To get from points B to A to F to C, one must still draw straight lines between the points, thus creating another linear paradigm, the only difference being that now corners have been added (which, come time for the final draft, are expected to more or less undergo erasure). An alternative view of the composing process might place added focus on the significant part chance plays in the realization and inclusion of material. By acknowledging that chance can occupy a major role in the construction of texts, the obligatory hierarchy surrounding the stages of draft creation and revision (where final drafts always overshadow preliminary ones) might be diminished; writers could come to view the composing process as something other than an activity geared toward the production of "polished" ideas borne out of "rough" thoughts. One might even postulate that there is never anything other than one draft, perpetually in a state of transition and renovation. In Ann Berthoff's words, writing is similar to a wheel already in motion—we neither hop on nor jump off, but simply experience the ride, our position(s) changing at every moment.[6] (This is not to imply that embracing elements of chance within one's writing automatically leads to a lack of sustained focus. Despite the choppiness evident in the above excerpt, Cage's essay on commitment does possess obvious recurring threads, not the least of which is his preoccupation with this term and its implications for human living.)

But now consider the following "book review" by Alan Davies, a text that deviates wildly from practically all conventions of standard essay writing. The following is "31 Assertions, Slowly," an unconventional review of a book of poetry by Christopher Dewdney; the piece has been presented here in its entirety so that the reader might experience the work in its segmented totality (or total segmentation).

Here language goes back to the spring we see it come out from.

The air is geology.

Eye is born in its sac.

Each integer vibrates the space between its neighbors, domains in line.

A star a dream of light from which a universe awakens.

Persons are volumes of live matter raised in meeting to 451° Fahrenheit, or cool in water.

Each version is solid eschatology.

In every passage a great whale blocks the sight from the sight but not from the whale.

Towns are beaches onto which wash.

Through these visions runs a tiny naked and frothing vision.

From the chosen vantage, fireflies are acres of light.

Large balls of silence roll past and through each other, on a border of nerves and delight.

Sense data fills cylinders with its saturated solution.

Each fossil a photograph of a comet, then, and also.

The literature phosphoresces in slow biologic warp, seeing desire untied of desire.

Dreams coat the inside of beings, the underside of sight.

Going out in air, the lungs envelop stone history.

A statement nearly restates another, it must be stating itself, must itself be stated.

Metaphor is one word for two: family resemblance.

History bumps itself off.

Preordination fosters statues.

Organisms are preferred which voice without breaking open their layers, rather case in them.

Far away objects are simple on protractor limits.

A body part is a testicle of motion.

The aliens are contentedly at home.

360° dreams 0°.

Inside brain a knot surfaces, to be solid text.

One mosquito syphons blood from the fucking body.

The future holds, sustains, each present in sounds.

Preference is an asterisk.

The author escapes from a paragraph, eloping along slightly bottomless discourse. (3–4)

Looking at a text like this, one might well question the appropriateness of calling it an essay at all. On first reading its only semblance of organizational coherence might be the fact that each fragment is a sentence, and the content one of relative obscurity.

Balls of science, lungs swallowing histories made of rock, fossil photographs—what have these things to do with a book review? How can anyone make sense of this? Couldn't Davies have simply stated what he meant, instead of reveling in seemingly intentional abstruseness? And while one might gain some slight comfort in the fact that Davies's subject is a text equally unconventional, a work full of lines like "Perihelion of the cicada through the brassy July sky, schemata of blue pepsis vectors" and "Feeding hairline crack a barn-storm translated into the propagation-lee of the glass machinery" (Dewdney 62), the question remains: is this an essay or isn't it?

To avoid the issue by lumping this piece under the label of "contemporary poetry" would be too facile; Davies is, after all, seeking to accomplish many of the goals sought by writers of conventional critical expository prose. His review, written in paragraphs (albeit a string of unindented, one-sentence paragraphs), praises the work under discussion by pointing out in distinct detail the type of imagery and landscape it evokes. An attempt has been made to grab the reader's interest by conveying the favorable impact the book had upon the reviewer. It would appear that Davies has been noticeably impressed; after all, composing a response like this can easily require more energy than hashing out a more conventional synopsis, and it's doubtful Davies would have gone to all the trouble had his impression been less approving. In addition, "31 Assertions" begins and ends with lines that sound something like introductory and concluding statements: "Here language goes back to the spring we see it come out from" eventually leads to "The author escapes from a paragraph, eloping along slightly bottomless discourse," lines that evoke a prefatory and conclusive air, leading one to realize that these assertions aren't carelessly jumbled together but consciously framed. (Note that the last line of the review happens to be an apt characterization of Davies's own text.)

Still, the question is a valid one: if this is an essay, then our academic definitions of this genre are debilitatingly constrained. But if it's not an essay, somewhere between Davies's text and the works represented in Donald Hall's anthology we have crossed some boundary of propriety. And though the former conclusion could easily scare away some readers because of its overwhelming implications for new limits of critical expression, opting for the latter raises serious objections. If Davies's piece is undeniably ineffective, bad, improper, and simply wrong for student imitation, we ought to be able to identify in detail the more blatant faults embodied within the grammar of this text. We should be able to hold up this review as an example of what good writers don't do: one shouldn't, for example, lump a handful of assertions together without binding them with transitional clauses. Single-sentence paragraphs should be used sparingly, if at all. A clear and coherent argument should run throughout the text, not a hodgepodge of impressions with little more than tenuous connections. One shouldn't overindulge with metaphor—at the very least the writer needs to provide readers with logical analyses that explain the more obscure metaphorical leaps. One should really avoid using words like "fucking" in one's text, and so forth.

Not that any of this is necessarily bad advice (throughout the writing of this book, for instance, I'm generally trying to adhere to some of these particular guidelines). But it is not unequivocal advice. My guess is that those likely to read my book are not avid readers of the more experimental of contemporary writings, and prefer a more systematic, conventionally organized and argued text, whereas a reader like Davies would probably find my prose painfully plodding, overburdened with unnecessary qualifiers and transitions. Since I'm trying here to make contact with other compositionists, not Language poets, it makes sense to play by a different set of rules than those Davies uses (or breaks). And yet as composition theorists we need to be wary of painting ourselves into corners, or assuming our favorite rhetorics are naturally the right ones for our students. When we don't make classroom environments where they can sample a patchwork of conflicting rhetorical philosophies, we steer our students into select literacy arenas; we prescribe for them hosts of silent rules that foreclose all kinds of textual construction.

Some might argue that the writers quoted above might be undeniably interesting, but only insofar as they are evaluated within the local confines of the literary communities they choose to interact with, whereas the assumed goal of the composition instructor is largely to help students gain access to much larger (i.e., "important") communities. But this logic doesn't help us escape the problem of what definitively constitutes the distinction between successful and unsuccessful prose. For if Davies and company represent valid discourse communities that are simply too small to entertain within our classrooms, we imply that in their stead we prepare students for something akin to a more "global" discourse community—always an obvious fiction—and that the prose of our profession, and the academy, is not itself marginal or indigenous but representative of universal motivations. Now, prose conforming to a linear-hierarchical structure is considerably more marketable, and thus a lot more visible, than the alternative prose forms touched on above. But is it solely the statistical popularity of discursive trends that should motivate our pedagogies? Should good writing be measured primarily by how easily it will be consumed by readerships trained to respond in ways resembling our own tastes and predilections? To teach discourse in our own image, and the image of our profession, is obviously beneficial, necessary, and probably unavoidable (students need, they *want* to learn how to communicate in ways that will make them look intelligent before their professors). But what gets lost when we refuse to entertain alternative rhetorics thriving beyond our favorite boundaries? What does it mean if teachers don't investigate the ideological assumptions that inform their pedagogies? To what degree are we capable of exhibiting "discursive freedom" in light of such restrictions?

Arguments have been made that the teaching of English, especially composition, is motivated more by unacknowledged ideology than anything else. Patrick Colm Hogan criticizes the deceptive manner in which composition can be taught in the writing course, where

> students are taught the 'proper' modes of argument. While claiming to teach valid argumentation, composition classes in fact function, at least in part, to inculcate ideologically defined 'limits of rational discourse.' Those who adopt theses which fall outside the problematic of dominant ideology, cite ideologically impure sources, etc., are swiftly informed that their 'writing' is inadequate. It does not take students long to learn what 'good writing' really is and to seek to conform their essays thereto. (177)

The issue, however, is not one of how to transcend our ideological shackles so that we might gain access to some romantic state of interpretive purity; if poststructuralism has shown us anything, it is that no one escapes the ideological webs of their own historical consciousness. Instead we need to learn how to nurture an ideology that delights in experiencing the comparative layering of unlike ideological grids.

Of the contemporary writers who champion increased tolerance of new composing practices, few are as eclectic in their defense of resisting rhetorics as Charles Bernstein. In his essay "Three or Four Things I Know about Him," he attacks the incapacitating notion of "imperial reality," i.e., the idea that

> the composition of reality is suprapersonal: the mistakes & plain takes of a person are not an essential part of reality's composition. Standardized spelling, layout, & punctuation enter into a world of standardization—clocks & the orbit of the moon & the speed of light. A social science epistemologically self-conceived on the model of the natural sciences becomes possible & grammar becomes a social science. Language is thus removed from the participatory control of its users & delivered into the hands of the state. Text is no longer regarded as requiring interpretation: rules for appropriate spelling & syntax are determined by consultation with generalized codes of grammar removed from their contextualized source in a text. . . . Decontextualized codification of the rules of language enforces a view that language operates on principles apart from its usage. These rules are not "picked up" but taught. Failure to produce appropriate language is regarded not as misperception but as error. The understanding begins to be lost that we are each involved in the constitution of language—that our actions reconstitute—change—reality. (*Content's Dream* 26)

What makes Bernstein's argument so powerful (and, ironically, largely ignored by popular literary and composition theorists) is that his prose is itself the manifestation of this need to challenge, subvert, and redefine the rules of discourse. The essay from which this passage is taken is a collage of fifteen sections, a blend of impressions presented the way paintings used to be shown in Victorian galleries—cluttered closely together on the same wall, held together as much by their proximity to one another as by any self-consciously maintained layout or curatorial motif. In "Three or Four Things I Know about Him" we find all of the following: quotes allowed to speak for themselves, presented without any overt follow-through; a portion of transcribed speech in a style reminiscent of David Antin's "talk/poems"; sarcastic commentary, like the snippet titled "TOILET PAPER CONSCIOUSNESS"; animated stream of consciousness ("switch, fug, cumpf. afraid to get down to it. avoidances: movies. i think it's rather boring already dAncInG with LaRRy rIvers . . . "); a brief, almost confessional interlude where the writer talks candidly of his relationships and insecurities ("I find it scary to give up that other security (which is power) by really trusting/needing/relating to others"); passages that more noticeably punctuate Bernstein's academic training ("Individual actions are depicted as reified instantiations fixed by the intersection of a variety of *theses*. . . . The hermeneutic indicts the scientistic with the charge that it has once again subverted the dialogic nature of human understanding with its behavioro-empiricism"); and tracts that are a composite of the above. The richness of this essay is due to the author's ability to repudiate linguistic uniformity by reconstituting language on his own terms. As one critic puts it, Bernstein's "stylistic indeterminacy" represents "a constant defusion of the idea of 'voice'. Style becoming, not a matter of authorial signature, not even a style, but a tactic, a strategy to get into the text" (Inman, "One to One" 224). To reach a point where one can dive into these otherwise alien rhetorical baths, and from them create powerfully innovative concoctions, can be remarkably liberating. Unfortunately it's a compositional state of mind students and their teachers rarely experience.

In some ways we've come full circle. This resistance to formalist scholarly discourse is actually very much in the tradition of the essay, at least as it was originally conceived by Montaigne, who has been credited with first developing the essay into a distinct genre. Kurt Spellmeyer reminds us that Montaigne, rebelling against the "exclusionary purity" of the scholastic tradition, opted for a self-consciously individualized approach to writing instead of the abstract impersonality of academic discourse.

Spellmeyer argues for reclaiming that early sense of the essay. As it currently is within our professional and classroom discourse, the essay now disguises "authorial fallibility and bias as well as the uncertainty of discourse itself" (264); if we were to return to Montaigne's initial desire, the essay would instead foreground "the speaker's movement from presentation to representation, from experience as 'fact' to experience invested more fully with personal, and with social meaning" (265). With Spellmeyer *transgression* becomes a central ingredient for powerful composition: "discourse that transgresses the propriety of discrete communities and challenges 'the unconditional priority of method' itself" (268). Viewed from this perspective, all of the above "experimental" writers show an affinity for the spirit of the essay as Montaigne originally conceived it; they all convey a need to experience written discourse as a manipulable craft, a medium lending itself to modulation and creative mutation. Their work identifies the fascination of observing the unpredictable manifestations, twists, and surprises that can occur in the composing process. Whether the text at hand is "true" criticism in any traditional academic sense is obviously not a primary issue—had they been more preoccupied with writing within the lines of academic propriety, these texts could never have existed.

The situation comes down to this: essays have been and continue to be written in an overwhelming variety of powerful forms, forms that far exceed the methods demonstrated by texts in Norton anthologies, the *New Yorker*, and *College English*. Our concern to teach students how to become proficient in the language of the academy all but ignores this wider view of composition, and as a result students develop no more than a highly selective perception of the possibilities available for writers. The central issue is not which discourse forms are ultimately right and which are wrong—a pointless question when considered outside of any immediate social community—but *why* certain forms are not permissible within the academy, and whether or not as teachers we wish to perpetuate such an exclusive club. Introducing students to alternative essays does more than provide them with means of experiencing a sense of play, the ability to generate more complex "voices" during revision, and the opportunity to review things from experimentalist points of view. By weakening the gulf between the discourse of the academy and the far richer mix of dialects rarely entertained in our classes, we loosen the prescriptive reins with which we censor student composition, and their thinking in general. By exploring a wider range of means by which human thought and expression are manifested in multiple rhetorics, students learn why certain communities and writers must, in order to survive intellectually, resist the laws of traditional academic discourse.

Beyond Eurocentric Discourse

*Being told to 'speak proper,' meaning that you become
fluent with the jargon of power, is also a part of not
'speaking proper.' That is, the culture which desperately
understands that it does not 'speak proper,' or is not
fluent with the terms of social strength, also understands
somewhere that its desire to gain such fluency is done
at a terrifying risk.*
—AMIRI BARAKA

*It is not the Black student who is wrong when he
expresses himself; it is the teacher who is wrong for not
recognizing and respecting the language that the student
uses.*
—STEPHEN D. CHENNAULT

*We must not forget that we're not just dealing with the
way a people talk or communicate, but how they're
taught to think.*
—HAKI R. MADHUBUTI

ALTHOUGH it has become chic for liberals
and self-proclaimed radicals to speak of enlarging the canon,
making literature studies more inclusive by incorporating works
by African Americans, Latinos, Native Americans, Asians, and
other "minorities" beside Shakespeare and company, not as many
recognize that another canon requires reconsideration: the canon
of discourse, our academic language canon. Issues of inclusion
pertain not just to literature but to composition as well—those
canons of rhetoric we claim to be essential, and those we render
invisible from our failure to take them seriously in front of our
students, within our profession. True, the canonical brews have

gotten spicier as contempt for discriminatory syllabi becomes more widespread. But it's still practically unheard of for philosophies of writing and communication indigenous to these overlooked cultures to be critically taught—and practiced—in classrooms.

Look at it in these terms: it's now considered gainful by many to have students read works by authors like Ntozake Shange, but not for them to write papers as colorful and performative in nature as Shange's texts. Students have more opportunity now to learn about the exploits of Coyote, but few are encouraged to write of the trickster figure with any sense of the chaotic play many Indian cultures privilege as an element of earnest, adult discourse. It may not be that uncommon anymore for the uniqueness of Indian and Asian views of temporality to be studied in conjunction with literatures from these cultures—so long as we articulate our responses in accordance with classical, traditionally Western privileging of linear, noncircuitous explication. Houston A. Baker, Jr., and Henry Louis Gates, Jr., can write detailed works on African American literary theory wherein they praise the improvisatory, blueslike nature of African American writings, so long as they typically cloak themselves in the highly theoretical garb expected of the contemporary theorist (Geneva Smitherman continues to be a welcome exception to this rule). Or to put it another way, introspective analysis of rap music is acceptable, but not creating one's own rap, or manufacturing an expository prose more jazzlike in design than academic. In essence, no matter how liberal and progressive the tenor of our new curricula, these non-Western, extra-European arts, philosophies, and literatures will remain forever delegated to the status of the other so long as we refuse to take them seriously by implementing them within our own writings and research, and enticing students to follow our example by becoming familiar with a wide volume of competing rhetorics. Otherwise, any alternative, non-Eurocentric literatures introduced into our curriculum might come to represent little more than slickly disguised tokenism.

This isn't to propose that writing should or shouldn't conform to any one of these overlooked perspectives, or that any version is any more valid than another—just that instruction in oral communication and the composing of texts must be offered from a relativistic point of view if, in fact, we're really committed to teaching from a critically multicultural framework to a culturally diverse student body. Obviously we have to make students aware of how different communities will reward and condemn unlike styles of expression. We have some obligation to make them conversant with the language of the academy, just as we simultaneously seek to make them aware of the conflicting ideologies implicit within discourses that are the site of academic and professional power. Naturally, any argument aimed at ignoring academic discourse would simply be another form of censorship, just as the academic who tells her students institutional discourse isn't worth learning perpetuates an obvious double standard. The languages of the academy are not enemies, but rather realities that students must at some level learn to negotiate.[1] The danger comes when Western, historically male discourses—be they current-traditional emphases formed from classical rhetoric, or more liberal expressionist stances valuing personal narrative—are the only extremes available to students.

I'm obviously not the first person to raise these objections. Geneva Smitherman, in her splendid and groundbreaking work *Talkin and Testifyin*, made this claim years ago (back when I was still in junior high school!):

> Generally, the framers of the recent multicultural approach focus on history, literature, folklore, and culture as the content of the curriculum. They tend to forget the most fundamental fact of a people's culture: their language. Thus language study should be an integral dimension of the multicultural curriculum design in black schools. (237)

(And, of course, not just black schools, but all American schools.) What I find most startling is that more than fifteen years later this profound theme in Smitherman's work, and all its radical implications, remain largely ignored within the field of composition, relegated to a past chapter in our profession when debates were waged over the validity of teaching Black English. Now, with the shift toward multiculturalism nearing its peak in American colleges, one might expect to see scholars turning their attention to the oral and performative discourse of their students and colleagues, and not just to the literatures they read. But the multicultural turn remains characterized, almost exclusively, by a preoccupation with literary texts, not the inclusion of cross-cultural discourses.

To try to define African American discourse according to any strict parameters would be more trivializing than beneficial. Just as Eurocentric rhetoric is itself a problematic term not pointing to any one style, but rather a hodgepodge of rhetorical leanings within which certain echoes and patterns predominate, the equally generic label "Afrocentric" signifies a loosely joined scope of psychological, philosophical, and artistic convictions articulated by Africans and African Americans resistant to traditionally Eurocentric views. While we should be careful about listing definitive rhetorical requirements for African and African American discourse, some primary contrasts can definitely be drawn between such discourse tendencies and the language conventions of the academy. Indeed, African understandings of discourse, performance, criticism, and even the nature of temporality itself, all of which have direct or indirect bearing upon African American discourse, are extremely different from European means of interpreting these themes.

To back up a bit, let's address the obvious: when the academy thinks of literature, it's no secret that texts by British and American men are what usually come to mind. The assignments we give, and our evaluations of student writings and classroom participation, are shaped in no small degree by paradigms foisted upon us during our own educational histories. Many of us have come to expect "appropriate" oral discourse to follow patterns and devices privileged by our past teachers (whether through their speech, their writings, or the texts they used), most of whom were schooled in compliance with fundamentally Euro-American standards. If what many of us know of literature stems from our acquaintance with canonical works, then it will be difficult for us to anticipate and evaluate student writing without such conditioning forever lurking in the background, quietly skewing our perspective. Perpetuation of Western literary and literacy canons sends a blatantly ethnocentric message to our students and the social, professional, and technological communities with which universities interact: namely, to learn standard En-

glish and academic discourse is essential, but to become proficient in ways diverse peoples choose to challenge academic criteria of discourse through creative resistance is not.

Yet such censorship flies in the face of the increasingly culturally diverse makeup of today's schools. There are more African
Americans in the United States than all of the citizens in Cana-
da, or Australia, for instance; the United States is at least the
fifth largest Spanish-speaking country in the world; in a matter
of decades whites will find themselves occupying minority status
in this country. Given measurements like these it has become
increasingly apparent that any system privileging a monocultural pedagogy of literacy leaves itself open to claims of cultural
discrimination.

A distressing example of how ethnocentric biases censure
other relevant methods of communication and textual construction is related by Dennis Brutus, in a discussion of how South
African students are taught literature and writing in their
schools:

> Blacks begin learning Shakespeare and Wordsworth in
> junior school ("Daffodils" is learned in almost every school).
> In high school blacks begin to read what might be called
> classics: Dickens' *A Tale of Two Cities* and Cooper's *The Last
> of the Mohicans* are included in high school reading. They
> might even read an early Shakespeare comedy. By the time
> one goes on to university, one is exposed to three years of
> English. If you are going to major in it, you go through
> the traditional kind of syllabus, beginning with Chaucer,
> through the Elizabethans (and perhaps the Metaphysicals),
> on to the Romantics and the Victorians, and perhaps read-
> ing a few of the modern poets as well. This pretty much is
> the range of exposure for an African being educated under a
> system inherited from the British university system. (6)

Although Brutus is discussing the literary canon, his insight tells
us a lot about the writing expected from these students; discussions of canonicity, after all, impinge closely on the teaching
of composition and literacy. "Indeed," remarks Brutus, "some
African writers have been criticized for a too-slavish imitation of
their English models" (7).

Such incidents of cultural homicide enacted in the name of intellectual enlightenment are well documented. Ngugi wa Thiong'o tells a typical story of what it was like to be caught speaking his native Kenyan tongue in his school system, and how African children quickly learned to adopt the British intolerance for African languages:

> It was after the declaration of a state of emergency in Kenya in 1952 that all the schools run by patriotic nationalists were taken over by the colonial regime and were placed under District Education Boards chaired by Englishmen. English became the language of my formal education. In Kenya, English became more than a language: it was *the* language, and all the others had to bow before it in deference.
>
> Thus one of the most humiliating experiences was to be caught speaking Gikuyu in the vicinity of the school. The culprit was given corporal punishment—three to five strokes of the cane on bare buttocks—or was made to carry a metal plate around the neck with inscriptions such as I AM STUPID or I AM A DONKEY. Sometimes the culprits were fined money they could hardly afford. And how did the teachers catch the culprits? A button was initially given to one pupil who was supposed to hand it over to whoever was caught speaking his mother tongue. Whoever had the button at the end of the day would sing who had given it to him and the ensuing process would bring out all the culprits of the day. Thus children were turned into witch-hunters and in the process were being taught the lucrative value of being a traitor to one's immediate community. (11)

It would be foolishly Europhobic to imply that the canonical works taught by Brutus's South African school system, or the English language taught to students like wa Thiong'o, are in and of themselves improper or wrong; but there is clearly something significantly wrong with the policies of censorship on which such curricular decisions are founded. An imbalance exists, and when this happens, communities are often being erased. This becomes more obvious when Brutus informs us that when South African students produced texts of their own making, their works were banned as quickly as they were published (this means anyone

found reading or quoting from an illegal text, or even in possession of the work, could be arrested and detained). Brutus
describes banned works like these as having moved away

> from traditional form toward a very conscious attempt at
> immediacy, at direct and unadorned communication. This, I
> fear, would suffer if it were judged by any academic canon,
> for it hardly conforms to accepted notions about the craft of
> poetry. They [the young black writers] would reply, quite
> frankly, that they are not interested in creating works that
> will endure, that they are not interested in creating works
> that will pass muster in the university; they would say
> instead that their preoccupation is with immediate and
> effective communication with the people around them. (7)[2]

And it's not hard to spot obvious parallels between the South
African student forced to read Pope but desirous of creating pro-
ANC propagandist poetry and the urban student required to
write research papers but more interested in fashioning raps
inspired by Public Enemy. While correlations between American
and South African educational systems might seem a bit extreme,
it's precisely this ethnocentric concept of the ultimate good that
condones racist perceptions perpetuating the belief that other,
outside discourses are automatically inferior, raw, and unworthy.

But how is it that intolerant ideologies like these lurk within
texts privileged by so many teachers, even those sincerely concerned with promoting liberal, impartial pedagogies intended to
"empower" students? W. Lawrence Hogue offers one explanation:

> Editors, publishers, critics and reviewers, who function as a
> kind of conduit for many of the dominant society's cultural,
> ideological, and intellectual wishes, impute literature with a
> defined literary experience. In presiding over the dominant
> society's literary tastes, these critics and editors are instrumen-
> tal in keeping certain ideas, social habits, myths, moral con-
> ventions, stereotypes, meanings of literary experience, and
> certain prejudices alive publicly—usually under the pretense
> of not wanting to upset the status quo, or offend the pub-
> lic. . . . They certificate those texts which have been judged to
> speak the discourse better; they repress nonconformist texts,

subjects, and perspectives as being inferior aesthetically for their inability to approximate established criteria—thereby effecting certain silences in literature. In short, they determine what is a "good" or "bad" literary text in accordance with the degree to which it effectively reproduces certain values and codes of the dominant society. The entire mode of literary production is really no more than a branch of the dominant society's social ideologies. ("Literary Production" 34)

This need to package anthologies and publish texts for a fiction-alized audience of generic proportions implies that the audience falling outside this category doesn't warrant our attention, which in turn "coerces writers with non-conformist perspectives and ideologies into writing for the 'hypothesized reader'" (Hogue, "Literary Production" 36). And though writing teachers (like myself) understandably have encouraged students to write for the "hypothetical reader" so that they might shift their gaze beyond the walls of the classroom, such hypothetical ghosts are always of a particular class, dialect, and culture—usually the "college pro-fessor" or, say, readers of the *Atlantic*.

A perspective like this becomes extremely alienating. The very emphasis on writing, for example, automatically eliminates many from the conversation. It's not uncommon for some cultures to harbor negative feelings toward written discourse in general, as for many ethnic groups the most desirable way to communicate is through face to face encounter. Ron and Suzanne Scollon tell of the Athabaskan Indians who had immense difficulty learning to write expository prose because the concept of fictionalization of both audience and writer was diametrically opposed to their need for the immediacy of face to face contact (Scollon and Scollon 48–49, 52–53). Leslie Marmon Silko writes of Pueblo Indian society where written texts were regarded suspiciously as slippery and ingenuine, whereas the preferred means of conveying state-ments of import was always oral (54). And Geneva Smitherman bridges this Native American discursive tendency with that of African Americans:

The black oral tradition links Black American culture with that of other oral "preliterate" people—such as Native

Americans—for whom the spoken word is supreme. The per-
sistence of the African-based oral tradition is such that blacks
tend to place only limited value on the written word, whereas
verbal skills expressed orally rank in high esteem. . . . Blacks
are quick to ridicule "educated fools," people who done gone
to school and read all dem books and still don't know nothin!
They have "book learning" but no "mother wit," knowledge,
but not wisdom. (Naturally, not *all* educated people are considered "educated fools," but if the shoe fits . . .) (76)

But this reluctance to undergo the necessary self-effacement
implicit in writing much essayist prose is antithetical to what
many compositionists consider to epitomize mature, successful
discourse. James Moffett, for example, has made an extensive
argument for highly abstract essayist prose as the culmination of a
writer's prowess, an argument that used to enjoy considerable
influence. Positioning various modes of written discourse on a
hierarchic scale intended to measure authorial control (grocery
lists being less advanced than the diary, which in turn is beneath
the published letter to the editor, etc.), Moffett and other writing
theorists sharing this view assume that the ability to fictionalize
one's audience into mythic, generic proportions, and then produce texts aimed at a mass of hypothetical readers, remains a
writer's highest mark of mastery. Such a conclusion is not so
much false as it is extremely culture-specific; it ignores many oral
cultures where the goal is not to fictionalize anyone, but to successfully interact with a concrete audience in the quickest manner possible—not an abstract dialectic, but one of immediacy
obtained via direct interpersonal performance.

As a result students have access in the classroom to little else
other than the academic dialect, which as some have argued is by
nature a "class dialect, essentially an instrument of domination"
(Sledd 669). It is not the teaching of standard English per se that
is so reprehensible, but the fact that no other dialects are allowed
to coexist alongside the language of institutional power. Alan
Dundes echoes this in the following:

In traditional American education, black students are penal-
ized for not conforming to white linguistic norms—one

recalls such terms as "Non-Standard English" or "culturally deprived." Moreover, the considerable verbal skills that black students do possess are not rewarded—partly because most white school teachers are almost totally unaware that Negro folk speech and verbal art have their own highly developed forms. (353)

When I first came across this passage, I realized Dundes was referring to me: I was one of those white school teachers utterly ignorant of other, equally sophisticated cultural discourses. Discursive tropes like "nommo," orature, signifying, call and response, "the dozens"—rhetorical considerations constituting an essential part of African American discourse—never played any role in my thinking of composition. As I continued to stumble across references to these worlds of discourse I realized that, if one was really serious about teaching within a multicultural framework, ignoring these "outside" worlds of discourse could no longer be possible.

I've tried to familiarize myself with some of the intricacies of African American rhetoric. What follows is not really valuable as any comprehensive overview of black discourse (readers looking for that ought to go straight to the primary sources—works by Smitherman, Baraka, Gates, Baker, Abrahams), but rather a trail of sources and information from which I've expanded my own awareness of discourse theory. Most of this material will be painfully obvious to many readers more aware than I of the depth of cultural discourses beyond those of the English classroom, and so I offer these initial impressions mainly to help underscore my claim that teachers of composition (using myself as an example) ought to be wary of how culturally myopic institutions of higher learning limit our perception of what makes for good discourse.

Négritude and the Black Aesthetic

My entry point into this consideration of African American rhetoric began with an examination into the motivations underlying two recent historical movements of particular significance: négritude and the Black Aesthetic. Négritude, an outgrowth of Haiti's "indigenism" and "négrism" in Cuba (Jahn

214–29), commenced with writers like Léopold Sédar Senghor (from Senegal), Aimé Césaire (Martinique), and Léon Damas (French Guiana). The movement was characterized by a collective desire to utilize language so as to foreground African themes and philosophical perspectives removed from those of traditionally Western orientation: "The aim . . . is to capture the African reality . . . the semantic, rhythmical and thematic achievements . . . as characteristics of a specific philosophy and attitude to the world, the conception of an African style and the unity of an African culture" (Jahn 249). Though controversial in its romantic mythologizing of the African continent (some see proponents of négritude espousing an overly simplistic view of a universal black solidarity, while certain African critics see texts by Senghor and others as Afro-European hybrids because of their reliance upon European, not African, languages [wa Thiong'o 26–27]), négritude warrants attention primarily as a measure of intellectuals who felt the need to express themselves in resistance to oppressive notions of linguistic standardization.[3]

Proponents of négritude give intriguing insights into the psychological matrix that supports writers of African lineage. Kenneth Kaunda argues that definite dissimilarities exist between an African and Western "psychology":[4]

> There is a distinctively African way of looking at things, of problem solving and indeed of thinking—we have our own logic-system which makes sense to us, however confusing it might be to the Westerner. If we were, from my own observation, to try to summarize the difference between African and Western psychology . . . I would say that the Westerner has a problem solving mind whilst the African has a situation experiencing mind. (Quoted in Tembo 193–94)

Léopold Sédar Senghor, one of the main spokespersons for the négritude aesthetic, painted a similar distinction between Euro-American and African thought processes. Although dichotomies like these can veer toward the prescriptive, what makes Senghor's work of value is recognizing his need to distance himself from cultural paradigms that silence rather than encourage diversely interethnic expression. Senghor identifies the African as fundamentally different from the Westerner in that the latter is typified by a pervasively analytical and objective orientation, one that interprets the world as so much material to be used, manipulated, and processed. The African's philosophical acclimation, he claims, differs in that one immediately absorbs objects and situations the moment they are perceived (echoes here of William Carlos Williams's credo "no ideas but in things" and other modernist workings drawn from the imagist movement). Senghor's sense of African philosophy stems in part from the research of German anthropologist Leo Frobenius, for whom the African's "intuitive" awareness of the universe contrasted sharply with the Westerner's "mechanistic" mindset—that is, a heightened, holistically spiritual emphasis on all lived experience as inseparably woven from the same cloth versus an awareness of the world as so many discrete, unlinked phenomena. Against the objective analysis of discrete events from a neutral distance typical in Western thinking, thinkers like Senghor, Kaunda, and Frobenius posit a direct and total encompassing of the world: immediate, spiritual inclusion within one's environment via any and all sensory perception, where the mundane and the habitual have profound implications.

Janheinz Jahn further distinguishes between Western and African thought:

> In African thinking, the universe consists of a network of living forces . . . all . . . related to each other and in continuous interaction. The universe is a unity, in which each part depends on the others, and no part is changeless. If you take possession of a part of a thing, you thereby participate in its life force. . . . For Europeans, force is an attribute: a being *has* force. In African thinking, force *is* being, being *is* force, a physical-spiritual energy and potency. The totality of all these living forces is NTU, Being . . . which, however, is never conceived of as separable from its manifestations. In NTU, the cosmic universal force, all single forces are tied together. (252)

A paramount concern for writers affiliated with négritude was to make this perceptual leap in their work: "In connection with this view of the world," writes Jahn, "the African writer has a very important function: he is word-magician and announcer, Africa's spokesman, sponsor and interpreter to the outside world, Africa's educator within" (250).

Négritude, though, has its share of critics, particularly for its tendency to romanticize the continent. Amiri Baraka, calling it a "bourgeois nationalist mystique," criticizes négritude's tendency to reduce all the inhabitants of an immense continent into some peculiar race bound by a mystical, genetic essence of shared cultural values. "Africa's cultural values when?" he challenges; "During primitive communalism, slavery, feudalism, or capitalism? During ancient Egypt? In Songhai, enslaved by colonialism, or up under the well-polished fingernails of black neocolonialism?" (288) Another obvious problem with négritude is its essentialism, forcing us to choose between viewing the world through Western or African eyes, permitting little room for rapprochement. In his essay "The Concept of African Personality," Mwizenge S. Tembo makes the Afrocentric position more inclusive of Western readers by advocating a stance whereby both extremes may exist in harmony:

> Even the physical constitution of the African predisposes him to respond to the external world in such a way that it becomes an engulfing experience in which the whole of the self is involved, and, by implication, no distinction is made between the physical and psychic self on the one hand and the external natural environment on the other. . . . Most Americans, it seems, cannot perceive a social experience such as a beautiful sunset, a meal, or the like unless they mention in advance that it is beautiful, nice, or looks good. It seems essential and an integral part of the experience to know and mention that one is experiencing enjoyment before he can perceive the enjoyment of ecstasy inherent in nature. My argument . . . is not that one or the other is better but that both should be regarded as genuine and legitimate perceptions of the social and natural environment. (200)

Likewise, when Addison Gayle in his study *The Black Aesthetic* proclaims that the black aesthetic "is a corrective—a means of helping black people out of the polluted mainstream of Americanism, and offering logical, reasoned arguments as to why he should not desire to join the ranks of a Norman Mailer or a

William Styron" (xxii), his argument is valuable not so much in its contempt for popular white novelists but its attack against racist educational institutions seeking to motivate students to write in specific traditions carefully selected and screened for them, instead of providing multiethnic traditions and ideologies reflecting a spread of competing cultural philosophies.

Writers affiliated with the Black Aesthetic movement have sculpted a hodgepodge of additional arguments expanding on the premises of négritude, among them the nationalist propaganda of the young Clarence Major, separatist and Pan-Africanist ideologies like those of Haki Madhubuti and Molefi Kete Asante, what Houston A. Baker, Jr., calls the "romantic Marxism" of Amiri Baraka and the early Stokely Carmichael, and more recent calls for experimentalist nonconformity by writers like Ishmael Reed and the later Clarence Major. It's this latter aspect, I think, that holds the most potential for all writers, black or otherwise. Ishmael Reed's call for "artistic guerilla warfare" by "mystical detectives about to make an arrest," for example, can be seen as the tone for the type of artistic inquiry necessary for fostering pedagogies of constructive resistance—serious critical questioning of the criteria that distinguish between rhetorics assumed as normative and those deemed dispensable. Look at Reed's agenda in following passage:

> I think the people we want to aim our questioning toward are those who supply the nation with its mind, tutor its mind, develop and cultivate its mind, and these are the people involved in culture. They are responsible for the national mind and they've done very bad things with their propaganda and racism. Think of all the vehemence and nasty remarks they aimed at the Black Studies Programs, somebody like William Buckley, that Christian fanatic, saying that Bach is worth more than all the Black Studies Programs in the world. He sees the conflict as being between the barbarians and the Christians. And, you know, I'm glad I'm on the side of the barbarians. So this is what we want: to sabotage history. They won't know whether we're serious or whether we are writing fiction. . . . Always keep them guessing. That'll bug them, probably drive them up the walls. (O'brien 179)

Inventive monkeywrenching like this (which has direct roots to African American tropes such as signifying and use of a double-voiced dialectic, discussed later on) is not a phenomenon unique to Reed's work, but indicative on a greater scale of African American vernacular in general. For example, it's evident in the powerful contemporary medium of rap. At its best, rap music (modern day versions of the African American "talking book") provides a nexus for the spontaneous, collaborative energies one finds running through so much African American discourse. As Houston Baker writes, it's this constant revamping of the vernacular that demonstrates the continuum of an Afrocentric urge, "the kind of holistic, cultural-anthropological approach implicit in the work of . . . spokesmen for the Black Aesthetic," "an interdisciplinary orientation and a tropologically active imagination— an imagination that ceaselessly compels the analyst to introduce tropes that affectively disrupt familiar conceptual determinations" (Baker, *Blues* 109–10). Although négritude and the Black Aesthetic are zones of discourse arguably more mythical than culture-specific in nature, it's exactly this mythic nature that permits such a wealth of communicative strategies to converge within a shared context: a continual remaking of communal vocabularies and grammars in opposition to standard English. "Without the belief in a common cultural heritage black writers would struggle fitfully for meaning and their literary community would break up into isolated individuals with artistic methods resembling private codes rather than communally raised songs. . . . Black artists have long recognized that any culture which exists as a self-communing entity must possess a mythology of some kind" (Benston, "Ellison, Baraka" 334).

Orature, Nommo, Call and Response

Circulating within much of this tradition is a profound attachment to collaborative oral communication. Many Eurocentric models of oral persuasion tend to favor succinct, linear argumentation, but an African American perspective could place equal or higher emphasis on rhythm, rhyme, repetition, alliteration, vocal inflection and modulation, and the manipulation of pitch, as well as what Smitherman calls "intonational contouring," "talk-singing," and "narrative sequencing," and other "tonal semantics" (Smitherman reminds us that West African languages are "tone languages," where speakers "rely on the tone with which they pronounce syllables, sounds, and words to convey their meaning" [135]). The total speech act, essentially, as oral artistry. More than just a critical tool for negotiation and persuasion, African discourse is almost always valued as an art medium, a stage for creative and spiritual expression, and less as a mechanics for creating static discourse-objects. ("Participation" and "communion," Sunday Anozie reminds us, are terms ethnologists have repeatedly used to describe black discourse [91].)

This emphasis on oral communicative power is what Molefi Kete Asante refers to not as oratory, which would refer to the eloquence of intellectual speech and debate, but "orature," beneath which is the driving force of *nommo* (*Afrocentric Idea* 83–86). Asante speaks of a "vocal-expressive modality" infiltrating and predominating the entire African world, in both contemporary and past cultures. Dance, music, and speech, not scribal discourse, are the primary measures of communication. Asante's argument is that the influence of classical rhetoricians like Aristotle, Cicero, and Quintilian, whose work shapes so much of the often unexamined philosophies operative in the writing classroom (despite the irony that such classical prescriptions were often intended more for oratory than for written texts), are simply inappropriate as models and standards to which multiethnic student communities must always unquestioningly adhere.

For example, in Western, classical rhetorical theory one is unlikely to find "magic" discussed as a fundamental component of the speech act, in contrast to African discourse, where language was not necessarily "a mere string of words. It had a suggestive power well beyond the immediate and lexical meaning. Our appreciation of the suggestive magical power of language was reinforced by the games we played with words through riddles, proverbs, transpositions of syllables, or through nonsensical but musically arranged words" (wa Thiong'o 11). *Nommo*—described as both "word magic" (Jahn 158) and the source of an African's "life-force" (172)—can be witnessed in a number of African American rhetorical tropes, particularly the practice of call and response. Having its origins in frequent rites, both public and sacred, performed within a tribal context (perhaps in the form of a shaman uttering a call to which others respond, or in the coded messages transferred back and forth between drummers at different locations), call and response is a distinctly African attribute that carried over most notably into slave spirituals and the blues. Both forms accentuate repetition as well as invocation of some higher force through a consistent "statement-response" structure, just as both the spiritual and the blues are sites for this means of expression—the spiritual from a nonsecular stance, the blues as a first-person monologue (Jahn 160, 166ff.). "Cutting"—that is, skipping back to names and refrains we've already heard—is a major ingredient here: naming not as mere recitation, but the actual spoken evocation of the people, emotions, and settings called forth; naming as nothing less than the actual *making* of the subject invoked. *Nommo* is when the speaker/singer/drummer/preacher seeks to go beyond interpretation and into a collaborative state of linguistic construction.

Call and response is an essential agent of other social arenas like church and the movie theater. Consider the difference between group dialogue in African American churches and that of non-charismatic white congregations. While many black worship services are sites for extemporaneous participation—the preacher serving as catalyst for expression within the entire group[5]—non-black services and masses might be more apt to feature unison prayer and communion, the priest often occupying a position hegemonically distant from the congregation, a leader and conductor of a quieter performance demanding a different kind of propriety. Roger D. Abrahams explains this by claiming that there is a greater degree of "psychic distance" between performer and audience within standard English than with blacks, who often "expect a high degree of complementary audience participation in answer to their efforts" (9).[6] This communal participation is essential for the magic of *nommo* to weave its effect. "To help itself, the community resorts to magic, mobilizes all spiritual forces, cites precedents, identifies with them, and exacts a full life for itself in communal ecstasy. Only the community can use these religious resources, whereas the Christian mystical experiences come only to individuals. To sing a Spiritual as solo would be absurd" (Jahn 161).

Scholars of African American rhetoric and communication also point to the movie theater as a social gathering place where Eurocentric and African American behaviors are at opposite poles. A film shown in a black neighborhood can be a noisy event because African Americans, Abrahams argues, are far more prone to collectively "talk back" to the screen. Asante echoes this when when he claims African Americans viewing a movie are participating in the events of that movie: far from passive viewers contemplating a remote narrative, the members of the theater confirm their own presence through vocal collaboration. Thus when an actor or actress is "being seen" on the movie screen, the "audience" is being seen too (*Afrocentric Idea* 67).

When we consider the tremendously interactive nature of African American discourse, "in which the subject and object are simultaneously the watcher and the watched, the agent and the acted upon" (Anozie 91), it becomes clear how insensitive many pedagogies are to African American principles of discourse; expecting ethnic students to accept and appreciate an educational system that privileges professorial lecturing over communal dialogue is to remain oblivious to the need for communal participation in such cultures. The professor who feels she is orchestrating a multicultural classroom atmosphere by lecturing a passive audience about Zora Neale Hurston's linguistic artistry could be seen as performing an unwitting act of cultural insensitivity; that is, to observe and analyze African American discourse in the clinical format of a traditional (Western) lecture is to forbid the dialogic interplay so vital to various cultural discourses. To teach works by black authors while permitting students to write of their experiences only within the rhetorical traditions of a fundamentally white academy not only misses the point of multicultural education, but could be interpreted as a cultural slap in the face.

Signifying, Double-Voiced Dialectic, Unnaming, and the Rhythmic Limp

The most multifaceted of African American rhetorical tropes is the distinctly African form of signifying—what Richard Abrahams has described as a "technique of indirect argument or persuasion," "a language of implication" used "to imply, goad, beg, boast, by indirect verbal or gestural means." Recently an obvious form of signifying has been heard in rap, the modern day version of "the dozens." A specifically African American form of verbal dueling where insights, barbs, and put-downs are directed toward an adversary within a public performative context, "the dozens"—a phrase now archaic and more recently replaced by terms like "sounding," "ranking," "bugging," and "snapping"—may be the most widely known form of signification, the term stemming from an eighteenth-century meaning of the verb *dozen*, which meant "to stun, stupefy, daze" (Gates, *Signifying Monkey* 71). Often quite ribald in its humor, the effectiveness of this oral sparring is not necessarily determined by the logical coherence of the argument, but more by the ability of the participant to quickly assemble a comeback, thereby gaining respect and prestige from the speedy manipulation of language. In general, signifying can

> mean any number of things . . . it certainly refers to the trickster's ability to talk with great innuendo, to carp, cajole, needle, and lie. It can mean in other instances the propensity to talk around a subject, never quite coming to the point. It can mean making fun of a person or situation. Also it can denote speaking with the hands and eyes, and in this respect encompasses a whole complex of expressions and gestures. Thus it is signifying to stir up a fight between neighbors by telling stories; it is signifying to make fun of a policeman by parodying his motions behind his back; it is signifying to ask for a piece of cake by saying, "my brother needs a piece of cake." (Abrahams, *Deep Down* 51–52)

Claudia Mitchell-Kernan expands on this by describing signification as not simply a rhetorical strategy but a language specialization indigenous to the entire black community:

> The black concept of signifying incorporates essentially a folk notion that dictionary entries for words are not always sufficient for interpreting meanings or messages, or that meaning goes beyond such interpretations. Complimentary remarks may be delivered in a left-handed fashion. A partic-

ular utterance may be an insult in one context and not another. What pretends to be informative may intend to be persuasive. The hearer is thus constrained to attend to all potential meaning carrying symbolic systems in speech events—the total universe of discourse. (314)

This distrust for institutionalized definitions can be witnessed in the well-known African American practice of continually changing and reshaping the vernacular, especially in the practice of reverse definitions: "bad" meaning superlative, "stupid" meaning innovative, a "freak" meaning a sexually liberated woman, etc. Though it is difficult to say if this linguistic reversal has its origins in slavery, when it was not only illegal for blacks to learn how to read or write but often forbidden (reinforced with torture) to communicate openly and extensively for much more than labor-specific purposes, signifying has obvious parallels with the brilliant communicative encodings found in slave culture. African American vernacular differs fundamentally from Western, academic discourse in that slaves were forced to develop a highly sophisticated language self-consciously intended to convey multiple messages—that is, to preserve the black community through inside jokes, advice, and support, while on the outside appearing to be not much more than nonsensical, primitive utterances.[7]

In *The Signifying Monkey* Gates traces the roots of signification not only to the ingenious monkey of African American folklore, but further back to Esu-Elegbara, the Yoruba deity depicted as having two mouths, the perfect symbol for what many linguists and African American literary theorists have described as a "double-voiced dialectic." The bidialectical nature of black vernacular indicates an understanding of both the dominating culture's language of institutional authority and one's own native, local dialect. Unfortunately, for the ethnic student to gain respectability in academic and professional circles, assimilation and indoctrination into the language of the academy becomes an unavoidable prerequisite. And though there's obviously nothing innately improper about standard English—*no* language system is necessarily more or less fertile for creative invention than any other—this imposed order of discourse creates confusion, antipathy, even hatred among those caught in the middle. Students aren't so

naive as to fail to recognize the power associated with being fluent in academic discourse, regardless of whether or not they can
speak the code. But at the same time they realize the discourse
they feel most comfortable with—that they, their friends and
families use and respect—isn't permitted in most classrooms,
thereby inferring that they themselves won't be respected until
they too adopt the academic voice. Because of these campaigns of
"de-creolization" (to use Smitherman's term), people quickly
learn to become double-voiced. The academy's problem is that it
fails to recognize the richness of such multivocality as it continues to stratify discourse according to culture, ethnicity, and class.
All of which resulted in what W. E. B. DuBois called a "double-
consciousness," a love-hate relationship with the dominating discourse—respect for what it can bring, disgust for its need to
obliterate alternative voices. Or what Smitherman calls the
"push-pull syndrome," the push toward Americanization coupled
with a pull back toward the African dynamic (10). A complex
sense of unfriendly competition between opposing discourse
modalities takes shape, making environments ripe for writers like
Michelle Cliff who, after realizing that in the course of writing
her dissertation the institution had successfully "tamed" her
dialect, rebelled by constructing a new kind of prose:

> To write as a complete Caribbean woman, or man . . .
> demands of us retracing the African part of ourselves,
> reclaiming as our own, and as our subject, a history sunk
> under the sea. . . . It means finding the art forms of . . . our
> ancestors and speaking in the *patois* forbidden us. . . . It
> means . . . mixing in the forms taught us by the oppressor,
> undermining his language and co-opting his style, and turn-
> ing it to our purpose. ("A Journey" 59)

Others, like Smitherman (*Talkin and Testifyin*), June Jordan (*On
Call: Political Essays*), and Verta Mae Smart-Grosvenor ("The
Kitchen Crisis"), have reclaimed the language in similar ways, by
combining black dialect and "standard" English within the same
textual space.

When members of a community, failing to see themselves represented in the language of dominant communities, seek to
undermine the oppressive conditions of that authorial discourse

by subverting it, a rebellion against the linguistic features embodying the politics of domination is taking place. Kimberly W. Benston calls this "unnaming":

> An act of radical unnaming sees all labels formulated by the master society ("they") as enslaving fictions, and implies further that no true black nation, no truly named black self, emerged from reconstructed post-bellum America. . . . Those who lost their fathers, mothers, priests and gods over the ocean have acquired a painful linguistic marginalia. . . . Former slaves are not easily turned into self-fashioning revolutionaries, for in what 'language' . . . except the master's would that demiurgic act shape them? ("I Yam What I Am" 151, 152)

This unnaming is rendered all the more graphic when we recall that the extremely important African practice of calling forth loas and orishas with sacred drumwork and dance was denied by Protestant slaveowners. To compensate for this, African Americans replaced drumming and dancing with an "inner dance," a mixture of swaying, hand clapping, foot stomping, shouts, unique cadences, slurring of words, paraphrases, and fluctuations in pitch, timbre, and intonation. African Americans continued to respond to this imposed unnaming by forming hybrid discourses that had no parallel in the language of white America. Houston Baker talks about this polyvocality of African American dialect in his insightful study of the blues as a primary source for African American experience. Characterized by the synthesis of diverse elements, Baker describes the origin of the blues in "work songs, group seculars, field hollers, sacred harmonies, proverbial wisdom, folk philosophy, political commentary, ribald humor, elegiac lament . . . an amalgam that seems always to have been in motion in America—always becoming, shaping, transforming, displacing the peculiar experience of Africans in the New World" (*Blues* 16).

But for me one of the most intriguing components of African American discourse is the aesthetic stagger, an intentional hesitation woven throughout the written, spoken, or musical text— what Nathaniel Mackey calls the phantom limb or fractured foot found in the discourse of African American poets, novelists, and jazz musicians, whose contrapuntal syncopation conveys "a rhythmic digestion of dislocation" (100), a "frustration with and questioning of given articulacies, permissible ways of making sense" (109). When force-fed a discourse where symmetrical clarity, romantic lyricism, and propriety were often assumed to be natural components of any well-bred person's speech, African Americans began to carve their own resisting signatures into the language by turning imbalance, asymmetry, and limping disruptions into measurements of aesthetic and intellectual power. This lilting stutter can be found as far back as the "lame blues" (Jahn 171), up to the "stammering articulation" of James Baldwin (Major 16), and even in the character of Smiley in Spike Lee's film *Do the Right Thing*.

What Mackey calls the "rhythmic limp" can be traced back to the rhythmic complexity of African music and its contemporary manifestations in contemporary jazz. Richard Waterman speaks of Africans having a "metronome sense" (cited in Chernoff 49–51, 96–97), an inner clock that maintains a central beat or rhythmic core, thereby allowing the drummer or dancer to vary the rhythm and introduce unexpected strains that might, to an untrained listener, appear to come from nowhere (parallels here with John Coltrane's "sheets of sound"), even though the musicians and performers are acutely aware of the underlying primary rhythms. "We can say that the [African] musicians play 'around' the beat, or that they play on the off-beat, but actually it is precisely the ability to identify the beat that enables someone to appreciate the music. We begin to "understand" African music by being able to maintain, in our minds or our bodies, an additional rhythm to the ones we hear" (Chernoff 49).

Unlike my musical education, where my high school music teacher insisted that we tap out a strict (although quiet) beat with our foot so we wouldn't deviate from the score that had been chosen for us—basically, teaching us to mimic machines— "some teachers of African music discourage students from tapping their feet because often the students tend to find a main pulse that eliminates the real rhythmic tension and conflict in the music. What the African drum teachers are afraid of is that their students are approaching the music by marking time from their own beats instead of from a beat which serves as their unsounded beat" (Chernoff 51). And while jazz (and by this I mean in particular what has at various times been called "New Jazz," the "New Thing," "Black Jazz," or "Black Art Music"—recent manifestations of the "jes' grew" discussed throughout Ishmael Reed's *Mumbo Jumbo* and which really broke loose in the sixties and seventies with the music of John Coltrane, Ornette Coleman, Archie Shepp, Pharaoh Sanders, Sunny Murray, Sun Ra, Cecil Taylor, etc.) is by no means an African music form, it does embody major elements of African discourse; its technicians do indeed possess this "metronome sense" where they focus on maintaining multiple, interwoven rhythmic relationships rather than spelling out a regimented beat:

> [Ornette] Coleman has said that one of the basic ideas in his music is to encourage the improvisor to be freer, and not obey a pre-conceived chord-pattern according to set ideas of "proper" harmony and tonality: *"Let's try to play the music and not the background."* However, his point is basically emotional and aesthetic, not technical. The music should be a direct and immediate *"expressing our minds and our emotions rather than being a background for emotion."* (M. Williams)

African Music, African American Discourse

The connection between music and discourse here is not insignificant; ties between African music and contemporary African American communication must be explored if we're to have any grasp of the workings of this discourse. Whereas European classical music—and ultimately classical rhetoric—developed into an aesthetics of organized and controlled complex harmony, African music—which *is* African discourse—is rooted within an organic concern for an aesthetics of *rhythmic* complexity.[8] In fact, the more we investigate African and African American music systems, the closer we come to understanding just how incompatible European discourse is with African, a point spelled out in the following passage from James Lincoln Collier's *The Making of Jazz*:

> For example, in European music a standard timbre is aimed for—that is, there is an ideal trumpet or violin sound that

the player, within narrow limits, aims for. In jazz, timbre is highly personal and varies not only from player to player but from moment to moment in a given passage for expressive purposes, just as European players swell or diminish a note to add feeling. In European music, each note has a fixed pitch (some slight variation is permitted the leading tone) that can be measured by a machine. In jazz, pitch is flexible to a considerable degree, and in fact in some types of jazz certain notes are invariably and deliberately played "out of tune" by European standards. European music, at least in its standard form, is built on the distinction between major and minor modes. The blues, a major building block in jazz, is neither major nor minor; it exists in a different mode altogether. In European music the ground beat is implicit in the melody itself; you can easily "tap your foot to the beat." In jazz the ground beat is deliberately avoided in the melody and must be established by some sort of separate rhythm section. Obviously, jazz operates on principles of its own; it simply cannot be understood from a European vantage point. (5)

Such fundamental differences need to be explored not only for the insight they give into cross-cultural rhetorics, but also because of the repercussions they have for our understanding of the nature of criticism itself. Though this isn't the place to enter into a discussion of the incompatibilities between academic literary theory and its possible African equivalent (that is, the role of ongoing communal criticism within African music), the distinction should be noted. John Miller Chernoff helps outline the discrepancies in his significant work *African Rhythm and African Sensibility*:

The fact that music plays such an integral role in African life means that if comparatively many people are artistic participants, many are also what we might call "informal" critics. Indeed, the absence of scholastic criticism is perhaps due in part to the fact that most people are too actively involved discussing what is going on to allow any specialist to tell them what to appreciate. There will be any number of complementary perspectives available at a musical event, and we may as well simply observe the "scene" as an index to musical quality: if someone executes an especially wonderful dance step and everybody watching smiles or cheers, we can be sure that the music has also reached a high point.

The essential criteria for distinguishing excellence in African music are . . . as much ethical as aesthetic. Yet African music does not become the subject of abstract and systematic discussions about morality and ethics, and people do not become analytical about the fundamental social themes displayed in their music: the point is to participate in the appropriate way. If the music is good, people listen, dance, and enjoy themselves. If it is bad, they will try to correct it in whatever way they can, perhaps by making fun of a vain dancer or anyone present with a bad attitude, perhaps by offering suggestions or encouragement to the musicians, perhaps by buying some beer, or perhaps, if their mood is hopeless, by being sensible enough to leave the place. . . . Since an African musical performance is so much a part of its social setting, we can recognize African critical standards by what happens in the situation itself. In such a context, everything one does becomes an act of "criticism": people express their opinions by participating. They make a contribution to the success of the occasion, and they behave with the understanding that what they do is an act of artistic participation as well. (92)

So whereas in the Western tradition we've grown accustomed to the idea of the academic and artistic "critic" who interprets literature, music, film, and art, this concept is glaringly absent in African cultures. People are too busy participating within the composition of the communal artistic discourse—too busy "enjoying themselves," really—to be bothered with investing some professional critic with the authority to interpret the artistic text for them. (Thus, for those literary theorists most concerned with viewing their world through a "multicultural" lens informed by African sensibilities, one of the quickest ways to achieve this end might be to abandon theory altogether and pick up an instrument! Or at least cancel those subscriptions to *PMLA* and *Diacritics*, and go out and buy some James Brown CDs.)

It can't be overemphasized how integral music and dance are to African rhetoric, and consequently its influence on contemporary African American discourse. As Chernoff reminds us,

> There are very few important things which happen [in African culture] without music, and the range and diversity of specific kinds of music can astound a Westerner. Ashanti children sing special songs to cure a bedwetter; in the Republic of Benin there are special songs sung when a child cuts its first teeth; among the Hausas of Nigeria, young people pay musicians to compose songs to help them court lovers or insult rivals; men working in a field may consider it essential to appoint some of their number to work by making music instead of putting their hands to the hoe; among the Hutus, men paddling a canoe will sing a different song depending on whether they are going with or against the current. . . .
>
> Moreover, as a group activity, music is a means for tradition itself to be organized and communicated. In many African tribes, different social groups have rights and privileges with respect to different types of songs. People organize themselves into musical associations and clubs. In the cities these groups are important not only as embodiments of tribal loyalties and continuities but often as organizations for political and economic actions; in the villages, creative effort in musical competitions becomes a way of discriminating status, obligations, and identity. (34)

Music, in fact, in African discourse, *is* language, not an accompaniment, a fact most obvious in the talking drums used throughout different African tribes. Here drummers do not send the African equivalent of Morse code to one another but literally recreate their spoken language, a feat made possible because so many African languages are tonal, where it is the pitch that creates meaning ("For example, the Yoruba word *oko* means 'husband' if both syllables are pitched the same, 'hoe' if the first syllable is lower than the second, 'canoe' if the second is lower, and 'spear' if both are low" [Collier 8]), thus lending itself to duplication by skilled drummers.

Plus, we must also keep in mind that any discussion of African music is also directly involved with the rhetoric of African dance, since "African music, with few exceptions, is to be regarded as music for the dance, although the 'dance' involved may be entirely a mental one" (Richard Waterman, quoted in Chernoff 50). Since, with the exception of talking drums, a great deal of African drumwork is not intended to convey any literal "meaning" save that of its rhythmic force,[9] the dancer is also the music, not simply because she might wear items that contribute to the sound (gourds, feathers, strings of cowrie shells), but because her movement is a physical launching—a "writing"—of those rhythmic vectors and counterforces into space.

For the Westerner, music, dance, and rhetoric occupy separate realms of activity. (Even a lot of dancing in Western culture exists as an isolated "text," in that the motions of the dance are often enacted without any overt connection to the music.)[10] African discourse, on the other hand, depends upon the tight interaction of oral, musical, and physical performance—a chain of discursive rhythmic modalities woven into a conglomerate of communal interaction. Music, within which coexist dancing, chanting, and oftentimes spiritual possession, is nothing less than the "social glue" of the African community (Collier 8), and as such must be studied as an integral component of African discourse, within which we find major threads informing contemporary African American communication. (As such, the African equivalent to functional illiteracy might not be someone who couldn't read or write, but someone *rhythmically* illiterate. While rhythmical illiteracy is rampant among non-African Americans, whether they can read or not, one might have difficulty imagining scores of Africans who lack the ability to sense and transfer rhythmic energies through performative discourse.)

In his essay "Literature as an Institution: The View from 1980," Leslie Fiedler lashes out at the academic homogenization of "the melting pot ideal: the instant WASPification and bourgeoisification of all Americans, whatever their class or ethnic origin" (81). Summarizing the state of English studies, Fiedler claims that "freshman comp has once more been openly revealed as being what it never ceased covertly to be: a last desperate attempt to impose on our multilingual, multidialectical population a single correct Anglo-American dialect, brainwashing us out of our various mother tongues—the demotic linguistic codes of home, street, and school yard" (82).

One step toward addressing Fiedler's criticism—still valid more than a decade later—requires a continued attempt to understand why other cultures meet Euro-American traditions and methodologies with resistance. W. Lawrence Hogue provides one explanation in *Discourse and the Other*, telling how writers like Ishmael Reed and Clarence Major had to negotiate the implicit correlations between the "dominant generic techniques" of standard academic discourse and the sociopolitical constraints, unstated or otherwise, that inform those techniques.

> They realized that the novel form serves as a vehicle for the winning and shaping of the consent of the ideological apparatus. Therefore, in their attempts to name other kinds of intelligences—Afro-American prediscursive and presystematic developments . . . these writers first had to defamiliarize the "naturalness" of established genres and languages by violating, breaking with, parodying, or playing on those conventions. (57)

Unfortunately, as such writers seek innovative and unconventional avenues of expression, their works run the risk of being tokenized, misrepresented, and ignored by the academy. "Seeking to control, sum up, or categorize the black world in phrases drawn from their own peculiar cultural discourse," Baker writes, white American critics "have seldom learned how to converse with the natives of black American culture. . . . They have failed to enlarge the American universe of discourse" (*Journey Back* 163).

And so what this brings us to is the necessity to develop pedagogies of negotiation, not censure. Ron and Suzanne Scollon offer an intriguing means of implementing this need for negotiation in a study highlighting the difficulties encountered when speakers of Athabaskan-English clash with Alaskan and northern Canadian educational systems founded on Standard English. The conflict is a classic one: oral cultures privileging face to face dialectic above "talking like a book" (52) clashing with mainstream educational policies preferring the fictionalization of the writer over the sophistication of immediate conversation; orality and oral culture meet literacy and essayist culture. A situation where, unless we learn how to teach understanding and appreciation for both sides of the spectrum, one version will always dominate, causing alienation and anger on one side, ignorance and intolerance on the other.

The answer, the Scollons argue, is to encourage cohabitation rather than appropriation for the sake of commonality: community among *un*equals, who are equal in a shared frame. The key to this pluralistic respect is what they call "deference politeness," not to be confused with "solidarity politeness." Basically solidarity politeness would be naive liberalism, the attempt to blend different communities by making each more like the other, thereby homogenizing "marginal" cultures as the scales are tipped in favor of the dominant community's goals and biases. Deference politeness, on the other hand, would try to avoid situations where one culture could exert more strength over another by making "distance, respect, and nonimposition" core requirements of any pedagogy:

> We must assume cultural, ethnic, and communicative pluralism as the only solution that will produce overall resilience of the communicative system. Difference and the resulting distance are essential for system stability. Our recommendation then is that deference politeness be cultivated in all cross-system communication no matter what the internal properties of the respective systems are. Only by showing a profound and sincere respect for communicative differences can the overall system gain stability. (201–02)

The concern echoes Geneva Smitherman's, when she insists that

> white students [must] learn the fundamentals of black communication [for] such a learning experience, if properly organized, will not only teach them to be able to understand and communicate with blacks, but in the process they will be turned on to other linguistic-cultural minorities within America. Such a perspective will go a long way toward retarding linguistic-cultural chauvinism, which is surely the greatest impediment to world citizenship. (235)

And yet, despite the rational logic behind these arguments, the seemingly genteel ring to a term like "deference politeness," implementing pedagogies of such pluralism requires an effort of substantial revision. How, exactly, might we generate change?

Later on I'll address some pragmatic modifications teachers might make in the design of the writing class; for now, I offer these few overarching possibilities for action. For one thing, scholars and teachers concerned with issues of literacy, composition studies, and the instruction of writing must acknowledge that alternative rhetorics do indeed exist; that these are intricately sophisticated modes of serious adult communication thriving, despite their lack of representation in academe, in our increasingly multiethnic national community. Let's admit it—it's embarrassing to attend the Conference on College Composition and Communication and hear thousands of white, middle-class theorists and teachers talking about "the universe of discourse." Whose universe? There is nothing universal about the popular contemporary debate between classical or current-traditional philosophies of composition and liberal expressionist, process-oriented pedagogies—a discussion distressingly narrow because both extremes of the polarity fail to consider a host of oppositional philosophies absent in the professional dialogue.

Teachers can begin by investigating more than non-Eurocentric literatures, and begin joining theorists like Smitherman, Abrahams, Chernoff, Asante, Baker, Gates, and others in studying the ramifications of African American and other cultural discourses. African American scholars have long understood the value—the necessity—of working both within and outside the academy: learning the academic grammar, but also keeping alive the ties with African American oral discourse. The rest of us would do well to match this versatility. Graduate students in composition, rhetoric, and literature could begin by writing dissertations on cultural discourses ignored within the field; scholars can write more articles and manuscripts that introduce alternative literacies to their colleagues. Numerous questions can be raised and wrestled with, like: what are some of the more pervasive rhetorical workings identifiable with Native American, Latino, and Asian cultures? what additional sophisticated rhetorics exist outside academic conventions? how do these complement and conflict with Western means of constructing arguments? how might genuinely cross-cultural rhetorics look, sound, read? how to pool various strategies for teaching these new modes of oral and performative composing?

Interestingly enough, such critical pursuit would have close parallels with the growing study of "contrastive rhetoric," where educators concerned with teaching English to English as a second language (ESL) and English as a foreign language (EFL) students do so by first learning the mechanics of various non-Western, nonacademic grammars. The goal of contrastive rhetoric is to investigate principles of composition used by other cultures so that we may thus isolate their rhetorical differences in order to make them more effective users of standard English. While this can be a valuable strategy where the instruction of non-Western students deficient in standard English is concerned, what I'm advocating is a sort of contrastive rhetoric in reverse: teaching students more or less proficient in English how to begin thinking and writing from perspectives found in other cultures. For example, where a primary (and, in my eyes, objectionable) goal for a scholar of contrastive rhetoric like Alan Purves is to teach students "the language of national literacy" and "develop language loyalty" (32), understanding contrastive rhetorics needn't push us toward such nationalist, monistic ends. One way to teach literatures, philosophies, and histories of other non-Western cultures would be to allow students to compose writings or oral performances in accordance with the precepts of those cultural values. The student of Japanese literature or culture, for example, might write essays using the *ki-sho-ten-ketsu* form, an interesting Japanese mode of expository writing where an otherwise standard linear-hierarchical essay form is made unique by the unexpected intrusion of a tangential aside approximately three-fourths into the work (Hinds 188). Or students studying Arabic cultures might compose essays utilizing the Arabic practice of incorporating intense repetition and accumulative paraphrasing into the text (Johnstone Koch 48). (Or, recognizing the logic behind the often cyclical, nonlinear understanding of temporality adopted by certain [Asian] Indians lends yet another means of composing the world for Western students unfamiliar with this "spiral" perspective.)

All of this is really about so much more than simply presenting students with "multicultural" classrooms. In many respects the issue at hand is one of survival. "To deny a people a right to determine their own cultural tradition is a type of genocide," writes David Mura (142), a Japanese American whose sense of alienation at the hands of a Eurocentric education in America is as strong as that felt by the South African students spoken of earlier by Dennis Brutus. "What I am now trying to do," states Mura,

> in both my writing and my life is to replace self-hatred and self-negation with anger and grief over my lost selves, over the ways my cultural heritage has been denied to me . . . over the ways my education and the values of European culture have denied that other cultures exist. I know more about Europe at the time when my grandfather came to America than I know about Meiji Japan. I know Shakespeare and Donne, Sophocles and Homer better than I know Zeami, Basho or Lady Murasaki. This is not to say I regret what I know, but I do regret what I don't know. (143)

In so many ways we perpetuate the nearsightedness of educational systems fundamentally ethnocentric in design. We do this by failing to respect, and validate, and experience, not only literatures from so many overlooked cultures but their rhetorics as well. And so Japanese Americans like Mura see themselves as victims of cultural genocide. Jamaicans like Michelle Cliff describe themselves as living fragmented lives, pulled simultaneously in conflicting directions ("I received the message of anglocentrism, of white supremacy, and I internalized it" ["A Journey" 158]). Black Americans "run the risk of becoming schizophrenic" in our country's educational systems (Baldwin 326). It even means whites like myself come to see themselves as ambiguously "American," not European Americans. (I once asked my grandmother what we were; she answered, "Pennsylvanian." In a way she's not too far off the mark: I know embarrassingly little of my Welsh, Irish, Dutch, and French—I think—ancestry.)

Actually, a pedagogy intent on applauding cultural diversity would find African American rhetoric a splendid example of a discourse that values the integration of multifarious influences and traditions: the highly performative, musical, improvisational, penetratingly sharp and mirthful essence of black vernacular could serve as an excellent model for a multiculturally informed, cross-disciplinary philosophy of composition. And the same could be true for Latino discourses—Carmen Tafolla points out that in Chicano literature "doubled possibilities for alliteration and double entendre [have been] found in concentrated mélanges of Spanish, English, 'Texan,' black English, even Mayan and Nahuatl word concepts. Imaginations exploded beyond limits, beyond conventions . . . [as] Chicano writers continued to indulge in 'language play'" (208), where "lexical creations sprang from an awareness of our own dually bilingual existence and from the discovery of new worlds of thought and literature—the Mayan, Aztec, Native American" (209).

When the academy refers to rhetoric it frequently has in mind something that began (and too frequently ends) with Aristotle's enthymeme. Talking drums, praise poetry, Iroquois circle dancing, and the "border writing" of Latin America[11] have no place in the current institutional understanding of literacy. Even literary theory, which often gives the impression of seeking out new corners of the "marginal," rarely resists *in practice* the institutional paradigms it pretends to critique—we have reader response, after all, not call and response. Unless the teachers of rhetoric and writing develop an intense respect for and start showing a keen interest in cross-cultural discourse traditions, the rallying cries for multiculturalism and diversity growing louder each year will remain compromised, compromised by an unwillingness to tolerate any serious coexistence between these alternative discourses and our professional habits of expression. One of the best ways to convey that respect is to start teaching these other discourses alongside the conventional, until eventually our current definition of "academic" takes on an entirely new and hybrid form.

When Male Means Marginal

*Who polices questions of grammar, parts of speech,
correction, and connotation? Whose order is shut inside
the structure of the sentence?*
—SUSAN HOWE

The struggle on the page is not decorative.
—RACHEL BLAU DUPLESSIS

Women, if you want to realize yourselves (for you are on the
brink of a devastating psychological upheaval) all your pet
illusions must be unmasked. The lies of centuries have got to
be discarded. Are you prepared for the WRENCH?

Leave off looking to men to find out what you are not.
Seek within yourselves to find out what you *are*. As condi-
tions are at present constituted you have the choice between
Parasitism, Prostitution, or Negation.

There is no half-measure, no scratching on the surface of
the rubbish heap of tradition. Nothing short of Absolute
Demolition will bring about reform. (269)

T H O S E words were written by Mina Loy in what
has since been referred to as her "Feminist Manifesto." She wrote
them in 1914.

Almost 75 years later, Nicole Brossard speaks these words after
a talk on "Poetic Politics":

It is hard for us to discriminate what patterns are human and
what patterns are male. Nor do we know what women's patterns are, since these have not been able to be made public
through art, writing, and so on. But we do know that male
psychic energy has fantasized—constituted—a corpus of

"knowledge" as to what is right and wrong, what is valued and what is not. This is what I am questioning: this *corpus* based essentially on a collective male subjectivity that gives us a culture or a civilization that has just one perspective on reality. But if we look at it from another angle, then reality is different. Had women, throughout history, been permitted to project their own fantasy, I think we would have for example, a different architecture; and probably we would have also a different kind of scientific reasoning process. I don't know how the world would be if women had been able to participate in the elaboration of laws, traditions, religion, etc. I just know one thing: patriarchal binarity has provided for systematic violence against women. (86)

These two quotes offer a glimpse into one of the more influential fissures running through twentieth-century writing: the advent of writers who began to suspect the duplicity inherent in terms like "standard," "normative," "acceptable," and "appropriate," especially when applied to the use of language; writers who came to recognize that such "givens" had never, ever been painted from neutral vantage points, were nothing less than the signatures of male institutions, powered by patriarchal and masculinist ideology. As if the "rules" of rhetoric and grammar, were they to suddenly acquire a voice, must bellow forth in timbres deep, low, loud and booming, accepting no alternatives, renouncing no authority.

The twentieth century has been distinguished by creative thinkers, female and male, who began searching for additional tones hidden beneath this overbearing masculine chorus. Intense resistance came to characterize the work of these active imaginations as writers tried to sketch the antithesis of whatever they identified as patrifocal language. "Man gives a notion of what woman is like at her worst," writes Madeline Gins. "A better way to say this is that all that has not been understood by or about 'man,' that is beyond 'man's' reach, is innately 'woman.' But this is not saying it either. How could it? I am using our communal language, which is man's" (91). And so the question of how gender influences the construction and dissemination of language comes to our attention; it's a question with deep significance for anyone involved with composition and rhetoric.

Our language is, to an extreme degree, the product of patriarchal ideologies and institutions; it reflects histories marked by male domination and the privileging of male modes of thinking, and in that reflection perpetuates the masculine biases from which it was formed. In their book *Women's Ways of Knowing* authors Belenky, Clinchy, Goldberger, and Tarule remind us that our country's educational structures, especially secondary and postsecondary schools, were built, designed, and controlled by men, for men. Even later women's schools were fashioned after these male institutions so that the education received by a woman would be equivalent to that acquired by the boys. Consequently, the authors write, "relatively little attention has been given to modes of learning, knowing, and valuing that may be specific to, or at least common in, women" (5–6).

Now some of the hypotheses in this book raise a number of questions. The authors' attempt to definitively outline how women "know," as opposed to how men "know," might lean toward a reductive tendency to polarize and, implicitly, hegemonize methods of interpretation within an overly generic framework. One is led to ask which women, exactly, are included under the assumptions of this work—all females on the planet? Do the suburban high school cheerleader, Simone de Beauvoir, Eskimo grandmothers, and Barbara Bush all share common sensibilities and thought processes indigenous to "women in general," ways of knowing inaccessible by males? Also, which segments of the female population are singled out for representation in this study? What rationale for excluding women of other cultures not interviewed for this work? And why the need for the universalist overtones of the all-encompassing title (a rhetorical technique, as I'll try to point out later, that many feminist writers might deem deceptively authoritarian).[1]

Yet these authors, in offering their own paradigms, do lend some useful considerations for the prospect of "feminine" writing. Their differentiation, for example, between "procedural" and "constructivist" means of making knowledge:

Women who rely on procedural knowledge are systematic thinkers in more than one sense of the term. Their thinking is encapsulated within systems. They can criticize a system, but only in the system's terms, only according to the system's standards. Women at this position may be liberals or conservatives, but they cannot be radicals. If, for example, they are feminists, they want equal opportunities for women within the capitalistic structure. When these women speak of "beating the system," they do not mean violating its expectations but rather exceeding them. (127)[2]

Interestingly enough, a great deal of the discourse we produce in the academy has its genesis in this "procedural" state of mind. We're conditioned to conform to our systems of higher education by writing in accordance with its commands, to make and teach texts grown from Euro-patriarchal ideologies. Our publications and dissertations, no matter how brilliant or transformative, are less likely to challenge the mechanics of the institutional machine than they are to conform to rhetorical styles arguably designed to help us gain further admittance into avenues of professional power.

If we weren't such experts in procedural knowledge, we'd be adopting what Belenky et al. term "constructivist" thinking: "to learn to speak in a unique and authentic voice," to "'jump outside' the frames and systems authorities provide and create [one's] own frame" (134). Constructivist thinkers, the authors continue, "show a high tolerance for internal contradiction and ambiguity. They abandon completely the either/or thinking so common" in institutionally male dominated ways of knowing. "They recognize the inevitability of conflict and stress. . . . And they want to develop a voice of their own to communicate to others their understanding of life's complexity" (137). Advocates of the constructivist angle, as evidenced in their calls for "Leaving the System" and "Moving Outside the Given," the authors of this work underscore resistance as a catalytic force necessary for creative, critical inquiry.

This constructivist approach, as one might guess, is in dramatic conflict with current pedagogies of considerable influence in composition studies—the stance, for example, chosen by David Bartholomae and Anthony Petrosky in *Facts, Artifacts, and Counterfacts*, who want

students to learn to compose a response to their reading (and, in doing so, to learn to compose a reading) within the conventions of the highly conventional language of the university classroom. We are, then, teaching the language of the academy . . . because we believe that the language of the university can be shown to value "counterfactuality," "individuation," "potentiality," and "freedom." (4–5)

Here we have the essence of procedural knowledge described in *Women's Ways of Knowing*. Surprisingly, support for canonical rhetorics historically determined by male educators has not only been advocated by critics like Bartholomae and Petrosky, but is symptomatic of many who argue for more "liberal" means of writing instruction, and whose pedagogies, carefully examined, might be seen to harbor overtly masculinized biases. Theorists who oppose the Bartholomae/Petrosky stance favoring academic discourse, for example, nevertheless have promoted attitudes about writing veined with curious assumptions unsympathetic to or unaware of feminist composing strategies.

For instance, it's not uncommon to hear writing described in bellicose terms, the labor of composing painted as an arduous, violent process of sweat and toil. Writing, to be sure, is often no picnic: we all know what it's like when ideas stubbornly resist manifesting themselves on the page. But it seems odd that the frequent lulls and impasses one naturally encounters—the necessary periods of hibernation often counterproductively labeled as writer's block—are so often portrayed as some initiation or gauntlet all good writers must hurdle if they wish to seek admittance into the upper echelons of real academic discourse. More than once the path toward good writing has been described as a sort of rite of passage: "the writing student has to be bloodied if he is to learn," declares Donald Murray (119), mandating that students must "respect" the subject-verb-object sentence (104).

And Peter Elbow, for all his nurturing attempts to make writing an enriching, moving investigation into the richness of one's personal experience, sounds more like an officer preparing his troops for battle than a reassuring teacher in this diatribe on revision found in his successful book, *Writing Without Teachers*:

Editing must be cut-throat. You must wade in with teeth gritted. Cut away flesh and leave only bone. . . . Force yourself to leave out all subsidiaries and then, by brute force, you will have to rearrange the essentials into their proper order.

Every word omitted keeps another reader with you. Every word retained saps strength from the others. . . .

Try to *feel* the act of strength in the act of cutting: as you draw the pencil through the line or paragraph or whole page, it is a clenching of teeth to make a point stick out more, hit home harder. Conversely, try to feel that when you write in a mushy, foggy, wordy way, you must be writing to cover something up: message-emasculation or self-emasculation. You must be afraid of your strength. Taking away words lets a loud voice stick out. Does it scare you? . . . It is no accident that timid people are often wordy. Saying nothing takes guts. . . .

Editing means being tough enough to make sure someone will actually read it. (41–42)

One could almost see students exiting their Freshman Expository Writing class bruised and battered after an hour of revising, their papers bloodstained and soiled (a correlation here, perhaps, with the use of bright red pens with which to correctively "bleed" student papers). It's important to hear the messages barely concealed in this passage: the writing process is closely aligned with violence, violence aimed at orchestrating prose into some "proper order";[3] points must "stick out," like spikes (phalli?) intended to snag readers as themes "hit home harder." "Fear," "strength," and "toughness" have become the vital ingredients essential for good writers.

Perhaps most interesting is Elbow's revealing use of terms like "message-emasculation" and "self-emasculation." Here he has gone further than describe good writing in typically patriarchal terms: not only must it be trim and spartan—what Richard Lanham calls the CBS style of composition (clarity, brevity, sincerity)—but effective writing must avoid "castration" at all costs. Bad writing for Elbow is that which is demasculinized, effeminized. But if that's true, how are women to succeed by Elbow's standards? Since his advice seems directed entirely toward men (men who supposedly fear asexualization), at best women must on some level imagine themselves as male authors.

And when Elbow describes poor writing as mushy and foggy, lacking strength, he keenly demonstrates the sexist trap many have fallen into when masculine-oriented terminologies are used to describe fine writing, while feminine adjectives epitomize the bad stuff. Frances Jaffer sheds light on how the vocabularies we use to either congratulate or criticize works of writing are extremely gender-specific:

> The language of criticism: "lean, dry, terse, powerful, strong, spare, linear, focused, explosive"—god forbid it should be "limp"!! But—"soft, moist, blurred, padded, irregular, going around in circles," and other descriptions of our bodies—the very **abyss** of aesthetic judgment, danger, the wasteland for artists! (DuPlessis, "For the Etruscans" 278)

Elbow isn't the only one who seems at times to confuse the teacher's role with that of drill sergeant. William Coles, Jr., as he portrays himself in his book *The Plural* I, offers an abrasive and affectedly macho interpretation of writing instruction. In this work Coles narrates in considerable detail a composition course he taught one semester, giving readers a lengthy monologue on the performance of his students in response to his unique teaching style. In the beginning of his book Coles mentions that although the class he used as a case study consisted entirely of males, the content of the course—the student writings and his teaching—wouldn't have been any different had there been any women in the class, an assumption that sheds doubt on Coles's awareness that women, compared to men, speak very differently in classroom environments, and could easily talk about subject matter far different from that discussed by male students, thereby drastically altering the classroom setting.[4]

Beyond this, consider the following comments taken from *The Plural* I, and their self-consciously confrontational tone (these are Coles's words to students, recounted from memory):[5]

> Come on, man. My God. . . . Is this only intended to be another god-damned paper for another god-damned English course. Come on, man. Come clean! (18)

> I'm not interested in having somebody say how sorry he is that he acted like a horses' ass on this Assignment. . . .

What I get is another batch of goddamned Themes. (72)

I am neither equipped for nor ready to assume the responsibility of posing as a parent, a priest, a psychoanalyst, a pal. I
am a teacher of writing. No more and, I hope, no less. (13)

I also draw a salary to do more than let my students bleed on
me. (35)

Coles's aggressive, badgering style seems aimed at bullying students into adopting equally "tough" personas, almost as if freshman composition were akin to boot camp for rhetoricians. It's
also relevant to notice how he exaggerates the hierarchic ladder
that situates him well above the status occupied by his students,
to whom he is at times patronizing and insulting ("writing, *even*
for undergraduates . . . is an art") (101, my emphasis). Coles's
stubborn attitude toward grading serves to unnecessarily reinforce
his authority: not only does he refuse any student the opportunity
to ask about grades during the semester, thus keeping them in the
dark about their classroom performance until the year's end, but
he has little concern for student questions and comments about
his evaluative criteria: "if the writer was offended" by Coles's
abrasive comments, "that was indeed his problem" (107).

To be honest I'm singling out writers like Murray, Elbow, and
Coles unfairly; after all, sexist overtones are rampant throughout
so many corners of academia, and I certainly don't wish to white-
wash myself as some enlightened exception. I am also being harsh
in criticizing these writers after examining in detail relatively
brief passages of their not so recent work, excerpts not fully representative of their pedagogies: whenever hearing Elbow speak, for
example, I've never heard the same aggressive overtones found in
the passages cited above. And Coles, at least in *The Plural* I, must
be given credit for laying himself on the line so, magnifying all
the mistakes and accomplishments of an entire course in such
detail—I doubt I would ever publicize the embarrassing moments
of my past classes with such candor. These teachers obviously
possess a serious commitment to transform their students into
what they deem successful writers, and I wonder if these masculinist overtones would surface today, given the degree to which
current educators are wary of voicing views that might be consid-

ered sexist or misogynist. (Conceivably, some might even admire the directness of Coles's and Elbow's masculine prose styles as more honest than a growing number of contemporary theorists whose hunger for the safety of political correctness has led them to overly sanitize their arguments, frightened of using language in any fashion that might be considered morally reprehensible as decreed by various left-wing dogma.)

Basically, I'm drawing attention to the peculiarities of certain liberal composition theorists to show how easily so-called empowering pedagogies can be coopted, laden with questionable, almost subliminal theoretical positions that collide with their intended claims. Practitioners like these have been hailed as excitingly progressive, offering liberatory complements to current-traditional pedagogies, and yet they can remain equally insensitive to gender issues and their intrinsic relationship to composition. The intolerance exhibited here for possible alternatives indicates just how surreptitious pedagogies are that envision the path toward intellectual achievement as tantamount to some athletic test of endurance, where only the fittest survive, thus maintaining conditions set forth by historically male-determined criteria.

Actually, masculinist biases in liberal pedagogies aren't all that surprising once we examine the nature of "academic discourse" in general. Despite the complex makeup of this abstract term, the "language of the academy" does indeed evoke a definitively masculine inclination. Walter Ong, cited by Adrienne Rich in her essay "Toward a Woman-Centered University," argues that the roots of academic discourse are specifically masculine:

> [Rhetoric] developed in the past as a major expression of the rational level of the ceremonial combat which is found among males and typically only among males at the physical level throughout the entire animal kingdom. . . . Rhetoric became particularly attached to Learned Latin, which the male psyche appropriated to itself as an extrafamilial language when Latin ceased to be a "mother" tongue (that is, was no longer spoken in the home by one's mother). Latin, spoken and written for 1500 years with totally negligible exceptions only by males, became a ceremonial language

institutionalizing with particular force the ceremonial polemic which set the style for all education until romanticism. For until the romantic age, academic education was all but exclusively focused on defending a position (thesis) or attacking the position of another person—even medicine was taught this way. (128)

More recently Olivia Frey, after reading more than 150 articles in *PMLA, College English, Signs, Critical Inquiry,* and the *New York Review of Books,* claims that in all but two of the essays she examined the authors resorted to what Frey calls "the adversarial method," an argumentative style ranging from mild refutation or correction of another's findings to sheer hostility toward a colleague's work. Frey's findings imply that the rhetorical combat described by Ong has continued to thrive long beyond the romantic period, remaining a standard for the public language of our profession (elements of which, readers will notice, are alive and well in my manuscript too). "What troubles me the most," she writes, "is the basic, unexamined assumption that the best way to know things about literature and to help others know things about literature is by presenting a thesis and making a case for it by answering counterarguments. . . . The implication [is] that if one does not argue well or argue at all, the writing is unclear, ineffective, and unconvincing" (511). Such adversarial rhetoric is much more than a chosen style; it would appear that one seldom has any alternative but to write this way if there's to be any hope of getting published in the journals of our profession or getting our dissertations accepted. Even Frey, though praising experimental attempts by women to reinvent conventional grammars, feels professionally obligated to avoid any attempt to discover her own version of exploratory rhetoric. "I hope I have the courage," she concludes, "to write differently next time" (524). Me too—but I wouldn't bet on seeing her results printed in most academic journals, which, though occasionally permitting critics like Frey to extol feminine rhetoric, are either reluctant to print the stuff or refrain from actively soliciting this kind of text, or any other prose deviating from the conventions of academic critical analysis.

These traditions of combative and adversarial rhetoric have

helped shape our current professional discourse, a mode of communication not without its critics. Robin Lakoff calls attention to the lexical traits she finds common among women's speech patterns—increased frequency of questions, a reluctance to convey hostility, a willingness to express uncertainty—and to how these mannerisms are often at odds with tenets of the fundamentally androcentric "academese," which often employs

> passives and impersonal expression, because they are more "polite," and technical terms as frequently as possible: a turgid prose style is amply rewarded. Many people have told me of being informed by their superiors, at early stages of their careers, that what they were saying was interesting and important but it was expressed too plainly (that is, too intelligibly) to be taken seriously by their colleagues. Moral: learn to obfuscate or you won't get tenure. (153)[6]

Academese is so powerful, Lakoff concludes, that women will continue to have a difficult time adapting to this style; and until more female role models enter the academy, the alternatives will be conversion or frustration—"hence, it is all the more important for women to play a significant role in the university system at all levels in the hierarchy, in order to clear the air and introduce some much-needed stylistic flexibility" (154).

But a lot more than simply increasing the number of women faculty and administrators will be necessary to achieve her vision of an academic arena more open to diverse rhetorical styles. It's now more than two decades since Lakoff's essay appeared, and while more women have entered the academy, the academic atmospheres seem almost as ill-ventilated as ever. (I seriously doubt today's dissertations are significantly more playful, experimental, and stylistically innovative than they were twenty years ago.) If we're serious about bringing a greater diversity of styles into the academy, waiting for the gender of our professional population to stabilize isn't enough. Academics, male and female, and especially those concerned with issues of grammar and style, will have to expand their awareness of rhetorical possibilities beyond the confines of academic tradition.

Beverly Dahlen, a contemporary poet, editor, and critic, has emphasized her need to break out of this tradition in search of new writing forms more conducive to articulating "the suppressed contents of women's lives." Although here she speaks particularly about the indoctrination of classical poetic forms, her contention can be applied to composition as typically defined in the classroom:

> The forms of power were what had been trotted out again and again in our literature courses. The identifiable package was always the beginning of the show and would turn up again on the final: the sonnet, the sestina, the rhymed couplet, *terza rima.* The parade of form, techniques, devices, the marshalling of strategies to capture the content—in short, a kind of military attitude towards writing was often what seemed to be implied. ("Tradition of Marginality" 72)

There is a struggle going on here, and it has to do with far more than one's favorite rhetorical style. For many women, and men, resisting patriarchal discourse is vital if one is to inscribe within language the shifting personalities, identities, emotions, and desires not represented or allowed within historically male-motivated rhetorics. Here we see conventional forms consciously rebuffed by twentieth-century women writers who, as one critic puts it, find such protocol nothing less than "straitjackets on the imagination . . . fussy Victorian 'knick-knacks' cluttering up the new mental spaces" (Burke 51).

Some, like Luce Irigaray, have gone so far as to charge that women's language can never exist, "phallocratic" civilization having sculpted every facet of the language available to us; to find an alternative language, she claims, would require us to imagine an ancient matriarchy with an utterly new discourse, an entirely new alphabet (101). But though constructing or even hypothesizing a brand-new language is an intriguing project to contemplate, it doesn't exactly offer a viable solution for many writers seeking languages of their own. And so, many choose to undermine "male" language by drastically altering it from within. Adalaide Morris frames the endeavor this way:

> If conventional language maps conventional terrain, voyages into the unknown and not-yet-recorded will generate writing that is, in some way, eccentric, extravagant, or

experimental. Customary language no longer suffices, and we must renew old words or create new ones. New or renewed words enable new habits and actions, habits and actions that will then, in their turn, generate new signs, new linguistic possibilities. (16)

But what exactly do these new maps look like? What are these linguistic cartographers doing that's so innovative? And how, specifically, does one come closer to defining the so-called masculine discourse rejected by these new rhetoricians? Writers have sought answers to these questions in unique ways, and after examining a variety of texts characterized by feminist, experimentalist impulses, it's possible to highlight some patterns prone to appear in a feminine rhetoric. Before doing that, though, I feel compelled to highlight what's at stake when using terms like "masculine" and "feminine" in conjunction with written discourse—the limitations and the benefits of this debatable terminology.

Personally, I don't think there's any such thing as a quintessentially "masculine" or "feminine" writing—at least, not in any sense that a text or rhetoric could be definitively measured as such. Perhaps I'm unwilling to buy into this essentialist reasoning because if, deep down, there really is a distinction, then by virtue of my sex I would have to remain forever confined to one side of the fence: though I might free myself periodically to roam (trespass?) into rhetorical landscapes new to me, I would have, according to this argument, sooner or later always to return to a (male) home base. And quite honestly I want nothing to do with being so categorized and compartmentalized, or to accept any dichotomy inferring that the active imagination must remain forever limited by gender.

Nevertheless, I think this dichotomy can be a useful starting point from which eventually to render essentialist terminologies like these void of their more pejorative connotations. Writers like Julia Kristeva, for example, have wisely denounced essentialist interpretations of *écriture féminine*; and yet, keeping in line with my own pragmatic agenda, I think using "feminine" as a working term might, for the time being, most effectively attract the attention of students and colleagues, and thus entice them into investigating this new realm of rhetorical possibilities—more than, say, such labels as Cixous's "vatic bisexuality" ("Laugh of the Medusa"), Kristeva's "sexual-symbolic difference" (478), or Luce Irigaray's *le parler femme*, translated by Toril Moi as "womanspeak" (Moi 144). Just because "masculine" and "feminine," when used to describe modes of composition, are labels that can't be summarily defined in that they point to no obligatory rhetorical techniques (writing from a self-consciously linear standpoint isn't intrinsically masculine, nor would a circuitous design necessarily indicate feminine style), these terms are zones out of which arise distinct patterns of influence. Though the labels are fictions, they stir up definite philosophical orientations with very real ramifications for how we teach writing. As Stephen-Paul Martin argues in his study of feminine reading and writing, *Open Form and the Feminine Imagination*, the "issue is not whether we are justified in calling the tendency to nurture, play, and be flexible 'feminine'; the issue is, rather, how to make these qualities more prominent in mainstream activities that are still essentially male-oriented" (5). Or, as Kristeva phrases it, "to nourish our societies with a more flexible and free discourse, one able to name what has thus far never been an object of circulation in the community" (482).

My aim is not to romanticize the study of writing by forcing it into a gender-specific polarity, though using gender-laden terms as a means of understanding ignored means of composition certainly invites such criticism (some have pointed out that "femininity" is itself a patriarchal invention, which pushes *all* women into the margins).[7] Rather, I hope to underscore contrasting patterns precisely in an attempt to integrate oppositional strategies within a shared frame: an attention to style and grammar, not a preoccupation with the biological origins out of which these stylistic traits might or might not emanate. "Women's writing will be more accessible to writers and readers alike," claims Ann Rosalind Jones, "if we recognize it as a conscious response to socioliterary realities, rather than accept it as an overflow of one woman's unmediated communication with her body" (374).

Best then to begin by painting the kind of linguistic landscape that would *not* likely be considered feminine rhetoric, at least by numerous writers who have sought escape from the paralysis of obligatory convention. When I talk of masculine rhetoric, for example, I'm thinking of writing that might more aptly be characterized as

firm
cohesive
temporal
sequential
rigid
closed
linear
strong
rigorous
controlled
hierarchical
authoritative;

expected to provide a primary thesis, concise conclusions, logical progression, and a self-confident tone.

A feminine rhetoric could differ drastically: it might be

nonlinear
ambiguous   atemporal   circuitous
meandering
permeable   open   polysemous
collaborative   nonauthoritarian   loose
playful   flexible
and organic;

emphasizing a conscious attention to fragmentation as an organizing principle, advocating a collage-like format, or presenting an impressionistic, deeply intuitive structure.

In response to the intensely male-dominated, patrifocal traditions that animate the writing theories circulating in our profession—whether current-traditional, liberal-expressivist, or social-constructivist—an increasing number of writers have countered with their own challenging rhetorical deviations. Collectively, these are the works of writers unafraid to try to sculpt their own linguistic frames of expression. I find the rhetoric of feminine texts frequently employing five predominant impulses: a

rhetoric of contradiction; a blurring of genre; heightened collaboration; a denial of hegemony; and an attention to silence as a
powerful rhetorical trope.

Rhetoric of Contradiction

Part of the difficulty in articulating a feminine composition is the question of whether or not one should abandon
rhetorics clearly founded in classical, and therefore masculine,
traditions. Is it, for example, hypocritical and self-defeating for
someone to discuss experimental writings in a format decidedly
conventional? The problem with a question like this is its assumption that one must adhere to a particular discourse: that deviation
from a familiar style, or any juxtaposition of unlike rhetorical
techniques, implies the taboo of contradiction, thereby weakening any premises of the writer. Feminine composition negotiates
this dilemma by embracing any and all angles of the rhetorical
spectrum, advocating a "rhetoric of contradiction" where a range
of polarities can be included within a writer's oeuvre. An eclectic
stance is encouraged, thereby extinguishing the possibility for
censorship of dissimilar rhetorical strategies. The more fences one
can hop, the better.

Susan Howe, a major force in the contemporary wave of
exploratory American writers, explains why a feminist consideration of language would have to allow for a plurality of voices:

> Yes, gender difference does affect our use of language, and
> we constantly confront issues of difference, distance, and
> absence, when we write. That doesn't mean I can relegate
> women to what we "should" or "must" be doing. Orders sug-
> gest hierarchy and category. Categories and hierarchies sug-
> gest property. *My voice formed from my life belongs to no one
> else.* (*My Emily Dickinson* 13, my emphasis)

The issue here is not to force anybody into adopting someone
else's chosen grammar, but to underscore how these divergent
communicative modalities are viable options, as "rigorous" and
sophisticated and seriously committed as any sense of stylistic
coherence found in academic expository prose. Not an erasure of

the phallocentric history of writing (for any such erasure would be delusory, simply another form of censorship), but a plowing forward into unique ways of constructing knowledge through all available organizational principles. Not an ignoring of inordinately prevalent male modes of discourse, but a concentrated effort to add to these traditions new options.

This penchant for welcoming contradiction can be found in Rachel Blau DuPlessis's concept of a "both/and" vision. Because the notion of obligatory rhetorical modes is offensive if not disabling to many writers, a feminine rhetoric would permit diversity of expression, which essentially would mean that neither academic nor nonacademic ways of writing would be favored but all extremes permitted. Forcing one to choose sides and toe some party line at any cost places the writer within a larger network where dichotomies continue to assert themselves. Irreconcilability between perspectives then remains the enforcing agent, not multiplicity of possibilities. DuPlessis's concept of the "both/and" vision fights this dualism by recognizing that our thought processes are seldom as rigid, clear-cut, and unwavering as the pointed arguments we're so often expected to manufacture. As communicators we are characterized by contradiction and paradox, fraught with conflicting views and motives, none of which might be "right" or "wrong." DuPlessis:

> A both/and vision that embraces movement, situational. (I don't mean: opportunistic, slidy.) Structurally, such a writing might say different things, not settle on one, which is final. This is not a condition of "not choosing," since choice exists always in what to represent and in the rhythms of presentation. It is nonacademic; for in order to make a formal presentation, one must have chosen among these: this is the rhetorical demand. Cannot, in formal argument, say both yes and no, if yes and no are given equal value under the same conditions. Either one or the other has to prevail. But say, in a family argument? where both, where all, are right? generates another model of discourse. ("For the Etruscans" 276)[8]

Consequently a writer might find it easier to influence an audience when contradictory claims are honestly given space within the same text. The writer might ask herself an array of questions, a decision that could simultaneously foreground a sense of intellectual inquisitiveness, bring to light issues and entry points into the subject(s) at hand, and also make the author's work accessible by virtue of its reluctance to dogmatically espouse any central thesis (maybe all, or none, of the possible theses could be supported—essays could conclude inconclusively, in an attempt to entice further readers into the dialogue). The essay as a prelude for further questioning, offering readers a handful of valid arguments, no matter how conflicting they might be. Rethinking critical texts as artifacts that don't have to nail down some polemic progressing T-unit by T-unit towards an inevitable conclusion, but rather can open up the further they progress. The finale of the essay as a blossoming of concepts tumbling into the reader's lap, calling out for continued assemblage.

As DuPlessis points out, appreciation for contradiction need not be identified with taking the easy way out. Of course a rhetoric of contradiction could easily lend itself to those who offer wishy-washy, noncommittal ramblings, or who use composition as a vehicle for self-aggrandizement rather than a process toward critically innovative thought. But no rhetorical approach is impervious to abuse. To condemn a rhetoric of contradiction on this basis would also require the denunciation of classical, formalist argumentation, since this too can easily be abused by sneaky rhetoricians who manipulate form to make questionable premises sound effective. In other words, paradox need not be the sign of weak intellectual capacities. Ever since Walt Whitman asked "Do I contradict myself?" in "Song of Myself," only to hastily reply, "Very well then I contradict myself, / I am large, I contain multitudes," critics have underscored those lines as evidence of the poet's ingenuity, an affirmation of paradox representative, some have said, of a new and brilliant American sensibility. Ironically, such praise falls within the safety of rhetorical arguments which view contradiction as an inadmissible characteristic of any worthy critical text.

Probably the most significant feature of a rhetoric of contradiction is that it could never summarily dismiss any compositional preference. Some writers might fashion texts after Quintilian, while for others Anne Berthoff's philosophies might be most appropriate; one might choose to use the much berated five paragraph theme for particular ends, with interesting results, while elsewhere adopting a Peter Elbowish preference for personal narrative. Or some writers might choose to orient themselves solely within specific traditions, whether romantic, Afrocentric, avantgarde, or classical, never desiring to deviate from these forms. Within the feminine focus, *all* of these options are viable. A rhetoric of contradiction, tolerant of all angles, would acknowledge and respect the legitimacy of unlike grammars.

Blurring of Genre

Another way of joining unlike elements within the same rhetorical field is the mingling of different genres within a shared textual space. Consequently a feminine composition could be many things at once: manifesto, tract, verse, didactic rant, philosophical inquiry, classical exposition, dialogue, interview, autobiography, epistolary, journalism (whether traditional or literary), or fictive musing. Shuffled within the same text, various genres might supplant each other as the writing commences, or even merge together to form new hybrids. Powerful writing need not always remain "purebred," faithful only to a shortened range of acceptable forms. On the contrary, one might actively pursue a more heterogeneous text, ignoring the debilitating academic assumption that "creative writing" remain a rhetorical entity isolated from serious, professional prose. An emphasis, in other words, on accentuating the procedural to an extreme degree, where process takes one back and forth not only through unexpected genres but into unanticipated modes of investigation.

Hélène Cixous's writings, it has been said, indicate a consistent drive to make writing reflective of the diverse spread of emotions embedded within any author, a condition marked by what many have termed textual *jouissance*: an obvious and flagrant pleasure, both sensual and intellectual, in the act of manipulating grammar and syntax. Writings like these become amalgams of journal entries, scholarly inquiry, poetry, fiction, manifesto, and autobiography; distinctions between genre dissolve, thereby calling into question the academic need to continually stratisfy discourse

"types." The works of DuPlessis epitomize this degree of polyvocality to an even greater degree; she describes her efforts as
attempts to

> erode some attitude toward reading and writing . . . to make
> meanings that [undo] hierarchies of decidability. I wanted
> no right/correct sequences of feeling emblematic in
> right/correct sequences of reading. The desire to create
> something that is not a complete argument, or a poem with
> a climax, but where there are ends and beginnings all over
> the work. A working work. ("Otherhow" 33)

DuPlessis's critical prose is characteristic of these impulses. *The
Pink Guitar*, a collection of essays written over a ten-year period,
is one of those books that give publishers and librarians
headaches because they're so hard to classify. An agglomerate of
poetry, literary criticism, feminist theory, and journal, all intricately spun together, *The Pink Guitar* is a courageous collection
primarily because the writings operate within, and thus perpetuate, the literary and aesthetic traditions under investigation. This
is critical writing that gets its feet wet — the work of a writer for
whom it's simply insufficient to peer into the convoluted terrain
of imaginative discourse from a vantage point entrenched in the
conventions of acceptable grammar. Instead, writers like Du-
Plessis are compelled to partake of the work they find so captivating: it is criticism that adds to the oeuvre under consideration.

Another account of disparate genres both fusing together and
dissolving entirely is found in Gloria Anzaldúa's analysis of her
compositional technique in *Borderlands/La Frontera: The New
Mestiza*, a work the creation of which Anzaldúa describes in this
way:

> In looking over [this book] I see a mosaic pattern (Aztec-
> like) emerging, a weaving pattern, thin here, thick there. . . .
> I see a hybridization of metaphor, different species of ideas
> popping up here, popping up there, full of variations and
> seeming contradictions. . . . This book seems an assemblage,
> a montage, a beaded work with several leitmotifs and with a
> central core, now appearing, now disappearing in a crazy
> dance. The whole thing has had a mind of its own, escaping

me and insisting on putting together the pieces of its own
puzzle with minimal direction from my will. . . . Though it is
a flawed thing—a clumsy, complex, groping blind thing—
for me it is alive, infused with spirit. I talk to it; it talks to
me. (30–31)

Anzaldúa's prose traces her desire to see writing as an act at once
sensual and spiritual, able, practically, to invoke states of perception akin to shamanistic experience. The result is a composition
of motion—not a unidirectional motion leading from introduction to body to conclusion, but a passage marked by turns and
metamorphosis: "thought shifts, reality shifts, gender shifts: one
person metamorphoses into another in a world where people fly
through the air. . . ." (35).

One of the more interesting effects of such stylistic interplay is
that the end product is often something totally unexpected,
sometimes deviating wildly from the original intent. In theory
this really isn't all that new a concept in composition studies,
certainly not among those who lean toward process-oriented
modes of writing instruction—"how can I know what I have to
say until I start writing?" goes the popular cry, as student writers
are encouraged to put pen to paper during the preliminary
"prewriting" stages of their composition, intentionally avoiding
too much forethought. But this approach toward writing is still
fairly conservative compared to the more wandering methods
proposed by people like DuPlessis and Anzaldúa. Chances are,
teachers who promote like-minded meandering within the early
stages of the composing process do so with an eye toward even-
tual closure, when the jaggedness of those early stages can be
smoothed out in retrospect to construct the illusion of some relatively seamless whole. And to be sure, this approach is unar-
guably valid, and essential—it would be silly to belittle the
writerly desire to bring ideas home in order to present some semblance of manageable, organized conclusion. But on the other
hand, "even the most seamless text consists of interruptions,
anticipations, predictions, retracings. . . . The difference between
intentionally fragmentary texts on the one hand and ostensibly
non-fragmentary texts on the other is that the latter attempt to
pass themselves off as naturally fit for smooth, untroubled access"

(Seitz 818). Instead, the issue becomes how to examine other viable ways of interpreting concepts of organization. And writers operating from feminist preoccupations are finding more and more that linear outlines and standard notions of incremental progression are all too often imperfect rhetorical tools. "When I begin working," writes Rosmarie Waldrop, "I have only a vague nucleus, an energy running to words. As soon as I start listening to the words, they reveal their own vectors and affinities, pull the poem into their own field of force, often in unforeseen directions, away from the semantic charge of the original impulse" (54). And keep in mind that when contemporary writers like Waldrop refer to poetry, they're often not envisioning poetic discourse as a realm that by definition must remain disjoined from critical, expository prose: this particular quote, for example, is found in an essay characterized by the very vectoral, quasi-chaotic momentum she highlights, the text bouncing among numbered theses ("Excursions" and "Alarms") that bring to the surface a mosaic of "doubts, complications and distractions" emanating from the subject at hand.

Communal Composition

Just as a willingness to entertain paradox finds itself closely aligned with a propensity to scramble genres, both of these methods leave the door open for a third discursive possibility: when multiple themes and styles coexist within the same text, collaboration between multiple authors isn't far behind.

A feminine emphasis might lead to communal texts—dialogic, not monologic scores. Assemblages of documents, voices, tapes, and quotations from various sources. A range of chromatics, all circulating in the same netting; multiple voices to reflect multiple backgrounds, cultures; an impatience with the myth of a "solitary" authorial voice responsible for propagating and codifying all information.

Collaboration, in fact, even to the point that the "final" text might read like a collage of notes, a chorus of fragmented (yet connected) voices conversing across the page. Works like *Women's Ways of Knowing* and Tillie Olsen's *Silences* are effective in part because of their polyphonic focus, the orchestration of numerous voices assembled by one or more authors.[9] Du-Plessis's "For the Etruscans" takes this need for community even further, her essay a pastiche of insights from women's journals, poetry, essays, and commentaries made in workshops and seminars so as to create "an emotional texture, a structural expression of mutuality" (275).

A similar focus is shared by the intermingled voices in the recent blending of autobiography, fiction, and manifesto *Tight Spaces*, by Kesho Scott, Cherry Muhanji, and Egyirba High. Equally difficult to categorize, this project is a collection of pieces by three women: fictions and recalled memories, poetry and autobiography, invectives against sexual inequality, and tracts for social change, all of which were triggered by, and written in response to, one another's texts. One lesson conveyed by writing like this is that the imagination is cross-disciplinary—and that to constantly, unquestioningly remain bound to the notion of adhering to a single genre, simply because to do so has been the traditional expectation within our academic institutions, is to risk stifling our creative faculties for the sake of conformity.[10]

Even the solitary author can devise "collaborative" texts by consciously underscoring a variety of personas within the same work—going back and forth, for example, between singular and plural vantage points within the same text. It has been observed that Cixous's prose often mixes pronouns, until "I" and "we" become interchangeable, her attempt to play up the multiplicity of emotions present at any time within the writer (Sellers 120). And Michelle Cliff, in the closing passage of her essay "If I Could Write This in Fire, I Would Write This in Fire," writes: "There is no end to this piece of writing. . . . As I read back over it, I see that we/they/I may become confused in the mind of the reader: but these pronouns have always co-existed in my mind" (81). Because Cliff's work is an attempt to convey the complexity of being a light-skinned Jamaican, a lesbian, and someone raised between conflicting colonial and indigenous traditions, referring to herself with a variety of pronouns is much more than an unusual rhetorical flourish; such fracturing is essential if the writer's feelings of alienation and kinship are to exist on the page ("as I am halfway between Africa and England, patriot and expatriate, white and black, I felt my use of language and imagery had sometimes masked what I wanted to convey" ["Journey" 61]). The struggle calling to mind lines from DuPlessis's *The Pink Guitar*:

> I am not writing the personal. The odd and somewhat debased notion of having a voice, or finding a voice, of establishing a consumable personality complete with pix, of engaging in self-revelation, even of engaging in autobiography is precisely the opposite of my deepest feelings about this work. I am not finding a voice, I am losing one. (72)

In this way the possibilities for self-collaboration blossom as one moves beyond the stasis, the myth of a solitary "personal voice" and into fields of new lexical possibility.

Denial of Hegemony

In the book *Writing Differences* Sarah Cornell posits "giving" as a key function in feminine writing: "*giving up* narcissistic arms of self-defence; *giving in* to the urge to let go and try to approach the text differently; finally *giving again* what we have received from the text to others" (Sellers 143). One of the more significant passages in *Women's Ways of Knowing* is when the authors state early on that their collective intention is to "share not prove" their observations (Belenky et al. 16). And then there is DuPlessis's concept of the "female aesthetic," where the writer privileges exchange and interfacing of ideas over verification of evidence. All of these attitudes reflect a shift away from the need to maintain jurisdiction over the text, and toward the cultivation of many-sided directives within the same compositional frame. Not only is this orientation closely allied with a willingness to admit contradiction into the rhetorical sphere; it also underscores a rejection of the implicit assumption that good writing must embody some degree of authoritarian control. Or at least it implies that authorial control needs to be defined in a variety of ways.

One might argue that there is something potentially positivist about writing according to academic tenets; no matter what one's writing may do, the proffered discourse must state a design, a motivation, a purpose or reason for its existence. It's not enough to simply share observations; in order for the text to become validated it must proclaim *why* its observations are worth sharing; ultimately, an idea or ideas must be sold. For many, the inability to encapsulate one's product within a topic sentence or concise abstrac translates into a sign of the writer's ineffectiveness (i.e., lack of marketability).

This traditional perspective—which obviously makes considerable sense in so much of our writing—is nevertheless in conflict with what DuPlessis calls the "female aesthetic," a positioning of oneself outside authoritarian structures:

> the production of formal, epistemological, and thematic strategies by members of the group Woman, strategies born in struggle with much of already existing culture, and overdetermined by two elements of sexual difference—by women's psychosocial experiences of gender asymmetry and by women's historical status in an (ambiguously) nonhegemonic group. . . . Meaning, a statement that is open to the reader, not better than the reader, not set apart from; not seeking authority of the writer. Not even seeking the authority of the writing. (Reader could be writer, writer reader. Listener could be teacher.) ("For the Etruscans" 275)

In other words women, having inherited a history distinguished by constant suppression, whose only access to self-definition is via masculine lexicons, and who are thus perpetually "under erasure" within the confines of patriarchal language systems, are not in any position to exert authoritarian modes of expression other than those handed to them by masculine institutions. Whereas women obviously have the capability to exercise, and abuse, authority as successfully as any male, such authority always carries with it the consent of an even larger phallocratic order. DuPlessis's "female aesthetic" represents an attempt to circumvent or at least undermine that order by pivoting the vertical ascendancy of hegemonic structure to a point where it is displaced by a more horizontal, pluralist field, a dispersion of voices and versions within a shared zone where the authoritarian impetus is rendered inactive.[11]

And yet, despite compositional strategies that grow out of a desire to subvert and deny hegemony within a feminine frame of reference, we should remember that effacing authority in any total sense is ultimately impossible. A published text is an authoritarian text, no matter how conventional or off-the-wall the material between the covers. The very nature of publication brands every published essay and book with an undeniable measure of authority, signifying approval by editors, publishers, printers, even copy editors, ingraining the work with "significance." The book jacket, the graphics on the cover, the copyright page, the spine, the heft of the cloth edition, the ISBN number, they all converge to proclaim that "this work is worthy," evidenced by the fact that people paid money to bring it to this stage. Publication creates money, and if not money, at least some degree of prestige to those involved. Even a manuscript handprinted and distributed by the author herself can't sever the text from a male-dominated capitalist structure—the hardware (typewriter, computer, desktop publishing software, paper, photocopier, etc.) necessary for any publishing endeavor won't allow it. Even the competency to assemble words into sentences that can be understood by others can cast a shadow of repressive authority over people lacking those same skills (functional literacy, in this sense, is never completely severed from certain "sexual politics").

One might well wonder at this point about the relevance of attempting to erase or scramble any semblance of authoritarian overtones within one's writing if in fact it's an impossible quest. If we're all prisoners of masculinist, capitalist ideology, why try to subvert that which can't be denied? Because there are indeed significant differences between rhetorical usage that willingly adopts an adversarial tone in order to confirm some argument, and that of the writer (or collective of writers) who undermine authority by exposing its presence, weakening its influence by encouraging a range of conflicting observations within the same text, thereby problematizing any writer's (or reader's) ability to "claim" authority. Since there are circumstances that make both poles worthwhile, there's value in exposing writers to both ends of the spectrum. It's a question of understanding the benefits of knowing how to stitch a rhetorical thread so fine as to make the text seemingly impervious to any cracks or flaws, as well as how to construct a writing that willingly exposes its fissures and paradoxes. Neither extreme is worse or better than the other; both ends of the duality represent legitimate means of expression.

Besides, there's nothing inherently offensive about embracing an air of authority within one's work so long, I would argue, as the writer has been afforded the opportunity and the skills to contemplate why that particular strategy was chosen over another. Again, the problem has less to do with one's preferred rhetorical methodology than with the habit of automatically imposing specific rhetorics while censuring viable alternatives. "Authority must not be conflated into a single ambivalent figure; we must constantly be on guard to differentiate realms and degrees of authority, specifically in terms of the type of control that is exerted" (Bernstein, *Politics of Poetic Form* 236).

Rhetorics of Silence

Capturing, preserving the gaps, lulls, and pauses— the silences that so much of our professional discourse tries to erase; the perforated, permeable texts—John Cage's inclusion of the silence that is never, ever really silent; double dashes, blank space, multiple parenthetical asides, words and lines under erasure, curious visual arrangements: all of these are echoes of attempts to foreground silence as an important part in composition, a rhetorical strategy complementing the desire to reject closure, and resist tying up texts into tight, clean packages.

A good share of academic discourse could be described as not only forceful, but often dogmatically overbearing—it is paramount to leave one's thesis loudly engraved upon the reader's mind. In opposition to this, other writers have tried, within their own texts, to articulate the silences running throughout their lives. According to the language of the academy, one would think it natural for all of us to cough up well-polished, finely honed arguments of considerable persuasive appeal on a regular basis. In reality, of course, we're constantly searching for words, stammering, hesitating, drawing blanks, and often at a loss to make logical connections. These are the silences present within all of us, and yet the command behind traditional academic discourse is always to pretend those silences don't exist.

Writers like Cixous resort to typographical techniques in order to convey the presence of silence: double dashes, excessive gaps in the text, parentheses containing no words, all of them attempts to contain the indescribable. Susan Howe finds it necessary to fill discourse with intentional fractures, "a stammering," "interruption and hesitation used as a force" ("Encloser" 192). Poet and critic Rae Armantrout specifies in further detail ways a writer might emphasize silence, thereby turning it into a powerful rhetorical tool:

1. She may end a line or poem abruptly, unexpectedly, somehow short of resolution.
2. She may create extremely tenuous connections. . . .
3. She may deliberately create the effect of inconsequence.
4. She may make use of self-contradiction or retraction.
5. She may use obvious ellipsis.
6. She may use anything which places the existent in perceptible relation to the non-existent, the absent or outside. ("Poetic Silence" 34–35)

Again, though here she discusses the construction of poems, Armantrout's techniques have relevance for expository prose, as she and other twentieth-century writers continue to reconceptualize language as a field where both "poetic" and "scholarly" investigations can merge, and coexist in the same rhetorical space, furthering the argument that dichotomies like the "creative/critical split" ought to be abandoned, or at the very least eyed with skepticism.

By "writing" in the silences, a reader can be compelled to become the writer, to imaginatively fill in the blanks. Although disconcerting to those conditioned to permit no loose ends or moments of "dead air" within a text, recognition of these silences might lead us to reexamine ourselves as more than mere interpreters and perceivers of information. We become, literally, the artist, for our imaginations are required to "complete" (i.e., continue) the work at hand. The focus shifts from a common expectation of "what will this text do to me?" to one of "what am I going to do with this text?"—a transition from passive readerly engagement to the reader as implied collaborator.

In spite of all these new ideas for composition, we should still be careful about romanticizing the possibilities for a feminine rhetoric. It can be too easy to make grandiose claims for writing styles that seek to undermine some notion of oppressive convention ("quite possible," as Mary Eagleton points out, "for a text to do this in the name of some right-wing irrationalism, or to do it in the name of nothing much at all" [202]). Nor are the writers who seek to articulate feminine grammars automatically immune to promoting their own idiosyncratic techniques as mandatory standards for all liberated women. Mary Daly and Jane Caputi's *Webster's First New Intergalactic Wickedary of the English Language*, for example, comes to mind, an alternative "Metadictionary" weaving a shifting series of "Word-Webs," linguistic maps of the authors' own concoction. On one hand Daly and Caputi's mock-reference manual is an encyclopedia chock-full of feminist word-play, a refreshing alternative for readers sympathetic with their unabashed desire to rewrite the dictionary, *their* way. The enterprise is an intriguing one, nothing less than manipulating language at its most elemental level—reconstructing grammar, defying repressive standardization, indoctrinating new vocabularies, all in hopes of creating a language system one can call one's own. At the same time, though, this feminist dictionary, taken in large doses, can come across as being as insistently dogmatic as the authoritarian "phallogrammar" the authors condemn; their new age neologisms are of formulas so rigidly imposed that there is practically no room left for deviation (in the *Wickedary*, "Feminism, Radical" is defined as "the Cause of causes, which alone of all revolutionary causes exposes the basic model and source of all forms of oppression—patriarchy—and thus can open up consciousness to active participation in movement, Transcendence, and Happiness" [75]).

Or take Hélène Cixous's brand of *écriture feminine*, characterized by a propensity to spew breathless, exclamatory prose, incessantly didactic and replete with phrasings intended to shock and embarrass purveyors of *phallogocentrism*.[12] On one hand, Cixous should be commended for helping rekindle the manifesto as a legitimate mode of argumentation: by engaging the somber forces of male academe in raunchy dueling, her unflinching satirical attacks breathe new possibilities into a professional arena where scholars might honor a satirist like Alexander Pope but are often reluctant to try their hands at the same sport.[13] (Certainly a great deal of our professional dialogue is argumentative, even nasty at times, as indicated by the frequent sparring in professional journals—but this is something far removed from the brilliant wit and craft found in works like *The Dunciad*.) But her larger argument comes under question as her call for individuality begins to sound more like a preacher's attempt to convert rather than liberate women writers; readers of "The Laugh of the Medusa" will notice how often Cixous claims women "must" do this or that. Fans of Cixous (and there are many followers) may have risked subverting their desire to undermine patriarchal authority by situating her (or any other feminist, for that matter) as a fundamental mouthpiece for any "authentic" woman's voice. The struggle to gain autonomy gets compromised by hero worship when theorists, praised for their ability to uncover and thereby topple authoritarian implications in various rhetorics, themselves become authorities, spokespersons for the marginal.

Nor should we make the mistake of thinking that advocating a feminine rhetoric, whatever our version of such an animal may be, can lead us to freedom or liberation from masculinist capitalist ideology. Cixous, for example, pretends that total escape is indeed possible: "let nothing stop you: not man; not the imbecilic capitalist machinery, in which publishing houses are the crafty, obsequious relayers of imperatives handed down by an economy that works against us and off our backs" ("Laugh of the Medusa" 247)—advice that, no matter how noble, is impossible to follow. The credulousness of Cixous's belief that one can indeed write free of patriarchal capitalist ideology is quickly apparent when we see how successfully one of her own novels was gobbled up by a publishing company that packaged its product for leering, male consumers, and Cixous becomes a victim of the "smug-faced readers, managing editors, and big bosses" (247) she so bitterly attacks. On the back cover of the 1985 London translation of her novel *Angst*, an anonymous narrative describes Cixous as "strikingly beautiful," having "immense intelligence," and invoking

"awe wherever she goes"—in that order. Three times her fiction
is described as that of a master: having "mastered different
media," she creates a protagonist who "master[s] her prolixity for
love" in a novel that is a "mastering of all that is most vulnerable
in the female unconscious." "All is laid bare on the page," the
text continues, going on to claim that men may be the ones who
get the most enlightenment from the book "because it will help
them realize the power and fascination that lies deep in every
woman." (One might even wonder how liberatory Cixous's novel
may have been if one considers that the number of readers who
read the jacket cover might very well have outnumbered those
who actually read the novel.) There is no escape from a capitalist
economy that perpetually generates such offensive, disempower-
ing ideology; and to think any form of feminine rhetoric can ultimately rid itself of this albatross is naive.

And so, given the richness, and the problematics, of a feminine
rhetoric, the most important question for the composition instructor now materializes: "Why teach it?" In one sense this is a
trick question, for there's no clear "it" there to teach—no way we
can set down penultimate guidelines for mastering these forms of
composition (just the prospect of a College Handbook of Feminine Writing seems absurdly oxymoronic). Even though I've
drawn up five loose groupings of feminine composing strategies,
one could easily add completely new forms to these divisions, or
maybe deny the lot of them altogether. To inscribe any regimen
of rules on my part would be utterly self-defeating: all of the
writerly decisions discussed here are alternatives reached at by
difficult, personal introspection and resistance by writers with
very different desires and agendas. Only one "rule," perhaps,
might surface when the possibilities of a feminine composition
are explored: that teachers and students maintain an open mind
toward languages and experiences so often ignored within our
educational institutions, and sample other legitimate modes of
writing and thinking with/in language.
    Just because the terrain described above remains largely
unmapped doesn't mean these rhetorics don't offer any lessons for
the scholar or student. Indeed the alternative—ignoring these
resisting writings just because they may seem odd, or because

they fit none of our most popular composing models—is far worse. As teachers and theorists of writing we're *expected* to be piqued and absorbed by the phenomena of writing; whether our concerns lie with issues of literacy, writing across the curriculum, writing center administration, or teaching developmental students, it should be presumed that the magnitude and complexity of composition in itself is on some level alluring, if not captivating, to all of us; consequently the inventiveness of a feminine composition is reason enough to warrant further study. But there's a lot more here than simply a new batch of rhetorical possibilities. The kinds of composition launched by these writers are a direct manifestation of the struggles and the successes of people for whom the reconstruction of syntax, grammar, and vocabulary is, again, nothing less than an act of intellectual survival. When Susan Howe asks, "Who polices questions of grammar, parts of speech, correction, and connotation? Whose order is shut inside the structure of the sentence?" we realize that this isn't all just some idle wordplay.

For roughly a century and a half, etiquette books outlined linguistic rules of behavior for American women—primers, basically, that spelled out correct linguistic conduct for the female sex. One study of these manuals points out that within these pages women were instructed to "avoid gossip, learn about male topics of conversation, not talk too much, smile, control their emotions, avoid slang, cultivate a lower-pitched voice, enunciate clearly, and above all, be a good listener" (Frank 49–50). If we examine such criteria we come closer to understanding the extreme degree of linguistic acculturation women have suffered at the hands of men (the primary authors and distributors of these guidebooks): the "avoidance of gossip" means to refrain from discussing topics relevant to an immediate group of confidantes, in favor of subjects more abstract in character. "Learning of male topics of conversation" implies that knowledge is intrinsically gender-specific, and that what might constitute "female" topics of conversation are of a knowledge order substantially lower than those of men. "Being a good listener and keeping quiet" enforces respect for authority, i.e., male talk. Allowing "displays of emotion" to enter into the conversation is impermissible, for it subverts the dialogic uniformity of abstraction. Even the woman's natural tone of voice had to be erased, in order to preserve the (so-called) deeper resonance of male speech.

To put it simply, feminine rhetoric—whether we define it as a disruption of the rational, and what Mary Ellmann calls "sudden alterations of the reckless and the sly, the wildly voluble and the laconic" (Eagleton 201), or Susan Howe's "shattering" of andro-centric dialectic, or Rosmarie Waldrop's incessant need for lexi-cal "surprise" as a life-affirming condition (70), or Kathy Acker's pouring of multiple genres into a textual blender so as to concoct hybrids of startling originality—however we describe it, these composings *demand* the attention of the writing teacher and the rhetorician. Nicole Brossard may have summed it up best:

> We cannot avoid questioning this cultural field of language, which both provides us with energy or deprives us of it. What I call the cultural field of language is made of male sexual and psychic energies transformed through centuries of written fiction into standards for imagination, frames of ref-erences, patterns of analysis, networks of meaning, rhetorics of body and soul. Digging in that field can be, for a creative woman, a mental health hazard. (75)

Contemporary Options

*Since in principle language belongs to everyone, we are
entitled to reappropriate it by taking the initiative to
intervene when it gives the impression of closing itself
off, and when our desire clashes with common usage.*
—NICOLE BROSSARD

*I'm extremely stubborn about what I write. I only want
to write things the way I want to write them. I think
that quality of stubbornness, of wanting to do exactly
what I want to do . . . I don't put that forward as a
virtue, although I certainly don't feel it's not a virtue,
but I don't feel it's necessary to put forward these kind
of views in a holier-than-thou or a bohemian dirtier-
than-thou way. These are simply things one does, finds
oneself able to do. And I'm not able, perhaps, to do
anything different than what I do.*
—CHARLES BERNSTEIN

Shatter the mirrors.
—IHAB HASSAN

Powerful similarities exist between the explorations of the new feminine rhetorics and forms associated
with early and late modernist writers like Gertrude Stein, Ezra
Pound, William Carlos Williams, James Joyce, Virginia Woolf,
and Charles Olson; Rachel Blau DuPlessis has commented on
these similarities, pointing out that "a list of the characteristics
of postmodernism would be a list of the traits of women's writing: inwardness, illumination in the here and now (Levertov);
use of the continuous present (Stein); the foregrounding of consciousness (Woolf); the muted, multiple, or absent *telos*; a fasci-

nation with process; a horizontal world; a decentered universe where 'man' (indeed) is no longer privileged" ("For the Etruscans" 286–87). Though the parallels between modernism and more recent feminist poetics have their limits—the insensitivity, for instance, Pound, Williams, and Olson showed for the struggles of their female contemporaries, and the sexist allusions in their work—it's understandable that a theorist like Julia Kristeva finds modernist authors, particularly Lautréamont, Mallarmé, and Joyce, to be "revolutionary" writers whose disruption of conventional grammars and syntaxes makes them models for the type of asexual, nonhierarchical writing she admires. "The modernist poem, with its abrupt shifts, ellipses, breaks and apparent lack of logical construction is a kind of writing in which the rhythms of the body and the unconscious have managed to break through the strict rational defences of conventional social meaning" (Moi 11).

But Kristeva's method of showing her desire to see writers break through such rigid defenses is as frustrating as it is encouraging. While praising the compositionist who highlights play, flexibility, and rhetorical subversion, Kristeva uses writers long dead in order to prove her point, ignoring a wealth of contemporary writers who continue to reshape the boundaries of composition. One reason for this may be that examining past innovators from the safety of historical perspective permits the author the illusion of disassociating herself from the forms under investigation, whereas to take a contemporary vanguard seriously is to indirectly beg comparison with one's own work— which in turn would make the prose of a modern theorist like Kristeva noticeably formalist compared to the current, ongoing stream of stylistically more imaginative texts published around her.

For there is no lack of innovative contemporary writing. All one has to do is thumb through a Small Press Distribution catalog or the latest issue of *Factsheet Five* to sample the thriving current of new writers exploring (and bending, and shifting, and smashing) the limits of composition.[1] In their introduction to *The L=A=N=G=U=A=G=E Book*, a slice of some of the more self-consciously exploratory writings of the late 1970s and early 1980s, the editors summarize their project as examining and supporting "a spectrum of writing that places its attention primarily on language and ways of making meaning, that takes for granted neither vocabulary, grammar, process, shape, syntax, program, or subject matter" (Andrews and Bernstein ix). But this characterization is hardly limited to those affiliated with the Language poets. The more one investigates the wealth of national and international catalogues, anthologies, zines, and manuscripts in circulation at any given moment, the more one realizes that the concept of "marginal" versus "mainstream" collapses, until there is no longer any mainstream at all—only a ganglia of unique communities with their own philosophies, aesthetics, and assumptions, coexisting perfectly well without each other. And yet, while an occasional theorist might briefly indulge in examining some modernist texts in order to test their relevance for composition,[2] for the most part composition and literary theorists have chosen to view the academy as a more or less self-contained entity wherein a select range of permissible rhetorics jostle for attention. That the walls of the university might be thought of as porous, receptive to numerous contemporary "postmodern" and underground rhetorical currents is an idea largely unexplored beyond a certain theoretical level (some of the work in cultural studies, as well as recent conversations pertaining to hypertext, where innovative composition philosophies of the twentieth century come into play, are noticeable exceptions to this). If this weren't so, the kinds of discourses touched on in the previous chapters wouldn't seem so out of place next to our more familiar current-traditional and liberal-expressive workings.

In this chapter I want to consider several issues relevant to the study and teaching of composition, issues that have been key preoccupations for contemporary writers investigating alternate modes of discourse—namely, the problematics of applying terms like "natural" to any compositional approach, additional considerations of genre and its various contemporary metamorphoses, alternatives to the spectator-participant dichotomy largely assumed in composition theory, new possibilities for rethinking the relationship between discourse and temporality, and the "rejection of closure" as a valid rhetorical possibility.

The Fallacy of the "Natural"

*Natural: the very word should be struck from
the language.*
—CHARLES BERNSTEIN

For those of us who grew up hearing teachers and
handbooks tell us that good writers know how to make sentences
that flow *naturally*, use language in *natural*, uncontrived ways,
and refrain from *unnatural* vocabulary and syntactic arrangement, Bernstein's words sound a trifle overstated. What kind of
writer, after all, seeks to construct a prose that is consciously
aberrant and off-key? (Many, actually, but we'll get to that later.)
If we want to persuade and educate readers, to argue and entertain with success and efficiency, doesn't it make sense to work
hard at developing a prose style that proceeds in a manner readers will find unobjectionable, pleasing, and familiar—i.e., natural? So what is it that provokes a writer like Bernstein to get all
bent out of shape over such seemingly . . . *natural* assumptions
about writing?

But to mandate what is and is not natural is simultaneously to
decree what is impermissible—what is ultimately wrong, inappropriate, bad, ugly, and undeserving of attention. To claim an
understanding of what is natural is to assume command over aesthetics in general, to cloak private, local ideologies under the
guise of some larger "norm." Even those rhetoricians and teachers
who claim to bypass this imposition of authority by privileging a
relativistic span of conflicting discourses nevertheless ordain
some sense of "the natural" via the tenor of their prose, the publishing companies they choose to represent their work, their lecturing style, the organizational structure of the classroom, and the
criteria they use to grade papers. An obvious example of this is
that, though I argue for accepting discourses that deviate in
extreme ways from the prose style of this book, I even undermine
my own argument as each successive sentence advances in a form
decidedly unlike any of the innovative rhetorics I'm pushing for:
I am here trying to sculpt a prose that not only reads with some
consistent "naturalness" (some academic audience's definition of
fluidity, consistency) when compared to the other sentences that

surround it, but also appears fairly acceptable—that is, natural enough not to scare readers away—to those who are most prone to pick up this book in the first place. But of course, my sentences are not natural in the sense that they reflect any global consensus of speakers or writers; rather, they result from centuries of powerful institutions that have mandated certain idiosyncratic aesthetic preferences as "standard" (i.e., normal) English. To assume or claim the naturalness of one's discourse is to forget that we live in a world utterly interwoven with diametric philosophies and aesthetics, many of them in dramatic opposition to one another.

Obviously, in order to communicate at all there must be shared and implicit guidelines—to get from A to B we need to know the same alphabet. Within local confines some sense of "the natural" not only makes perfect sense but is absolutely essential for the most elemental of communication. It is natural, for example, that Charles Bernstein says the word "natural" ought to be banished from our vocabularies because this reasoning fits in with his pluralistic philosophy and the sentiments of the community of writers he associates with. Any relationship, family, classroom, and bureaucracy must invariably agree on some shared dialect(s). Discursive agreement and shared convention are necessary for our survival; we need the commonality of our local discourses in order to coexist.

But there is a radical difference between our everyday adoption of local dialects and the writing instructor who takes on the responsibility of unequivocally defining for her students the incontestable boundaries of "natural" discourse. Whether conservative or liberal, I think most composition instructors and writing programs at least claim to operate on the principle that students can benefit from learning how to write powerfully and influentially for at least several audiences: the professors and professionals they're most apt to encounter, and the students themselves. To do this often requires a fictionalizing of discourse so that it can be described in a global rather than local context. Even liberal and Marxist pedagogies seeking to help students locate their own "voices" while encouraging them to critique the assumptions inherent within institutional constraints can perpetuate the natural/unnatural dichotomy, as the rhetorical strategies represented in assigned readings, the discursive style of the instructor's speech, the manner in which the instructor describes her assignments, and the prose style found in the marginal notes written on student papers all quietly but powerfully reinforce a notion of the natural belonging to the teacher and the institution, and not necessarily to the student. In fact, the single most powerful lesson that occurs in most writing classes might very well take place on the first day of the semester when the course syllabus is handed out, the only time many students ever read something of length written by their instructor. This brief document can be tremendously influential. Students, understandably assuming any text created by a writing instructor might be indicative of what good writing is, could interpret the prose of the syllabus as appropriately representative of academic discourse. Regardless of whether the thematic content of the syllabus conveys a strictly authoritarian tone or one more "user-friendly," any decisions inherent within the instructor's grammar, subtle or overt, can easily underscore a particular version of literacy.[3]

Let's look at the assumptions made in the following statements: when a writer "shapes his experience into a verbal object, an art form, in order to communicate it and to realize it more fully himself," claims James Britton, "he is seeking to recapture a *natural* order that his daily actions have forfeited" (66, my emphasis). Judith and Geoffrey Summerfield assert that successful texts are those that best create an illusion of "naturalism" (62). And in her book *Writing the Natural Way*, Gabriele Lusser Rico spends considerable time defining for her readers the correct process for "natural" writing, which "occurs as follows: nucleus word leads to clustering, clustering to an internal pattern awareness, pattern awareness to the emotionally charged trial-web shift, trial-web shift to the impulse to write" (93). What this shows is that even liberal educators like these are not immune from elevating their own ethnocentric, culturally restricted preferences into universal prerequisites. Why must the white middle-class professor's notion of "the natural" be synonymous with that of the freshman from El Salvador, the black urban student, or even another white middle-class professor down the hall? How can any male definitively characterize what is natural for women? In that case, for what reason are we to believe that viewpoints informed from heterosexual identifications are always commensurate with those of gays and lesbians?

Arguing that there is no such thing as a natural writing style, Charles Bernstein explains that the academic taste for various forms of expository prose results from a relatively recent historical need to separate discursive tendencies into simple, easily manageable schisms—valuable versus disposable, normal versus abnormal:

> It seems to me that, as a mode, contemporary expository writing edges close to being merely a *style* of decorous thinking, rigidified and formalized to a point severed from its historical relation to method in Descartes and Bacon. It is no longer an enactment of thinking or reasoning but a representation (and simplification) of an eighteenth-century ideal of reasoning. . . . At a certain historical moment certain paths were chosen as to the style that would express a quasiscientific voice of reason and authority . . . a voice that was patriarchal, monologic, authoritative, impersonal. The predominance of this authoritative plain style (taught in such guides as Strunk and White) and its valorization as a picture of clarity and reason is a relatively recent phenomenon. (*Content's Dream* 221–22)

Consequently it is not that the academic expository essay embodies valuable traits lacking in other compositional forms, but simply that some form has to serve as the machinery through which the dominating elite must enforce its agenda. It matters little which coat of arms the ruling aristocracy displays on its flag; what matters is that the same banner be flown everywhere in the dominion. "The crucial mechanism to keep in mind," continues Bernstein, "is not the rules of current preferred forms versus possible alternatives but *the mechanism of distinction and discrimination itself* that allows for certain language practices to be legitimized (as correct, clear, coherent) and other language practices to be discredited (as wrong, vague, nonsensical, antisocial, ambiguous, irrational, illogical, crude, dumb . . .) (*Content's Dream* 223). That is, it's not so much the standard as the machinery of standardization that determines the enforcing discourse of power.

To use some idea of the natural without identifying the problems inherent in such terminology is basically to say that "this is natural because I say so." If only a disclaimer were introduced into this assumption, to make it read: "this is what *some* people might consider a natural way to write, so let's investigate what it can and can't offer us, and then move on to other interpretations," the argument would become one of potential encouragement, not commanding dogma, and thus pedagogically more accurate and beneficial; hence the reason why so many twentieth-century writers are motivated to remind us of the necessity of scrutinizing any "claims to naturalness and objectivity carefully to find out what or who is being suppressed" (Armantrout, "Mainstream Marginality" 144).

The Spectator/Participant Dichotomy

An interesting feature of many theories of composition is their tendency to situate the thinking and writing process within a conceptual framework confined by two "natural" poles: immediate involvement versus reflective distance. James Britton's understanding of composition, for example, relies heavily on his belief that authors must invariably perform as either Participants or Spectators within their written work, with Expressive language serving as a doorway into either realm—a sort of roving catalyst bouncing between the two extremes. In the participant mode we communicate in order to get things done: conversation, reports, memos, shopping lists—all these are products of transactive discourse. On the flip side is the world of poetic involvement, those contemplative moods where we operate as spectators, whether in meditative expository prose or poetry, and "stop the world in order to get off" (Britton 77). One of the byproducts of this objectification is the ability to "globally contextualize," a term Britton uses to refer to moments when we "reconstruct the verbal construct" and make it our own—moments when we get the big picture, so to speak, as opposed to the "piecemeal contextualization" we experience while living in the transactive mode.

Other theorists lend support to Britton's binary orientation: Judith and Geoffrey Summerfield strongly emphasize the major role paratactic and hypotactic modes of discourse play in our communicative processes, using these terms in much the same way Britton describes participant and spectator; Louise Rosen-blatt similarly discusses how we write in terms of aesthetic and efferent effect, her equivalent of poetic and transactive aware-ness. Donald Murray's description of this dichotomy centers on his notion of internal revision (inner motivation and personal speech) pitted against external revision (attention to form and convention), views that have been shared by Donald Graves and Janet Emig. And Peter Elbow summarizes his idea of the compos-ing process in distinctly Coleridgian terms involving an interplay between first-order and second-order thinking.

As a pedagogical tool this design has definite value. As a con-ceptual opposition of purely dialectical value, and not necessarily intended to denote phenomenal experience, the spectator/partic-ipant dichotomy can be effective in making students aware that becoming a hypothetical spectator is not only advantageous but necessary if one wishes to anticipate and interact constructively with "outside" audiences. Since inexperienced writers often con-sider their writings from egocentric perspectives, by urging them to adopt the myth of an introspective viewpoint the teacher can help such writers anticipate how other audiences of differing interpretative backgrounds might regard their work.

Taken too literally though, this way of splitting the world runs the risk of honoring a static formula, an overly simplistic and classically romantic view of the cognitive process as subject to some metaphysical toggle switch that forces writers to situate themselves in one extreme or the other. Not that Britton, the Summerfields, Rosenblatt, et al. necessarily claim their dichotomies to be epistemological truths in this reductive fash-ion; still, taken to its extreme such a model is reducible to this inert duality. And apart from metaphysics, in practice many writ-ers portray the relationship between themselves and their envi-ronments according to a less polar scale.

The notion of the detached observer, for example, has prob-lems: is there, after all, any way we can really become total specta-tors, and remove ourselves from the flow of information and activity we wish to examine? For we are always inescapably partici-pating during every moment of our experience, no matter how we choose to define the process of that experience—and how else can one observe and contextualize without becoming actively engaged? There is no definitive way for any of us to "freeze" the climate at hand, and put our written texts on hold (Britton's "stopping" of the world) while we sort things out; procedures of summarization and evaluation never exist in vacuums, but are always inseparably conditioned by the flow of time; as such our writings are always in some state of flux. Whether we call it reflection or participation, we never occupy an "exterior" vantage point from which we can detachedly observe the continual procedural flow of incremental momentary perception. Or, as one writer puts it, "we do not first have some sensation or impression and then order it; rather, we do not have a cognition at all until ordering has happened . . . the verb (to know, to be aware, to perceive) comes first and it produces the noun which is consciousness" (Brummett, 84).

Composing Time through Different Lenses

This desire, in fact—to globally contextualize from a retrospective point of view—reveals the residue of a larger Euro-romantic privileging of analytic distancing and passive objectification. Global contextualization, as well as the objective distance required in order to magically metamorphose from participant into spectator, are concepts rooted in what Milic Capek has termed a "Newtonian-Euclidian subconscious," a sensibility of temporal consciousness grounded in the linear-sequential paradigm where past, present, and future can be thought of as spatial coordinates plotted across a linear continuum.

> Our subconscious is far more conservative than we are willing to admit, and this is true not only of our emotional subconscious but of the intellectual one as well. That is why Newtonian-Euclidean habits of thought will—if not always, at least for a considerable time—appear more natural to mankind than the new modes of thought which require so much effort and vigilant analysis. (181)

Which isn't to say this Newtonian residue is "wrong"; we rely upon the metaphoric notion of a time line constantly; indeed, it's hard to imagine lifting ourselves outside of this orientation for any length of time (in fact, it's difficult enough to verbalize temporal consciousness without divulging the deep-rootedness of our linear metaphors, evident in using expressions like "*length* of time"). Rather, the problem is that this perspective fails to anticipate alternative cross-cultural and twentieth-century interpretations of temporality, and how these philosophies might further reshape our understanding and making of written discourse.

An interesting component of writers promoting various African philosophies is their resistance to Western depictions of time. Léopold Sédar Senghor offers the following description of négritude's understanding of temporality: "While modern Indo-European languages emphasize the abstract notion of time, African languages emphasize the *aspect*, the concrete way in which the action of the verb takes place. These are essentially *concrete* languages" (84–85). John Mbiti makes an argument for not three but two dimensions of time indigenous to African understanding: "potential time" and "actual time." "The linear concept of time in western thought with an indefinite past, present and infinite future," he states, "is particularly foreign to African thinking. The future is virtually absent because events which lie in it have not taken place, they have not been realized and cannot, therefore, constitute time" (cited in Anozie 53). This characteristic is confirmed by Geneva Smitherman, who emphasizes the fact that the concept of "progression"

> occurs only into the past world of the spirit. Thus the "future" is the past. In the community, then, one's sense of "time" is based on participation in and observation of nature's rhythms and community events. (In the African conception of "time," the key is not to be "on time," but "in time.") (75)

This substitution of a three-part temporal structure with one binary in form recalls Benjamin Lee Whorf's portrayal of time in Hopi culture. Whorf also found the Hopis lacking a threefold temporal structure, in its place a tension between what he called "manifested" (or "objective") time and a "manifesting" ("subjective") state of being. Describing manifested time as the equivalent of both Western concepts of past and present, Whorf conceived of manifesting time as a peculiar cognitive dimension where the future as we perceive it is indistinguishably fused with "all that we call mental," where both the imagination and awareness of future are somehow folded into the same perceptual plane. Although Whorf's assertion that nowhere in the Hopi language is there to be found any reference to time, either implicit or explicit, has since been disproved (Malotki), others have pointed to similar Native American oppositions to Western time: Paula Gunn Allen comparing the "achronicity" of the Indian's understanding of time as cyclical as opposed to the sequential characteristic of Western views; Leslie Marmon Silko characterizing the Pueblo's communal discourse structure as not linear but closer to a spider web in form, where threads radiate outward in multiple directions and intersect at various moments: "As with the web, the structure will emerge as it is made and you must simply listen and trust, as the Pueblo people do, that meaning will be made" (54).

Feminist theorists have also actively sought nonlinear metaphors for composition. Julia Kristeva, in her essay "Women's Time," proposes a division of temporal understanding sympathetic to female consciousness, where "monumental" time, a more cyclical frame of reference that Kristeva links with female subjectivity, is offered as an alternative to linear or cursive time. Monumental time "retains repetition and eternity" (473), a locus for female intuition, whereas linear time is described as a progressive unfolding of moments. Linear (masculine, historical) time might be characterized as a succession of particles, whereas a wave would be more appropriate to symbolize the flow of Kristeva's "Monumental" time. Elsewhere, Nicole Brossard echoes this attraction to the nonlinear as she remarks how within her writing she "started to use new metaphors to understand things: the spiral, the hologram, metaphors which would help me to drift away from a linear and binary approach" (78).

Anthropologist Roy Wagner does a splendid job of exposing the logic at work within these nonlinear, presence-saturated means of interpreting temporal consciousness. To do so, Wagner focuses on two schools of thought regarding the perception of time. The first viewpoint is one probably most of us share, and it is the basis of both the spectator-participant and prewriting/writing/revising models popular in composition theory: the phenomenon of what Wagner calls conventional "clock time," which is measured spatially, as opposed to "epoch" or "organic" time, which is a matter of duration. Clock time—"unreal time," Wagner calls it—is inevitably spatially oriented, its measure recorded by the movement of the sun and moon, the sweep of the second hand, sand sifting to the bottom of the hourglass—all physical objects traversing space. "We measure space and call it time (or, more precisely, we measure space as the 'time' of our measurement)." What's curious about this measurement, Wagner shows, is that "we have no good empirical check, beyond the synchronization of other and different spatial analogies, on whether the 'thing' that is being measured and analogized exists at all, much less whether it 'flows' at the measured and uniform rate that our instruments suggest it does" (83).

What Wagner calls "epoch" or "organic" time, on the other hand, "does not accumulate (and *count*) like intervals; its events are in themselves relations, each one subsuming and radically transforming what has gone before. Each unit, then, *differentiates* the character of the whole beyond anticipation, assimilating what has preceded it into its own relation, a 'now' that supersedes, rather than extends, its 'then'" (81). "A memory of childhood," he continues, "an episode from the Middle Ages, or a fantasy of the near or distant future: each is a piece of figurative time that belongs to a flow of analogy—a 'now' that remembers or imagines itself into (and out of) other 'nows'" (90). As a result, the only nonmetaphoric time that exists is nothing less than the duration of our lives: "Life," writes Wagner, "is in fact the only 'kind' of time that we have, and literal time is a mere translation or common denominator of it" (84).

The African distinction between potential and actual time, Whorf's manifested versus manifesting time, Native American views of time as cyclical or spiral as opposed to sequential, Kristeva's concept of Monumental time as an answer to masculine cursive time, and Wagner's "clock time/organic time" distinction—all of these reflect a need to leave behind the potential oversimplification of the linear model and in its place postulate a more complex balance between the two poles of conventional (formalist, abstract, historical, institutional) and experiential (nonlinear, shifting, active, organic) temporal consciousness.[4] They also have close parallels with the concept of "twoity" developed by mathematician and founder of the Intuitionist School of Foundations of Mathematics, L. E. J. Brouwer. In a lucid introduction to difficult material (see the Introduction to *Being = Space x Action*), Charles Stein outlines some basic principles underlying Brouwer's accomplishments in mathematics and mysticism. Brouwer calls attention to the fact that our fundamental intuition of "point-instants" operating within a linear continuum is an impossible reduction in that such a linear paradigm is itself born out of temporal experience, and consequently an abstraction that simplifies the complex fabric from which it derives. Instead of this "move of time" that implies "a linear continuum of point-like moments of infinitesimal duration, which vanish as they arise and are replaced spontaneously by successor moments" (C. Stein 15), Brouwer replaces the concept of the point-instant with that of a "twoity":

> a dyad with the following characteristic: each moment of consciousness spontaneously splits into two parts— 1, the trace of itself surviving as a spontaneous memory; 2, the succeeding moment. This new moment repeats the process, similarly splitting into the trace of itself and its own successor. Both the dynamic character of time and the way consciousness is bound up with temporality are thus built into the fundamental concept. (16)

Stein points out that this isn't just a more representative model upon which to base our understanding and construction of time; to understand the import of twoity requires each thinker to perform "a deliberate concentration of consciousness on its own streaming" (16), to enter into a private, intensely contemplative, meditational state of mind; otherwise this "bi-unity" remains just another analogue, hypothetical and unrealized. This need to immerse oneself in an experiential embrace of the durational flow of our lives recalls Gertrude Stein's concern for what she termed the "continual present," a concept positing that any sense of experiential closure or finality is unattainable, and that the only option any of us have is to continually begin, again, and again, and again. "The composition is the thing seen by every one living in the living they are doing, they are the composing of the composition that at the time they are living is the composition of the time in which they are living. It is that that makes living a thing they are doing" (G. Stein 516). Instead of getting bogged down in the romantic trap of encapsulating human experience within zones of perception independent of one another, of which one must either be objectively or subjectively aware (the distortion of the Wordsworthian attempt to harness emotion recollected in tranquility), the implication of Gertrude Stein's philosophy is that our only recourse is to proceed: to continue, alter, and thereby create and recreate anew whatever activity we are engaged in. One is never turning back, but always already beginning, redefining. Composition, in other words, not as the revision of past artifacts, but as the perpetual construction of starting over.

Each of these alternatives to the Western (arguably masculine) insistence on depicting time as unidirectional linear progression could have major and largely untapped implications for composition theory. As we further refine our knowledge of how writers create texts, and as we expand our understanding of the nature(s) of composition theory, the metaphors we use to help approximate the complex ways writers and readers make texts will have to keep pace with contemporary and cross-cultural philosophies relevant for our discipline. We now have access to a host of different metaphors and paradigms with which to interpret temporality and its relation to the creation of discourse. Given the increasing attention to cross-cultural and "postmodern" texts and literacies, how will we compensate for discourse philosophies that regard temporality and its effect on communication in non-Newtonian, non-Western forms? Can those of us still holding onto the participant-spectator dichotomy, for example, a split that must inevitably separate the "poetic" from the transactive, effectively critique the work of compositionists for whom such divisions are, if not obsolete, often irrelevant? If our composing models are influenced by linear paradigms, how will we respond to the writer interested in subverting such linearity through avoidance of closure, fragmentation, circular organization?[5] Do we have an obligation to introduce students to these additional forms, or should composition theorists confine themselves to addressing the construction of discourse along more provincial lines?

The Cross-Fertilization of Genre

From the found texts and chance compositions of the dadaists and surrealists, to the visual scripts of the Russian constructivists, to more recent cross-disciplinary and "postmodern" accomplishments, we can now point to hundreds of writers and performers who have made it their business to investigate, and in so doing reconstruct the possibilities for written and performative discourse. Accompanying these ongoing explorations are new philosophical orientations that can drastically affect the ways we think of composition. Two areas especially cry out for reconsideration: our habit of separating various writings styles according to specified genres, and our frequent expectation that closure remain an essential component of successful written discourse.

The shock effects of poststructuralism are behind us. Deconstruction, once philosophy's newest cutting edge, now occupies the status of the most recent chapter in our big book of theoretical moments. "Postmodern" is a term that has come to characterize any number of phenomena: an emotional shift away from romantic modernism; self-reflexive, self-questioning poetics; analyses of late capitalism and its shaping (or negation) of twentieth-century culture; newfound fascination (or despair) over the omnipresence of ideology and the metanarrative; confusion in the face of an unknowable deluge of perpetual information, signifying the death of metaphysics; paralysis in trying to comprehend what it means to live in a state (and State) of constant environmental and social violence, kitsch, mass consumption and destruction; and so on. As "postmodernism" was quickly gobbled up and digested by the media—what with the airing of "Postmodern MTV" in 1989, and film critics calling movies like Madonna's latest autodocumentary "the essence of postmodernism" shortly thereafter—the word came to signify little more than the latest marketing cliché, and consequently its own death. As such, the question before us now (at least the one that interests me) is: what remains for the compositionist after the debris of deconstruction, in the wake of our preoccupation with the postmodern moment? What insights can we garner from the theoretical turmoil of the past several decades and use to reshape our pedagogical needs and desires?

One of the more fascinating upshots of poststructuralism and the attention to the postmodern is that the matter of genre has forever been called into question. Where does one genre end and another begin? If the boundaries that separate poetry from prose, biography from fiction, science from journalism can no longer be drawn with the same degree of confidence we once knew, then how do we continue thinking about writing? It was so much easier to discuss composition when the boxes were self-contained and autonomous: when creative writing looked and sounded a certain way that expository prose didn't, when critical theory was clearly distinct from autobiography.[6] Now we no longer have boxes, but multiple stylistic planes that freely overlap each other, texts like various layers of colored acetate randomly honeycombed, sandwiching and separating at the whim of the writer: in some sections single colors filter through, while elsewhere tints fuse together in complex patterns. Of course this kind of text is still quite rare in most of our academic arenas; there is no lack of academicians insistent upon preserving conventional genre distinctions, as practically all of our professional journals attest. But it has become difficult if not impossible to ignore the influence of texts that do resist such traditional categories. Works like Derrida's *Glas*, Nabokov's *Pale Fire*, Cixous's "Laugh of the Medusa," Ihab Hassan's *Paracriticisms*, Borges's essays, Wittgenstein's notes, the prose of Roland Barthes, Norman O. Brown, and Blanchot, recent work by Michelle Cliff, Rachel Blau DuPlessis, Charles Bernstein, and Eduardo Galeano—all of these have already gained too much attention to be dismissed as the occasional expository oddity. Writers like these remind us that such manipulation of genre has been going on for more than a century, from the prose of Whitman, Baudelaire, Lautréamont, and Mallarmé, to that of D. H. Lawrence, Stein, Pound, and Williams, to the texts of Duchamp, Cage, and Olson.

As compositionists continue to embrace terms like *heteroglossia* and *bricolage* we discover the increasing fascination many have with those conglomerate texts and theories that are mosaics of unlikely sources and influences, defying conventional categorization in order to present readers insights unobtainable in more standardized discourse. Genre, for many writers, has simply vanished. Richard Rorty, showing a similarity with theorists like Robert Scholes and Richard Lanham, urges "that all writing should be viewed as a seamless whole. . . . A piece of writing can have motives and effects not predictable from the genre it follows. . . . Even the writer may be mistaken in expecting only one kind of result when he or she is trying to work out a certain problem" (Kolenda 47).[7] Continuing in this direction, Michael Davidson talks of "palimtexts," his term for texts that aren't literary objects or genres but "writing-in-process" utilizing any number of textual sources, works that are at once original concoctions as well as the residue of past tracings and influences (78). Here the text is perceived not as a finely wrought artifact carefully framed and controlled, but as the manifestation of its own unfolding, unending genesis—the text *is* the process of its own construction, rather than the product of a contemplative imagination reorganizing, from a distance, prior drafts into palatable wholes. Davidson claims the "palimtext" doesn't "represent the mind thinking; it *is* the thinking itself, including its marginal references, afterthoughts and postscripts" (80). Or "the desire," as Bernstein puts it, "for writing to be the end of its own activity, its very thatness" (*Content's Dream* 68).

This desire to foreground the ceaseless flux forever characterizing the evolution of the written word was imaginatively captured by Ihab Hassan in his work *Paracriticisms*, a theoretical collection of musings that advocated abandoning genre in favor of what he calls "speculations"; in an attempt to compose not a dialectic but a "multilectic" (xii), Hassan's paracriticisms were intended to reflect "the erotics of participation . . . the perpetual effort of self-creation" and the "playful discontinuity" he considered to be primary concerns of the contemporary critic (24). Within *Paracriticisms* the reader finds a mixed bag of textual forms and styles, including the following: "acceptable" scholarly prose; font changes to indicate where more fragmented notes have been brought into the text; poetry; bibliographies tossed out at unexpected moments; dialogue between fictional personas (Hassan playing the roles of Reviewer, Professor, and Literary Cynic, all of whom criticize Hassan's previous manuscripts); codas; and chapters preceded by dozens of epigraphs. "Typographic variation and thematic repetition, serialism and its parody, allusion and analogy, query and collage, quotation and juxtaposition," all coexist in the final composite (xii). The result is not criticism imitating art, but the results of a critic digging into the possibilities of his imaginative voices.

Writers like these have in common the shared assumption that to grapple with human experience in all its forms requires one to seek new means of articulating that adventure; to assume that all such experience can be told within our most familiar genre distinctions is not only ethnocentric, but an insult to the imagination. Permitting no subversion of these boundaries denies the exhilaration that can come from composing thoughts across a variety of expressive paths; it distorts the flexible character of experience, what Rorty calls "tissues of contingencies" forever in modulation. This isn't to deny the validity of acknowledging or even teaching traditional genres; the complexity of composition and its infinite manifestations frequently require us to agree on standard boundaries, so that we might better fathom the evolutionary flow of rhetorical forms that have shaped the work of past and current writers. Such perspectives are especially valuable for immature writers, who can easily conflate all of writing into some incomprehensibly amorphous mass of sentences and paragraphs that "good writers" just automatically know how to manipulate. But there are limits to how far teachers ought to enforce these social and institutional boundaries; clinging to conventional stylistic patterns ignores the abundance of texts that defy such pigeonholing, foreshortening the compositionist's ability to imaginatively fashion language in new ways.

Embracing those types of writings that refuse to fit neatly into our most comfortable notions of genre, and encouraging our students to taste the effects of exploring their ideas along similar lines, might bring us closer to the spirit of William James's "philosophy of plural facts," what he called a "mosaic philosophy" (46): ideas and information not seen as grounded in any metaphysical bedrock but rather joined at the edges, revealing a mosaic of multiple surfaces—strings of continuums hinged not by any larger, totalizing categories of genre, but by their interaction with one another. In other words, meaning made not by any abstract compartmentalizations of discourse, but by the constant bumping together of language, resulting in both familiar and unusual patterns.

Most importantly, this confusion of genre breaks down one of the more debilitating dichotomies sustained within the academy: the separation between poetry and prose. To maintain this schism is to sustain a dichotomy rendered archaic by the constellation of writings that cross between the poles, thereby transgressing and dissolving common genre lines. Since Baudelaire we have had poetries in prose; since Pope there has been criticism in verse. Lately we have seen the development of what Benjamin Hollander calls the "analytic lyric," that is, intuitive criticism in forms that blur the distinction between poetry and critical discourse:

> A critical interpretation of a text can itself constitute an analytic lyric rather than simply a normative or explicative approach to a work: an analytic lyric (by which I mean a writing) that can inhabit a site where poetry and the methods of examining it converge in a critically informed music; a writing moved to a dramatic and participatory lyric gesture by the occasions and/or poetic texts which provoked it. These kinds of writing remain outside the canon of the critical establishment—primarily because they break down the status of the expository, essay form as the singularly adept critical method—and they represent the work of such seminal figures as Robert Duncan (*The H.D. Book*), Paul Celan (*The Collected Prose*) and, more recently, Susan Howe (*My Emily Dickinson*). (Levi Straus)[8]

Again, some might make the mistake of assuming that writers like Duncan, Celan, and Howe, in addition to others discussed here, hold little or no significance for the field of composition studies, which is after all generally concerned with the expository essay, not poetry. But the term "poetry" has become so expansive as to include far more than the traditional forms with which it was once associated; better to regard such people as investigative, experimental writers, authors interested in exploring written discourse along infinite paths, whose working space can no longer be characterized by conventional understandings of the term "poetry." Contemporary writers like these are our most extreme example of the probing compositionist, the writer continually plumbing the shifting intricacies of syntax and grammar in order to further articulate the possibilities of critical expression.

The Dissolution of Closure

Why insist that knowing is a static relation out of time when it practically seems so much a function of our active life. . . . When the whole universe seems only to be making itself valid and to be still incomplete (else why its ceaseless changing?) why, of all things, should knowing be exempt?
—WILLIAM JAMES

THE OPEN TEXT

A significant side effect of contemporary works that distort conventional distinctions of genre is that such writing might tend to undermine any semblance of total resolution; and so the idea of closure, for the conglomerate text, becomes problematic.

A great deal of writing instruction, whether interpreted through current-traditional or liberal filters, eventually gets down to the business of helping students create texts that embody some sense of closure. Even those who grimace at the rigidity of five-paragraph themes and other traditional skeletons generally seek to make their students learn ways of composing texts that indicate some aura of completion. Excessive tangents are discouraged because they can make a text seem too meandering, too uncharted. Rhetorical style is expected to remain more or less consistent so that the reader is not halted by confronting unexpected grammars, vocabularies, and phrasings at every turn. Even the instructor who prefers not to force students to generate thesis sentences and hierarchical outlines nevertheless often wants students to develop texts that show evidence of some intentional central core, some "primary idea"—I know I frequently do, for instance. But what other options are there available to the contemporary writer, and thus the student?

If a text consciously jumps from genre to genre, shifting say from autobiographical anecdote to critical analysis to verse to drama to parody—or capitalizes on any of these forms within the same compositional space—any stylistic "spine" within the work becomes convoluted and twisted. The text is no longer a central skeleton clothed within a uniform skin, but more like a shifting mobile, an assemblage of various impulses collected in the same space but no longer hegemonically displayed. Though texts of this kind still revolve around a few primary overriding themes— John Cage's "Lecture on Commitment," for example (see chapter three), though a hodgepodge of anecdotes and insights, neverthe- less continually harks back to the central issue of the title—the polyphonic character of these works becomes a fixed component of their overall content. And so texts that mix genre are restrict- ed from obtaining the same kind of closure associated with more conventional expository prose. In fact, for some writings "any attempt to explicate the work as a whole according to some 'higher order' of meaning . . . is doomed to sophistry, if not overt incoherence" (Perelman, "Plotless Prose" 28).

Instead, what we have are writings that might be described as "open texts," taking our cue from Lyn Hejinian, who refers to compositions as either "closed" or "open." By closed Hejinian implies a text "in which all the elements of the work are directed toward a single reading of the work. Each element confirms that reading and delivers the text from any lurking ambiguity" ("Rejection of Closure" 270). Hejinian doesn't mean this in a pejorative way. The Dickens novel and the detective story, both of which Hejinian admires, are examples of closed works in that the reader is led toward a specific point, an inescapable conclu- sion (i.e., "the butler did it"). This is not to imply that as readers we fail to have multiple interpretations. We can, after all, dissect *Great Expectations* through various lenses—Marxist, feminist, psy- choanalytic, deconstructive—but no matter what our orientation each of us will essentially be referring to the same linear trail, the same basic narrative plot within the story.

The "open" text is something else entirely:

> It invites participation, rejects the authority of the writer over the reader and thus, by analogy, the authority implicit in other (social, economic, cultural) hierarchies. It speaks for writing that is generative rather than directive. Reader and

writer engage in a collaboration from which ideas and meaning are permitted to evolve. The writer relinquishes total control and challenges authority as a principle and control as a
motive. The open text often emphasizes or foregrounds
process, either the process of the original composition or of
subsequent compositions by readers, and thus resists the cultural tendencies that seek to identify and fix material, turn it
into a product; that is, it resists reduction and commodifica-
tion. (Hejinian, "Rejection of Closure" 272)

Resisting the "chain reaction" effect typified by the hierarchical,
propositional structure of expository prose where clause A antici-
pates B which precedes C and so forth, the open text produces an
opposite reaction: each new sentence or "text island" is unexpected, jarring the reader's attention and sending her off into
unpredictable directions: X precedes A precedes L precedes D,
etc. But whereas past avant-garde writers have deliberately
emphasized chance as a compositional technique by randomly
cutting and pasting texts into nonlinear arrangements, Hejinian
is concerned with the kind of open text that, from beginning to
end, emphasizes a less affected nonlinear progression rather than
the intentional fracturing associated with surrealist pastiche.
With the open text the spaces between the sentences force us to
make conscious leaps, while the spaces between sentences in a
closed text do their best to stay out of the way, blending into the
woodwork so as not to jolt the narrative "flow." In the open text
the "sentences are workers. All parts are studios. . . . Much of the
litter that goes into production is left lying intact (or in pieces,
depending on the reader's response)" (Rasula, "What Does This
Do . . . " 66).

Instead of the closed texts we are accustomed to, where the
composition is a seamless unity carrying forth a limited number of
intended, primary messages, and where all embodied sentences
and paragraphs work in unison to achieve that sense of unity, the
open text seeks to rekindle a vivid sense of presence attainable in
the act of reading. With Hejinian's brand of open text, it is difficult to separate ourselves from the work in order to synthesize
any overarching gestalts or themes, for each sentence immediately, drastically pulls us into its own composite field. Not that the

writing lacks harmony; as we read we do become aware of residual tones and moods. But these impressions surface not from any hierarchical structure but from the complex juxtaposition of diverse elements. The result is a multivectoral collage where each sentence is its own thesis, as opposed to the conventional system of subordinate clauses branching out from a central trunk.

An example, from Hejinian's autobiography *My Life*:

> Last night, in my dreams, I swam to the bottom of a lake, pushed off in the mud, and rising rapidly to the surface shot eight or ten feet out of the water into the air. I couldn't join the demonstration because I was pregnant, and so I had revolutionary experience without taking revolutionary action. History hugs the world. The Muses are little female fellows. To some extent, each sentence has to be the whole story. It is hard to turn away from moving water, where the tiny pebbles are left along the shore. Being color-blind, he could not tell if they were brown or grey. Romance says, "Come away with me," but neglects to say whence, or is it whither. Writer solstice. Let's listen for the last of the autumn frogs. (67)

As readers we're conditioned to expect most sentences to pick up the narrative thread left off in the previous line, unless they begin a new paragraph or section. But here every new line plops us into an entirely different landscape, each segment an alternate key-hole offering us unanticipated scenes. With Hejinian's writing we are permitted to register the images and implications of each line only momentarily for the duration of that sentence, for each successive clause, with its completely new orientation, impels us to concentrate on its new content, creating a tension with the preceding, growing string of sentences. And yet we are never completely successful in attacking each new sentence with a clean slate, for vestiges of earlier lines remain in our minds, casting hues across each new phrase. The work comes to take on an aura of intense polysemous activity, unique in that the sentences become a synergism of disjointed particles, simultaneously splintered and connected.

An increasing number of writers have found it necessary to make writings that draw on this fractal technique.[9] Ron Silliman, for instance, makes open texts that utilize what he prefers to call "the new sentence." The following is from *Tjanting*:

> Airplanes swim thru the night sky like sharks with flashing lights. Shot rock thru a pile of poppies. In baseball, each ankle serves a different function. Twitching at the door, the landlord stood in anger. Think of the act of writing as a sitting, minimal dance. If it revolves, even the referential word will have a revolution. She returnd to find 3 small birds, confused, exhausted & hopelessly trappd in her studio, & they willingly let her touch them. This is role memory. The idea of kids as an audience. This is what skin does to your coffee. If this notebook were lost. The waterfall becomes a skylight when it rains. My body a slab like a huge bar of soap. & we sat around this laughing table, smoking the kitchen pipe. The warp of the line in the room. These words write pen's shadow also. A Maurice Sendak kind of morning. (111)

To the unaccustomed this sort of prose can appear confusing and annoying, and understandably so since we've rarely been taught to read texts that are so intentionally nonlinear. We expect linear narratives created for some semblance of a passive, unobtrusive audience; we're conditioned to expect the text to do most of the work for us (the common definition of a good writer as one who weaves words in a pleasing manner readers can follow with little resistance). The concept of reader as "writer" of the text, creator and manipulator of the ideas housed therein instead of a passive recipient for someone else's information, remains a relatively recent concept. Reluctant to lead readers carefully by the hand throughout the composition, announcing and recapitulating premises and themes at every turn, authors like these are interested in undermining their authorial sovereignty by enticing readers to join in the creation of the text, to "fill in" the gaps and leaps between images. These open texts have a smorgasbord quality to them; their power derives from what might be likened to a variety of semantic dishes, which may either be bypassed or returned to for seconds. One may read a book like Hejinian's or Silliman's from any point, picking up the narrative at random, reading backward or forward at will. But the reader must serve herself; she cannot wait passively for the author to bring her a narrative unfolding in a series of logical courses.

And while at first these excerpts might seem to have been written in the surrealist tradition of automatic writing, where each and every thought is allowed to rush out in an attempt to uncover the chorus of ideas and images forever bubbling away "beneath" consciousness, there are major differences between surrealism and this more recent move in composition. The surrealist technique of automatic writing easily lent itself to obligatory formulas and rituals: many of the compositions were intended to convey the character of a waking dream. Just mentioning the term "surrealism" evokes a particular subject matter—Salvador Dalí heaving cats through the air, carp flying through windows, melting watches and men with beaks. Though the open text can echo the surrealist technique of psychic automatism, these contemporary works are not the products of any school or church (the formation of which was André Breton's ultimate goal). The drive, rather, is to seek out an environment, an orientation with the writing act where the author can immerse herself as completely as possible into something similar to Stein's "continual present," engaging the ongoing construction of composition in an intensely intimate, self-reflexive, and tactile manner.

Actually, though works like these might seem affectedly avant-garde to the unsuspecting reader, disconcerting in their seemingly deliberate incoherence, we're more used to nonlinear paths of reading than we might realize, as in our daily lives we are constantly reading texts, scribal or otherwise, in ways that disrupt their intended linear flow. Viewers often watch television by "zapping" back and forth between dozens of channels, using the remote control to initiate fractured paths of viewing. (Even to watch TV without switching channels is to encounter a text startlingly surreal in its odd juxtaposition of scenes: Dan Rather lauding allied forces and their obliteration of thousands of Iraqi children segues to a housewife gleefully singing with cookie-making elves, followed by actual footage of a drug bust made in Miami, then a local used car commercial—each linked in a matter of seconds, without any logical transition. We're so used to this that, were we to come across a channel where the camera shots did not switch to another angle or image every three seconds, but stayed trained on their subject for five or more minutes at a time, the result would be noticeable indeed, and probably unsavory, even uncomfortable to most viewers.) Or take our reading of the newspaper: rather than read every article to its conclusion, chances are we skip around from one article to another while still on the same page, reading a patchwork of texts, many of them left unfinished as we abandon lines mid-sentence to jump to a neighboring text. In fact, our everyday patterns of thought are themselves less "linear" than they are floating arrangements of spontaneous accumulative impressions. Though it requires a conscious effort to notice it, the progression of our thoughts takes us on flights of imagination, demonstrating how our thinking process is nothing less than a continual, unending open text driven by chance: one moment I look forward to cooking dinner, which for some reason triggers a memory of my father breaking his toe, a contemplation replaced almost immediately with concern over the heat bill, which leads me to think of Chichén Itzá, and so on. Whether following connective threads or hopping unexpectedly into new lines of thought, the character of our day-to-day contemplation constitutes one mammoth, infinite open text. And just as the unpredictability of our meandering thought trains is the catalyst through which we mold new ideas, so too can the fractured text provoke readers into assembling interpretations unattainable while reading the steady rhythms of conventional prose.

In addition to the "new sentence," journals, diaries, notebooks (even blue examination books)[10] are also open texts since their organizational structure relies upon no preformed outlines; the daybook, we might say, is composed only of what many consider "prewriting"—the writer can't go back and revise an entry from the previous week, but must start anew with each successive entry. Though journals are filled with recurring themes and contemplations that orchestrate into their own unique patterns and refrains, the primary organizing principle is the flow of temporal progression; the passage of hours, days, weeks, or seasons is the only outline. In this way closure is never attained, only postponed until the writer either abandons the journal, or dies.

This is precisely the tack recent compositionists have taken with the journal form, an approach particularly appealing to those sympathetic with feminist concerns for circumventing the obtrusion of authority within the rhetorical construct. Beverly Dahlen's A *Reading 1-7* is such an example, a powerful journal/poem of epic dimensions:

> watching him arrange the flowers: dark stemmed iris, the blue flag, everything speaking, not a word, where does language end? what limits? an idea whose time had come, for that he got a bullet in the head. the relationship. the revelation of structure. don't ask, don't ask what you can do for your country.

> love, what is it, under late high capitalism, under gas bills, armor, slaughter, what is it. a lyric episode, an inarticulate babbling, not one word in the whole lot. deconstruct that. go deconstruct that language.

> this was a kind of writing. of speech. tonguing. how could he say how wrong that was? because words take the place of another, pretend, the violence of the word intervening. blessed or damned. 'no book ever ruined a girl's life.' I don't believe it. books ruined my life. my life is a ruin of books. I would give it up forever, go catatonic. and still there is a language. it is given, damn it, given, eat it. it's the same thing, overthrow it, if you love him go to him, what is it? what is love? what do we know? (67)

This impulse to fracture authority is even more noticeable in the work of Hannah Weiner (*Spoke*; *The Clairvoyant Journal*), whose compositions are kaleidoscopic accounts of multiple interior voices constantly interrupting one another, stuttering across the page in horizontal, vertical, and diagonal vectors to such an extent that the content of the work focuses as much on the opacity of the alphabet as the subject of the writer's fractal narratives. Weiner's texts embrace an absence of closure on several levels: the journal format, with its open-ended space; the inclusion of multiple personas, generally three or four that flit mothlike through and across one another; and the constant interruption not only of voices but words, which break apart and leave off unfinished as new ideas push themselves onto the page. All of these techniques converge in an amazing spatial display, at once schizophrenic and yet intimately rhythmic in its splintered chorus, making her work some of the most persuasive reflections of stream-of-consciousness captured in print. With so many compositionists intrigued with the process of writing, the flux and play of thought as it manifests itself on page and screen, one might think the meandering scripts of writers like Weiner, Hejinian, Silliman, and Dahlen would surface more frequently in the work of modern composition and literary theory. Their collective resistance of closure, their reconfiguration of expository prose in ways subverting authorial control, and especially the ways in which they underscore the porous, interactive possibilities of writing, make experimenters like these particularly valid for those probing the possibilities and limits of composition.

EMBRACING CONSTRAINTS

In their search for a migratory compositional activity responsive to free-associative links, modern writers have willingly entered the gray discursive spaces existing between poem and notebook, lyricism and critical analysis, journal and fractal narrative. This weaving of rhetorical styles, though, doesn't mean the open text is free of rules or procedural regulations. These innovative writers, recognizing the impossibility of ever composing free of rules, forms, and ideologies, actually embrace constraints; their work is as formal as any academic text, the primary difference being that the standard organizational logic has been substituted for others.

A text like Hejinian's *My Life*, for example, adheres to some hard and fast rules. In her autobiography Hejinian first of all requires that her sentences be grammatically correct in accordance with standard English. More notably, Hejinian arranges her text within a strict numerical structure: depending upon which edition of *My Life* one reads, Hejinian's sentences are presented in either 37 or 45 sections of prose, each of them containing 37 or 45 sentences respectively (the number of which corresponds to the author's age at publication).[11] In addition Hejinian causes certain sentences to resurface regularly throughout the book, creating a gauze of lyric refrains that evoke a subtext of shifting echoes circulating throughout the book. In a similar way the diaristic writings of Bernadette Mayer (*Memory*; *Studying Hunger*), though on first reading appearing as loose and unrestricted as any stream-of-consciousness text, are confined within rigid temporal boundaries, entries made within the strict parameters of a single day or a single month in order to reflect the trail of thought within a defined place and time, resulting in a portrayal of memory's polylogue, hopping among the zones of present and past contemplation.[12] Likewise most of Ron Silliman's work is orchestrated according to rigid mathematical constraints—in *Ketjak* each paragraph within the text is double the length of the previous one, containing all previous sentences and supplementing them with an equal number of new lines, whereas the numerical structure for his book *Tjanting* is based on a Fibonacci series where the number of sentences in each paragraph is equal to the sum of all sentences in the previous two paragraphs, etc.

What we realize from these various restrictions and unconventional rules is that the open text, at least as it's defined by these writers, doesn't derive from some romantic yearning for discursive freedom located "beyond" the fetters of rigorous form. These writers acknowledge that no discourse is without its laws, that language is always a system of checks, rules, and restrictions. Flexibility, even "empowerment" (if we can use such an abused term) results not from eliminating grammar but assigning it our own signature; that is, through our own conscious manipulation and restructuring of syntax and vocabulary. "It is NOT that grammar, per se, which is an abstraction, a projection, is repressive," quoting Charles Bernstein, "but that societal conditions are repressive and that these repressions are *reflected* in grammar, can be spotted in that particular mapping" (*Content's Dream* 418). In rejecting obligatory closure, linearity, and the compulsory need to conclude, summarize, and seal up a writing with the equivalent of so much rhetorical packing tape, the writer is not necessarily denying constraint. If anything, those writers who reject traditional means of composing are deeply concerned with codes and restrictions: "The classical playwright who writes his tragedy observing a certain number of familiar rules is freer than the poet who writes that which comes into his head and who is the slave of other rules of which he is ignorant"

(Raymond Queneau, in Motte 18). The fundamental difference is that on one hand there are writers who adhere to laws and constraints without reflection, while elsewhere there are those who value the ability to communicate within traditional grammars and logics, and those startlingly unique. Lyn Hejinian phrases it this way:

> I perceive the world as vast and overwhelming; each moment stands under an enormous vertical and horizontal pressure of information, potent with ambiguity, meaningfull, unfixed, and certainly incomplete. What saves this from becoming a vast undifferentiated mass of data and situation is one's ability to make distinctions. Each written text may act as a distinction, may be a distinction. The experience of feeling overwhelmed by undifferentiated material is like claustrophobia. One feels panicky, closed in. The open text is one which both acknowledges the vastness of the world and is formally differentiating. It is the form that opens it, in that case. ("Rejection of Closure" 271)

But the spokesmen (most of them are men) most dedicated to extolling the virtues of self-fashioned, self-imposed compositional constraints are those affiliated with the Ouvroir de Littérature Potentielle, Oulipo for short, which translated means Workshop (or Sewing Circle) of Potential Literature—a small collective of mathematicians, scientists, musicians, poets, professors, and technicians who in the early 1960s made it their business to seek out, research, and invent new forms and structures for composition, and then disseminated those forms to interested readers and writers. Oulipians were engrossed with constraints, which were seen not as hindrances but liberatory techniques, so long as they remained self-imposed. Inspiration, long considered by many as the source for all art, was the enemy of the maker of potential literature. The idea was to free oneself from inspiration and throw the muse, which was never more than the aesthetics of a dominant ideology thinly disguised, out the window forever. Oulipians championed the conscious, voluntary use of self-conceived combinatory systems as an important avenue toward truly original composition, in contrast to the romantic reliance upon the aleatory and the myth of the talented, enlightened artist which, they claimed, too often spelled creative death for the writer. In other words, once we realize that all self-aware inventors of contrived, preferably ludic linguistic systems perpetuate some kind of poetics, then being a poet is no longer contingent upon talent or chance, a concept articulated in one of the Oulipo's first manifestos by François Le Lionnais:

> Must one adhere to the old tricks of the trade and obstinately refuse to imagine new possibilities? The partisans of the status quo don't hesitate to answer in the affirmative. Their conviction rests less on reasoned reflection than on force of habit and the impressive series of masterpieces (and also, alas, pieces less masterly) which has been obtained according to the present rules and regulations. . . .
>
> Should humanity lie back and be satisfied to watch new thoughts make ancient verses? We don't believe that it should. That which certain writers have introduced with talent (even with genius) in their work . . . the ouvroir de Littérature Potentielle (Oulipo) intends to do systematically and scientifically, if need be through recourse to machines that process information. ("First Manifesto" 27)

To get a picture of the impulses behind the Oulipian philosophy we need to consider the quintessential Oulipian text, Raymond Queneau's *Cent Mille Milliards de poémes* (One hundred thousand billion poems). At first glance an unassuming set of ten sonnets, Queneau's series of poems is a work of *potential* literature where the first line of the first sonnet may be followed by the second line from any of the ten sonnets, then by the third line from any sonnet, etc. So, for each of the first ten lines ten different second lines can be added, resulting in 10^2 possible combinations for the first two lines alone. Since there are fourteen verses, the total number of combinations reaches 10^{14} (one hundred thousand billion). "According to [Queneau's] calculations, if one read a sonnet per minute, eight hours a day, two hundred days per year, it would take more than a million centuries to finish the text" (Motte 3). Queneau's system quickly provoked Oulipians to invent their own combinatory systems, incorporating algorithms, anaglyphic texts, haikuization, homomorphisms, Latin bi-squares, lipograms, palindromes, "snow-

balls," and other mathematical systems (geometry, matrix algebra) applied to linguistic structures. Like mathematics, language
is an architecture built from within; Oulipians saw themselves as
the "rats who must build the labyrinth from which they propose
to escape" (Lescure 37).

Given the Oulipians' emphasis on unlimited potentiality and
indeterminacy, plus the importance they placed on always foregrounding a sense of play in their word games and collaborative
systems—qualities that would seem to mirror the poststructuralist preoccupation with *jouissance*, multiple readings, deconstruction of narrative, and absence of closure—it's curious that their
enterprise hasn't caught the attention of literary theorists in the
past three decades. Certainly one reason lies in the fact that, by
and large, poststructuralists have preferred to apply their deconstructive skills to the traditional, the canonical, and the linear,
veering away from the radically avant-garde and exploratory
since the latter, when juxtaposed against the work of the theorists, can easily make otherwise "cutting edge" criticism appear
impenetrably academic, conventional, and tedious. The Oulipians, however, did consider it important to keep abreast of theoretical advancements made within the academy, even though
they took pains to dissociate themselves from any academic
movement or "serious" school, pointing out, for example, the
fundamental differences between academic structuralism, which
they viewed with some suspicion, and their own very different
definition of "structurElism" (Le Lionnais, "Second Manifesto"
29; Roubaud 93). The Oulipians, like "Language" poets and
other contemporary experimental writers, have continually
defied the tenets of our most fashionable critical theories, and
therein lies their relevance for the compositionist. From
Gertrude Stein to the Oulipians to Hannah Weiner, writers have
composed within philosophical orientations that continue to
resist our most basic assumptions about writing. Readers might
find these experiments tremendously liberating, intolerably
annoying, or simply boring; but whatever our reaction, our
understanding of composition theory will lack depth of field if
these ends of the spectrum remain ignored—especially if it's simply because they don't fit neatly into our most familiar pedagogical frames.

HYPERTEXT

> *Why should a writer be forced to produce a single,*
> *linear argument or an exclusive analysis of cause and*
> *effect, when the [hypertextual] writing space allows a*
> *writer to entertain and present several lines of thought*
> *at once?*
> —JAY DAVID BOLTER

Not only did the Oulipians devise radically new methods of composition before the deconstructionists started generating their related (albeit significantly less playful) theories within the academy, but they also recognized early on the significance of the computer for imaginative writing, a correlation many literary and composition theorists have yet to explore. Early texts by Oulipians Paul Fournel and Italo Calvino, for instance, outlined means of making creative literature with computers, while Raymond Queneau's "A Story as You Like It" is an early model of a hyperdocument.

Parallels between Oulipian narrative experiments and hypertext are not unusual; a good many twentieth-century writing strategies, with their emphasis on fractured narrative, nonlinearity, collaboration, multiple genres, and mixed media, operate according to the same techniques found in contemporary electronic discourse. In fact, hypertext is nothing less than the next logical step in a century of compositional exploration. Some have pointed out that hyperdocuments are primarily a literary conception, the issues and problems they raise closely related to those evoked by twentieth-century poetry (Slatin 112);[13] others have shown that writers like Sterne, Joyce, Woolf, Faulkner, Borges, Robbe-Grillet, and Barthes were significant precursors to the medium (Bolter 131–39; Moulthrop 119).[14] And the concerns of artists like the cubists, the Russian futurists, and particularly Marcel Duchamp, who were interested in investigating the "hyperspace" of four- and n-dimensional geometries, anticipated the hypertextual dilemma of imagining multidimensional texts beyond the limited two-dimensionality of the computer screen.[15] If we are to grasp the philosophical underpinnings of hypertext, its current state, and its implications for writing instruction, compositionists need to acknowledge the importance of the nontraditional, nonlinear (or alternatively linear) composing practices that laid the groundwork for this recent technology.

First, it's worthwhile to understand the distinction between hyper*text*, and hyper*media*. While a hypertext can and often does incorporate visual and sometimes aural messages within its primary text, "hypertext" still generally refers to linguistic texts that are constructed and read in accordance with nonlinear, interactive frameworks (by nonlinear I don't mean that the reading of such texts doesn't proceed in a consecutive manner; just that there are multiple options as to where the reader can go—sort of a "broken linear" or "shattered linear" approach, as opposed to the "straight linear" format present in most traditional "hard" texts). "Hypermedia," on the other hand, can denote electronic discourse capable of incorporating scribal, visual, aural, and, in the case of virtual reality, tactile and other sensory information within the same context: chunks of words, graphs, illustrations, animation, video displays, and audio could all factor into the grammar of hypermedia. Three-dimensional flow charts might appear, reassembling themselves to the accompaniment of a voice-over (a film clip of Amelia Earhart pops up when the appropriate window is selected, bagpipes sound when a certain path is triggered, and so on). As for written hypertext, it too can assume a variety of forms. There can be a central core out of which shoot a complex series of diminishing branches, much like an extended series of multilayered footnotes. Other texts are more aptly characterized as crisscrossing webs in which a constellation of text chunks (nodes) might link up or remain isolated from one another, depending upon the whim of the reader. There is no rigid spine to this kind of hypertext, its form forever modulating in response to the reader's predilections. Instead of the classical hierarchical outlines we learned to make in grade school, a more appropriate metaphor for the hypertext might be that of a textual amoeba that extends and retracts in accordance with the stimulus provided by reader-turned-author (the "nucleus" of the amoeba being the reader's input coupled with the memory of the computer). This dissolution of any central core is cleverly portrayed in the following message, found in the depths of Jay David Bolter's *Writing Space:*

The Computer, Hypertext, and the History of Writing (hypertext version):

> You have reached the center of this text. But the central point of this text has been that an electronic text has no center. In this new technology the distinction between one text and another, between primary and secondary texts breaks down. Electronic "footnotes" can have the same importance as the "body" of the text; a reader's notes can have the same status as the author's pronouncements. An electronic text works by association as much as by hierarchical arrangement, and its unity is achieved through a dynamic interplay of potentially equal elements.[16]

(It's interesting to recall how earlier writers like Pound, Williams, and Olson, in anticipation of this decentering technology, made extensive use of marginal comments, footnotes, and asides, as the nature of their material demanded a variety of different textual levels.)[17]

Hypertext has received considerable attention as a decentering approach to discourse where a nonlinear intertextuality shapes the writing environment—a topographical "writing space," as Bolter calls it, where shifts in voice, variable arrangement, and reader manipulation of text become key rhetorical ingredients. Unlike the bounded, finite book, much of hypertext is without anchor, a community of nodes adrift in an online space navigated by online operators. Rather than chart an inflexible course to which the reader must remain faithful, the writer of hyperdocuments is more concerned with supplying readers tools and information with which they can make their own maps. Again, Bolter:

> In the computer medium, where texts cannot achieve the same fixity, authors cannot speak with the same abiding authority. Instead, the computer offers as its ideal a kind of universal library, in which all texts are electronically connected to all others and through which the reader can browse without restriction. Furthermore, the reader can at any time become the author—by cutting and pasting texts of interest or instructing the computer to remember the path

that led from one text to another. The texts that come and go across the reader's computer screen are neither perma-nent nor inviolate.[18]

The linear-hierarchical expository essay, with all its transitions, subordinates, and its facade of seamlessness, is subverted by hypertexts that are wide open spaces where readers may alter, expand, and reconfigure the text into paths more to their liking. "Expository prose, with its linear and propositional structures, has been too much identified with the privileged form of reason itself" (Delany and Landow 7); as a result the hypertextual envi-ronment might be viewed as nothing less than "an assault on a central concept of Western culture—the book itself" (Barrett, *Text, ConText, and HyperText* xv).

"Afternoon," a work of interactive fiction by Michael Joyce, is one of our first marketed forms of hypertext, and has been described as similar to

> a video game in which the player pilots a spaceship around planetary obstacles that each exert a gravitational force. Readers of "Afternoon" move along paths with their own inertia, while at the same time experiencing the attraction of various parts of the fiction as they move by. It is easy to fall into an orbit around one set of episodes, one focus of the story. Readers find themselves returning to the same episodes again and again, trying to break free by giving different answers [to the text's prompts] and therefore choosing differ-ent paths. When it succeeds, this strategy may then push the reader into another orbit. (Bolter, *Writing Space* 125)

"Afternoon" is a text that provides *readerly* interaction; that is, multiple paths are offered for readers to follow, but the text remains relatively "locked," therefore preventing most readers from rewriting, removing, or reprogramming the text. *Writerly* interac-tive hypertext, on the other hand (the hypertext version of Bolter's *Writing Space*, for example), is "unlocked," designed not only for reader consumption but also for reader collaboration, inviting readers to become contributors, allowing them to "reach into" a malleable, impermanent text where the material may be edited, rerouted, supplemented, or changed according to individual desire.

Just as a great deal of avant-garde and experimentalist composition of the twentieth century—the work of the Oulipians, for example—has received little serious attention from literary theorists, so too has hypertext been largely ignored, a fact conspicuously ironic given that so much poststructuralist theory and postmodern critique capitalizes on the very elements that make hypertext distinct from conventional print. Bolter has pointed out how postmodern theorists "uncannily" seem to preconceive electronic writing, yet rarely, if ever, make the computer a central focus of their study (156). Others claim that hypertext, practically in one fell swoop, deflates much of the poststructuralist appeal by putting into immediate practice ideas that had existed only in abstract theories, creating

> an almost embarrassingly literal reification or actualization of a principle or a quality that had seemed particularly abstract and difficult in its earlier statement. Since much of the appeal, even charm, of these theoretical insights lies in their difficulty and even preciousness, this more literal presentation promises to disturb theoreticians, in part, of course, because it disturbs status and power relations within their—our—field of enterprise. (Delany and Landow 10)

While plenty of educators are examining and developing new pedagogies in response to the new writing technology—classes and workshops using such programs as Storyspace and Reading-space,[19] communicating and collaborating via email with other students and institutions[20]—the theory and practice of hypertext, despite its tremendous significance for composition and literary studies, remains, at least as of this writing, a marginal preoccupation in comparison with the bulk of scholarly and pedagogical work undertaken in the rest of the profession.

That talk of hypertext is sometimes met with resistance and skepticism is not all surprising. Bolter warns that hypertext could easily go the route of television, the electronic arena turning into a programmed path offering no substantive interaction at all, just "the illusion of perceptual experience" as readers simply become another hypnotized consumer (98). Indeed, hypermedia will inevitably (if it hasn't already) turn into the media's latest marketing strategy (it doesn't take too much to imagine software packages sponsored by Pepsi-Cola distributed to schools, featuring video interviews with General Colin Powell amidst virtual maps of Kuwait and Iraq as various narratives aim to indoctrinate passive viewers with the latest national ideology). Even Bolter's infectiously excited overview of hypertext and its untapped potential in *Writing Space* has stirred up reservations; in an early review on *EJournal*, Joe Amato expresses skepticism that Bolter's vision of an interactive electronic community of human nodes linked to one another, all of them communicating with only their mice and keyboards, poses a real risk of further homogenizing people who have already become dangerously dehumanized at the hands of contemporary culture. Hypertextual interaction, while breaking down traditional authoritarian rhetorics, doesn't guarantee that the politics of sexuality, ethnicity, and culture will be foregrounded any more successfully in an electronic forum; if anything, it might be easier to hide behind our screens, abusing the "invisibility" of interacting with online networks in order to type out representations of ourselves that might be gross distortions of our everyday actions. (But then, one might easily question whether communication through printed media was ever any better at safeguarding against such misrepresentation and alienation; rhetorical deceit can just as easily lurk in a printed journal as it can in electronic mail or hypertext.)

Others have criticized hypertext on the grounds that most readers simply don't want to waste their time on fractal texts. Joseph Jaynes, for example, has argued that writing, if it's going to teach us something, *must* be synthesized within a unifying structure, not a smorgasbord of nodes disrupted by changing vectors. Readers must have "limited freedom," for they want to be led down a finite, linear path leading to fruition, not get "lost in hyperspace"; to "'enter and explore,'" Jaynes argues, "is a condemnation, not a solution" (159). And true enough, hypermedia does have the potential to be confusing; if writers of hypertext don't develop ways of helping readers constructively navigate the textual web, the experience can be unnerving, sometimes exasperatingly chaotic. But Jaynes's argument, which is probably the most popular form of condemnation leveled at those quick to praise the virtues of hypertext—and ultimately most of the exploratory critical texts discussed in this book—can't go unaddressed. For such an argument is misleading in that it assumes proponents for nonlinear, collaborative, experimental discourse—electronic or otherwise—are by definition enemies of all that is linear, hierarchical, and conventional. The creative potential of hypertext, or any other experimental discursive technique, lies not in its destruction of convention but its opening of new alternatives; simply put, new rhetorics provide access to new modes of critical thought. Linear rhetoric, obviously, can achieve astounding results; we've all had the experience of reading texts where an argument has been fashioned step by step with crystalline precision, culminating splendidly in a brilliant finale. But most proponents of hypertext are not claiming that we banish this particular mode of communication, only that we refrain from maintaining this discursive style as our *only* viable option.

It's important to fully recognize the logic that leads a critic like Jaynes to cavalierly dismiss the experimentalism represented in hypertext, a logic that is most evident in his likening the difference between linear and disrupted text with the tension between representational and abstract art, a problematic comparison in that it assumes an incontrovertible separation between (Western) "reality," and the imaginative, or "unreal." Hypertexts, reasons Jaynes, with all their dislocations, are similar to "abstract paintings [which] do not 'teach' in the same way that representational paintings often do. This is not to imply that they are without value or somehow less worthy of our appreciation; only that such abstractions create a sense or mood rather than a lesson" (158–59). This line of reasoning is common among critics of abstract and avant-garde workings, but within it are embedded significant misunderstandings. First, "representational" art is no more or less abstract than nonrepresentational art; if anything, a great deal of abstract art may be seen as more representational, or at least "honest" in that it claims no representation other than itself (Jackson Pollack's drip paintings are "about" dripping paint), whereas the "lifelike," representational landscape is wholly contrived, static and two-dimensional in comparison with the shifting, three-dimensional environments we interact with at every given moment. Second, "representational" art is a culturally specific term that has no meaning once we shift beyond a local context: Renaissance perspective is fundamentally different from

Eastern depictions of depth of field, just as Norman Rockwell's representation of human beings has nothing in common with those of cubists or the Navajo. Third, to say that representational art "teaches us a lesson" while abstract (and, by implication, non-Western) art merely conveys "a mood" is an awkward proposition. Part of the difficulty with this agument is that it is never specified what "a lesson" means, or even why the sole objective of any educational discourse is to teach "lessons," as if such things were uninfected by the social and political ideologies that shape the communities within which they're generated. In fact, might not a fair share of our teaching be characterized as little more than the transference of vague moods and sensibilities rather than isolated lessons or bytes of information? There is no scarcity of lessons, i.e., information; the challenge is to form environments where we might translate some of that information into immediate, relevant knowledge. We quickly discover that criticism like this is little more than one critic's plea for a personal aesthetics, as Jaynes simply doesn't like texts that are "free-form and specifically random"; he considers them "failures": stream of consciousness narratives (which for him parallel the organization of hypertext), though "interesting and of great literary value . . . do not teach us useful things except indirectly as we can puzzle them out" (160). Readers, he claims, need to decipher puzzles, not make them; there is no place for writers who seek to put readers through such acrobatics.

The problem here is not with this critic's aesthetic preferences; no one, obviously, is obligated to appreciate either "abstract" or representational discourse, whether visual or written. But biases like these against the nontraditional have too often been proposed as natural assumptions that ought to be maintained in our teaching: the linear and the conventional text remains "normal," while those that are spiral, intentionally fractured, and experimental are dubbed "weird," and thus significantly less important for the student to discover and emulate. But to pit "normal" against "weird," of course, is to hammer home unimaginative dichotomies determined more by institutional bias than any comprehensive attempt to assess a broader scope of composing philosophies. And the pedagogy that preserves such facile opposition is not only unbalanced, but instills within the student a foreshortened understanding of contemporary discourse that is simply erroneous and reductive.

Back in 1926 Gertrude Stein published an essay, "Composition as Explanation," that contains the following observation:

> Those who are creating the modern composition authenti-
> cally are naturally only of importance when they are dead
> because by that time the modern composition having
> become past is classified and the description of it is classical.
> That is the reason why the creator of the new composition
> in the arts is an outlaw until he is a classic, there is hardly a
> moment in between and it is really too bad very much too
> bad naturally for the creator but also very much too bad for
> the enjoyer, they all really would enjoy the created so much
> better just after it has been made than when it is already a
> classic. . . . It is so very much more exciting and satisfactory
> for everybody if one can have contemporaries, if all one's
> contemporaries could be one's contemporaries. (514–15)

During a presentation I once gave at a Conference on College Composition and Communication, I happened to mention that for me Gertrude Stein was far and away the most important composition theorist of this century. Though the comment drew its share of raised eyebrows from the audience, I was serious. If we are not, each of us, articulating our own modern compositions, then we become little more than clever copycats, mimics trying to simulate the shadows of past innovators. As it is, an overwhelming amount of "the modern composition" never makes its way into our professional conversation. Even the "modern" compositions of those long dead—the rhetorical accomplishments and questions raised by writers like Stein, Pound, Williams, Woolf, Joyce, and Olson—are still ignored as discursive quirks, irrelevant oddities immaterial to the serious business of teaching students how to write and read and wear the literacies of our institutions. We forget that for the modernists (i.e., symbolists, fauvists, cubists, expressionists, futurists, constructivists, dadaists, surrealists, imagistes, and vorticists) and "postmodernists" (which can include surfictionists, Oulipians, Language poets, and now the makers of hyperdocuments), ludic experimentation has always been a serious business. The unfamiliar gyrations identified with modernist and postmodernist rhetorics are not the products of bored, elitist fancy; these new composings, from the earliest modernists to the most contemporary writers of hypertext, are nothing less than the signs of inventive resistance brought on by the need for intellectual survival. Such struggles warrant the attention of composition studies.

Stein was right: it *is* infinitely more exhilarating, more rousing—more *fun*—to acknowledge the latest directions of our contemporaries while the transformations occur; otherwise, we're just wandering through lexical museums informed by philosophies and aesthetics generated in past eras. Though conventional rhetorics, whether classical, neoromantic, or intentionally authoritarian, without a doubt produce powerful results, these are not the only forms of discourse at our disposal. Without an opportunity to examine the richness of contemporary discourses thriving beyond the ivory tower, the academic conversation will not be measured by its receptiveness to creative change, but on how well it continues to preserve its status quo, no matter how liberally defined.

One of the most common complaints I've heard faculty make is that too many students demonstrate lack of imagination. Their topics are dull, their papers wooden, their participation (when it exists) lacking excitement; so many of them seem committed to an antiintellectualism where critical risk-taking and playful inquiry are to be avoided at all costs. While my experience, fortunately, has been just the opposite—most of my students really are a delight to work with—I have of course witnessed that same stoic inertia my colleagues refer to. But students are not born with the seeds of indifference; teachers like us plant them. Students, no matter how much they might lack ingenuity and spontaneity, will always be mirrors of the educational systems they've slogged through for the greater part of their lives. How can we demand originality if our understanding of composition belies a distrust of the most original writings of this century? If we shy away from daring writing philosophies, and stick with defining composition according to paradigms that fail to reflect the healthy mosaic of styles constantly transforming into newer, fresher hybrids, why then should we expect students to get tired up over the immediacy and malleability of discourse? When so many of us openly admit the incredible dullness characterizing so much of our academic discourse—the prose that *we* make—why seek student writing that is fresh and imaginative? If so many of us don't look forward to reading dissertations or *PMLA*, why should student texts be any better? If we want to see students stop writing lifeless prose, we should introduce them to some of the most invigorating and infuriating, fertile and controversial texts of our time. Open texts, nonlinear prose, mutations of genre, and hypertext are just a few of the new directions in modern composition. The challenges they offer might stimulate us to make new constructions, or they might confuse and infuriate us beyond description—but whatever our reactions they will, if honest, remain legitimate responses to drastic shifts in contemporary writing, reactions that require continued discussion and debate. Students ought not be denied access to these contemporary discussions.

Implications for Practice

*I'm asking simply to be exposed to, and informed about,
the full range of compositional possibilities. That I be
introduced to all the tools, right now, and not be asked
to wait for years and years until I have mastered
right-handed affairs before I learn anything about
left-handed affairs. That, rather, I be introduced to all
the grammars/ vehicles/tools/compositional possibilities
now so that even as I "learn to write" I will have before
me as many resources as possible. I'm asking: that all
the "ways" of writing be spread out before me and that
my education be devoted to learning how to use them.*
—WINSTON WEATHERS

THOUGH theory and practice are potentially
two sides of the same coin, one gets anxious when theoretical
musings aren't translated into at least a few tangible proposals for
quick usage; if interesting theory doesn't readily lend itself to
something one can actually *do*, soon, in the classroom and with
colleagues, innovative hypotheses risk leaving in their wake the
residue of cynicism. At this point I'm obliged to examine these
new composing methodologies from a practitioner's perspective:
namely, looking for how members of English departments and
writing programs—including full-time faculty, adjuncts, graduate
students, chairs and directors—might begin integrating the above
insights within their daily work, or at the very least, work toward
turning the academic landscape into one more tolerant of these
alternative discourses. The ideas I've in mind range from the
long-term and idealistic (some might say naive, and perhaps
they're right) to the more pragmatic and immediately accessible.

The first and by far the most extensive of the ideas I have in
mind pertains to widespread curricular reform:

1. Drastically revamp current writing curricula by abandoning the one-stop composition course, replacing it with a series of lower- and upper-level writing-intensive courses that teach significantly divergent rhetorical methodologies. At a time when higher education is being strangled financially, what with shrinking budgets, course cuts, and teacher layoffs, combined with ridiculously large teaching loads and class sizes, I can already hear readers squirming with impatience at yet another proposal calling for additional classes. And given the frightful economic conditions bleeding our profession, not to mention the firmly entrenched elitist disdain so many professors of literature continue to harbor for even the most formalist of composition classes, a call for more writing courses—and especially the kind I'm considering—might come off as obnoxiously quixotic. Yet while fantasizing like this admittedly involves some degree of self-indulgence, I really think periodically outlining our most idealistic models is necessary if we're to maintain some tentative grasp on where we want to be headed. Offering short-term, pragmatic proposals is vital—and I'll get to some of those shortly—but they have to be developed within a larger pedagogical context where the ultimate goals and desires are articulated in some detail. This is why I begin here, with a proposal to significantly revise the idea of a writing curriculum.

For starters we might think of composition and rhetoric in a fashion similar to how the teaching of literature is most commonly conducted, where a conglomerate of differing historical and cultural literary zones are brought together under the unifying rubric of "English studies," beginning with survey courses, then branching off into specialized classes focusing more directly on a range of genres, authors, and literary theories. Just as different English faculty could easily, within their separate classes, teach *Beowulf*, *Wuthering Heights*, *Finnegans Wake*, and *The Color Purple* during the same semester, so too could a wide sampling of rhetorical possibilities coexist within courses offered during the same academic year, available to both beginning and advanced students. For example: just as students are gradually introduced to a selective assortment of conflicting literatures and genres in their Introductory Literature class, they could also take a course in Theories of Composition, where students would spend a semester getting acquainted with three or four broad yet uniquely different approaches to composition and discourse. Having taken this course, students could then choose from various writing electives highlighting academic, expressivist, ethnorhetorical, experimental, "feminine," technical, and computer-oriented modes of discourse. In addition to this, shorter writing courses or periodic workshops (perhaps one or two credits) would be offered within each localized discipline—writing for the biology major, writing for the accounting major, and so forth.

Let's take a detailed look at these courses and what they might involve:

Theories of Composition: This would be the first writing course students take upon entering their freshman year of college (unless they are in need of considerable developmental help, in which case they'll most likely need additional support, which I'll discuss later on). The primary goal would be to show students that the effectiveness of one's discourse—whether written, oral, or performative—is largely, oftentimes entirely determined by the audience that will receive, and probably evaluate, the communicated text. For example: if a student is writing solely for herself, then she might judge her writing according to certain internal, subjective standards. If she writes a letter to a friend, many of those same standards will give way to other criteria more appropriate for that particular audience, criteria that in turn might modify yet again if she writes another letter to, say, her grandmother, or a boyfriend. Now if she writes a term paper for her history professor, all of the above criteria will probably give way as she substitutes an entirely new set of standards that will govern the shape and content of her prose. Furthermore, if her professor is a cold disciplinarian, the prose she uses in her research paper might be rather different from that contained in the journal submitted to the professor who is humorous and flexible. Students need to see that the skilled writer is one who can adapt to multiple audiences, changing her style in subtle and overt ways to suit different situations and readers.

The problem is, in many composition courses we don't go far enough with this. While many of us do indeed teach students ways of anticipating different audiences, the range of potential audiences covered can to be quite limited. In my experience students typically start by writing short texts that are more personal in nature, that is, grounded within some self-consciously autobiographical frame of reference, after which they might develop longer, complex essays that read more like critical analyses— arguments, critiques, appeals, reviews, and assessments aimed at a hypothetically wider audience. In other words, the student begins from a local, subjective context, then gradually branches out to a point where she can adopt a supposedly more objective and distanced perspective, and throughout it all learn various techniques of invention, revision, and editing. (This is how I've often heard teachers describe the basic skeleton of their entry level writing courses; at least, no one I know travels in the opposite direction.) And yet, in such classes the student is always writing for a local audience: namely, her professor, sometimes her classmates (if a workshop format is used), and, if she's not too preoccupied with producing exactly what she thinks the professor wants to read, herself.

In an attempt to expand the student's awareness of additional audiences and discourses, the Theories of Composition course brings additional rhetorical perspectives into the classroom, where students examine, model, and critique a number of conflicting styles. The course is divided into three or four sections, each one marked by a different generic compositional focus. During each section students read essays that reflect in some way the compositional orientation currently under investigation, discuss the techniques and assumptions housed within those texts, and finally write texts that are evaluated to some extent on how well they adhere to similar writerly objectives. Then, with the beginning of a new section, students switch to an entirely different compositional approach. In a sense, the course is like several miniseminars contained within one large class.

When teaching as an adjunct several years ago (and blatantly envisioning the classroom as some experimental lab, the students and myself as guinea pigs—which, in some circumstances, can be the best a young adjunct might hope for), I tried teaching a version of this course on several occasions, and in a nutshell this is how it worked:

During the first week of the course I had students discuss selections from a book by Raymond Queneau, *Exercices de Style*. My attempt was to convey the idea that the sound, shape, and feel of a composition are governed largely by the intended audience; and since the variety of potential audiences is practically limitless, so too the range of possibilities for writing. The trick was, how to identify, understand, critique, and enter into those multiple possibilities. First published in 1947, *Exercices de Style* tells the true account of a man who gets on a bus, observes a minor altercation between two passengers, and several hours later sees one of those same men involved in a conversation about a button—and that's it. The brief story is undoubtedly one of the most insipid in the history of prose, except that Queneau tells the tale ninety-nine different times in ninety-nine unique styles: narrative, notation, awkward, official letter, philosophic, exclamatory, tactile, telegraphic, haiku, sonnet, free verse, precious, mathematical, logical analysis, passive, casual, medical, and so on, variations that, for the most part, are refreshingly witty and imaginative (although, it must be admitted, at times tiresomely sexist).

After this I had the class observe an event lasting five minutes or so (me doing various odd things in front of the class), during which they were to take specific, detailed notes. After having the students brainstorm until they came up with at least fifty additional stylistic possibilities and genre forms that Queneau did not use within his ninety-nine, I had them rewrite the observed event half a dozen times using six approaches from this list. (The students quickly came up with more than enough ideas that, though certainly not what most rhetoricians would consider traditional or legitimate discourse forms, were varied and lively enough to capture their interest in the assignment. Some of the genres and styles they came up with, for example, were to rewrite the event using the language of a sports announcer, rapper, mystery or horror novelist, school catalogue, Presidential address, Jamaican patois, Sunday school teacher, college newspaper editorial, drill sergeant, etc.) This exercise, while nothing all that spectacular in conception, did seem to set an effective tone for the rest of the class (well, at least that given week, anyway), emphasizing the fact that experimentation was to play a heavy role in the course. More importantly, I think it helped me get across the idea within the first week that one didn't necessarily need a thrilling subject matter to make an interesting piece of prose, but could accomplish this by imaginatively reconfiguring the rhetoric used.

After this warm-up, I divided the semester into four sections, each roughly three weeks long. In the first quarter I taught writing from my impression of what an expressivist perspective might entail, making extensive use of pre- and freewriting, requiring students to keep a journal, and having them write autobiographical sketches and personal narratives (approximately three pages each) leading up to a "personal essay," which had to undergo at least two revisions. In the meantime students read four or five essays by writers like Frederick Douglass, Black Elk (with John G. Neihardt), Virginia Woolf, Malcolm X, Joan Didion, James Baldwin, Michael Ventura, and Maxine Hong Kingston. For each assigned essay they had to write a personal response, which had to have two sections to it: one where they offered their own personal commentary (they were free to write whatever opinions they had, so long as they tried to justify them and used specific details rather than generalizations to explain the rationale behind their reactions), the other part devoted to a rhetorical analysis where they picked three things from the essay that they liked, didn't like, or were confused by—the writer's use of terse sentences, colorful vocabulary, staccato paragraphs, parenthetical asides, etc. (This rhetorical analysis was what students consistently found most difficult, since few of them had ever been encouraged to investigate texts from this perspective.) At the end of this quarter I gathered up their writing into portfolios, all of which I'd commented on previously but not graded, and gave each student the first of four grades.[1] While the grade was based on a number of criteria, I tried to evaluate their personal narratives in part on how well they embodied some of the same characteristics found in the essays they read—for instance, how effectively I thought they used description, how vividly they described their characters and settings, how well they managed to underscore the primary themes that were important to them, how well they anticipated the reactions of the students with whom they shared their papers during workshops, etc., in addition to how well they utilized processes of revision, whether or not they incorporated prewriting and freewriting within the creation of their texts, and the like. Throughout, I consistently urged students to seek ways of enticing some primary "idea" or theme or focus to surface from their prose, the import of which would not only be obvious throughout the bulk of their essay but of potential relevance to hypothetical readers other than their immediate family. And although I personally have little interest in the type of narcissistic narrative easily created in this phase of the course, I do think it a considerably helpful "passage" for many less experienced writers. Besides, the goal at this point is not to create a text I'll want to put on my bookshelf, but rather to show students the complexity inherent in writing seemingly simple autobiographical accounts.

During the second quarter I shifted from an emphasis on personal narrative to "academic" discourse. Here students wrote one medium-length paper (eight to ten pages) in which they had to cite sources from at least one journal and one book received through interlibrary loan, and use either MLA or APA style format. The main emphasis for this assignment was to show evidence of sustained critical analysis and some semblance of an argument circulating within the text. (Much of this section was spent addressing various common flaws of reasoning in student papers—getting them to see the weakness of black and white dichotomies, non sequiturs, ad hominem attacks, assumptions disguised as evidence, and so forth.) After taking it through a number of revisions, and making at least one required appointment with the college's writing center, I graded this paper using a different set of standards, based primarily on how many other faculty at the college evaluated student texts (which I knew something about, based on my many conversations as a counselor with students about their writing assignments, plus seeing the syllabi, assignments, and corrected papers of several dozen professors in a range of disciplines). I assessed what I thought to be the effectiveness of their overall analyses, the development of the introduction and conclusion, their use of hierarchical, linear argumentation, correct and appropriate use of citation, proper bibliographical form, etc. I allowed only a limited number of errors per page, and I did not accept any late assignments— requirements I personally object to, but which were in line with what many other faculty in various departments at this particular college required. Whenever possible I had students pick a topic that could also be used for an assignment given by a professor in another class, whereupon I would meet with the student individually to help them ascertain what exactly that professor was looking for. In addition they continued to make their two-part responses to assigned readings, only this time I asked that their commentaries be more formal than casual in tone. The essays we read were originally intended for academic audiences, by writers like Adrienne Rich, Dennis Tedlock, Barbara Myheroff, W. E. B. DuBois, and occasionally a passage taken from a textbook used in one of their other classes. On several occasions I had students read essays that some of their professors in various disciplines had published in a small journal distributed among the faculty.

During the third quarter we switched to African American discourse; they continued to read essays but this time they were texts that either addressed different elements of African American rhetoric or utilized African American discourse directly within the actual essay—selections from Geneva Smitherman, Roger D. Abrahams, Verta Mae Smart-Grosvenor, and Amiri Baraka. We also read fiction by Zora Neale Hurston and Ishmael Reed. As for their writing assignments, I had them write responses to the music we listened to in class (blues, jazz, and rap), which I tried to relate to their readings by Smitherman and Abrahams. Finally, I had them attempt a study in which they analyzed the types of discourse used within either their own immediate family or some club or group with which they were intimately connected. (If I were to teach this course again, I would at this point also have the students record and transcribe their spoken texts, in an attempt to identify the rhythms inherent in their own speech; see Ethnorhetorical Investigations, below.) The writings for this portion of the course were largely in the form of journal entries.

Finally, we explored a sampling of odd, avant-garde, and experimental texts—manifestos, collages, essays, and scores by H. D., Charles Olson, John Cage, Charles Bernstein, Hakim Bey, and Michelle Cliff. During this last quarter I evaluated students on how much effort they put into creating an imaginative paper where they were expected to create a text that utilized any of the alternative forms we discussed during these last three weeks. (In the future I would at this point have students read selections from portions of Winston Weathers's *An Alternate Style*, discussed later on, and select from his list of options for composition one or two techniques to use within their final papers.) At the end of the semester, I had them write a short paper where the goal was to put into some kind of perspective the various forms of discourse we had peeked into, explaining which forms were more interesting or aggravating to them, and why. At the end, I tried to leave them with the message that nothing we did in class would necessarily ensure them of a good grade in future classes, and that if they wanted to get the best possible grades on their future papers, the best advice I had for them was little more than common sense: (a) start writing rough drafts and notes for the paper the moment it's assigned; (b) make frequent appointments with professors to try to get a clearer idea of what it is they're looking for; (c) make frequent appointments with the writing center for help on multiple revisions; and (d) do whatever necessary to ensure that as many errors, inconsistencies, and ambiguities within the text have been weeded out of the final product; i.e., proofread it half a dozen times, then have a friend or tutor read it over, especially since many professors will penalize students for what might seem to be a relatively few casual mistakes.[2] Finally, I encouraged students who were eager to continue writing in alternative styles to seek out professors who were known for their flexibility, but to do their best to adapt in situations where this would be impossible or inadvisable. And, if they were ever in a situation where they wanted to deviate from the enforced conventions but were not permitted this freedom, I encouraged them to speak candidly with their faculty in an attempt to explain their point of view. Ultimately, while I want to help students learn when it's important to adhere to certain imposed rhetorical forms, I don't want to teach them to become submissive and simply accept whatever a professor requires of them without any discussion. Since as an undergraduate I was forever trying to work out "deals" with my faculty ("Professor Moriarty, if I write a one-act play instead of the compare-and-contrast essay, and preface it with a detailed, five-page introduction and analysis, will that do?"), and as a result enjoyed parts of my education a great deal more, I also encourage students to do the same, so long as they're aware that sometimes it'll be more prudent, and perhaps beneficial, to work within the professor's constraints rather than create their own.

As for the overall structure of this course, throughout the

semester we had a workshop about every two or three weeks, and during the rest of the time discussed either the essays being read at that moment or the various perspectives associated with the areas of discourse under investigation during that quarter. For their final grade I averaged the four portfolio reviews together, sometimes raising the grade a notch for students who worked exceptionally hard and showed dramatic progress (in this way a student who was a fairly talented writer but lazy and apathetic might well end up with a lower grade than a developmental writer who really took the workload seriously).

In all honesty my initial attempt at this compositional survey course was a mix of exciting discussions and writings along with confusing transitions. There are bugs with this kind of course, to be sure. For one thing, it asks a lot from students, and from the instructor. Not only do they have to do considerable reading and writing, but they also have to switch gears just as they're getting into the swing of a particular form of writing. On one end the traditional composition course that privileges a particular theoretical orientation (whether expressivist, formalist, or social-constructive) permits students more time to "get the feel" of the constraints and ideologies circulating within that orientation. But it also dupes students into thinking that other legitimate discourse alternatives don't exist or don't matter. A version of the Theories of Composition survey course, on the other hand, can expose students to legitimate cross-cultural, feminist, and experimental ways of composing the world, and possibly help them develop a tolerance and respect for opposing philosophies of discourse—something extremely important if there's no opportunity for something like this to occur in the rest of their courses. The downside to this is that students can have trouble adapting to the sudden changes in this class, or comprehend these different rhetorical "zones" in little more than a cursory manner. Also, if the college admits many developmental writers but fails to provide them with the appropriate developmental assistance, such students can find a course like this daunting, to say the least.

But as long as composition is treated as a one-shot course where students are expected to "get into shape" in anticipation of the academic writing demands they'll encounter over the next four years (always a ridiculous assumption, since different profes-

sors and different disciplines have always had conflicting expectations for the written word), choosing between the two versions
won't be an easy decision. At any rate, it'll be one each teacher
will have to make on her own, depending as it will on a host of
factors, not the least of them being the support of her English
department, writing program, colleagues, and administrators; her
job security; and whether or not she has the time to commit to
the preparation and work necessary for this type of course.

Some will argue that the writing course that fails to offer students the necessary tools they'll need to survive in academe and
beyond is fundamentally, even inexcusably flawed. But *no* composition course does this, no matter how concentrated its focus, any
more than the student who has sat through two semesters of
Introductory Lit courses understands the depth and complexity
embedded in the term "literature." Even graduate students of literature—indeed, their professors as well—do not comprehend
"literature" in any totalizing form, but only from behind an idiosyncratic lens ground by one's tastes, the particular English
departments one has encountered, the aesthetic privilegings of
one's professors, and the availability of certain texts. If we spent
every hour of each day reading as many different volumes and
collections of literature from as many countries as possible, we
would, at the time of our deaths, have surfed only a small piece of
an ever-shifting sea of words. As Buckminster Fuller put it, the
days when humans could be considered specialists are gone forever, as computers have taken over that role; from here on out we
are all generalists, selecting our way through an incomprehensible flood of information, our paths governed only by taste and by
chance. And what is true for literature in this case is also true for
composition, rhetoric, and discourse. To expect students to exit
their one or two writing classes more fully aware of what "writing" is all about is disconcertingly naive. And if they do leave
such limited course offerings confident that they somehow possess all the insight necessary to understand, interpret, respect, and
interact with the complex, cross-cultural audiences surrounding
them, then we've taught them to be equally naive as well.

Of course, the Theories of Composition course, with its introduction into various composition philosophies--academic,
expressivist, cross-cultural, feminine, experimental, whatever—is

not going to provide students with the time to fully understand how these different rhetorics originated, how they relate to the academy, or how they can be negotiated and explored more fully. By itself, the Theories of Composition course is basically just an extended, watered down introduction, an attempt to turn upside down the formulaic, ethnocentric, and unimaginative definitions of writing students learn through osmosis in twelve years of institutional education. Ideally, it should be followed by composition classes of greater concentration, places where students could explore in detail the historical rationale behind certain discourses, and imitate different rhetorics while critiquing the ideological assumptions behind them. How many of these courses could be offered, and how frequently, would depend upon the particular needs, strengths, and weaknesses of the department. But since at this point I'm still imagining an ideal curriculum, consciously ignoring real problems like limited (or nonexistent) department funds, lack of qualified or interested faculty, and so forth, what follows are some hypothetical courses that could be offered to those who have already taken the composition survey class.

Introduction to Traditional Academic Discourses: This course might begin with selections from works like Aristotle's *Rhetoric* or Cicero's *De Oratore*, highlighting parallels between classical rhetoric and current-traditional revivals—distinctions between judicial, deliberative, and epideictic arguments, etc.[3] From here students might branch out into an examination of such popular academic practices as the five-paragraph theme, linear-hierarchical organization, thesis statements, preliminary outlines, objective tones, and appropriate methods of citation, reference, and footnoting. The class could make rhetorical analyses of the kinds of prose typically associated with academic discourse, including interdepartmental memoranda, passages taken from textbooks used in core courses, graduate dissertations, conference papers, and journal articles. Students would practice writing a variety of "academic" essays, from short pieces designed for essay exams, to "position papers" or reviews of academic articles of medium length, to longer research papers that would measure, among other things, how the student incorporated outside sources into the body of her text, how footnotes and endnotes were developed, how charts or diagrams were threaded into the work, how the structure modeled itself according to forms of linear, incre-mental progression, how accurately documentation of sources followed appropriate styles, and so on. As for the latter, the stu-dent's specific major could determine the style to be used: En-glish majors in the class could adhere to MLA style, while psychology majors could use APA format, etc. (Faculty from each of the different departments might drop by for one or two class periods and work in small groups with those students majoring in their field, showing them specifics and advice about how to use the appropriate style.) Students could be encouraged to study arguments for and against conventional modes of academic dis-course, comparing what proponents of classical rhetoric claim in contrast to those who urge the pursuit of more recent composing philosophies.[4] Students could prepare oral presentations that would be evaluated according to what typically constitutes an academically effective public speaking style: eye contact, suc-cinctness and clarity of presentation, organization of materials, use of visual aids and handouts, and the ability to field questions and facilitate discussion. A combined emphasis on oratory and written presentation.

Or, instead of having one single Introduction to Traditional Academic Discourses course, three separate courses or seminars might be given, each for maybe one or two credits. Distinguishing between various academic discourses with courses like Writing for Courses in the Humanities/Social Sciences, Writing for Courses in Business, and Writing for Courses in Science would be important since the compositional atmospheres presented within these broad arenas are frequently at odds with one another (the art history professor's definition of "good writing" will not neces-sarily serve for the professor of business law or biochemistry). In fact, any attempt to teach students "academic discourse" without the support of other departments and a strong Writing Across the Curriculum program is going to be seriously compromised, for no single-semester course can give students anything but a severely limited understanding of what "academic discourse" might entail in its entirety; and few faculty have the expertise and pedagogical savvy to teach students such an overwhelming and conflicting range of rhetorical styles. The professor who spends most of her time reading and writing prose that falls under the heading "sci-

entific writing" is simply more knowledgeable about this discourse than most writing instructors in an English department,
although obviously the two can collaborate in order to identify
classroom strategies for teaching such writing. Consequently, the
various courses in academic discourse would have to solicit the
help of faculty from different departments in order to identify the
rhetorical criteria that should be covered. Faculty from each
department might compile lists of what they considered to be
necessary components of successful student and professional
texts, which might then be offered as basic guidelines to be used
within certain courses or divisions. In addition, these three versions of Introduction to Academic Discourses could be team-
taught by faculty members in various related departments, along
with composition specialists: the Writing for Courses in the
Humanities/Social Sciences class, for example, might have a philosophy, sociology, and history professor working with a compositionist in order to develop and evaluate assignments.

Writing Personal Narrative: Many compositionists balk at the
constant emphasis on academic discourse, claiming it's more
important that students get in touch with their different voices.
The more students are permitted to tell their own stories, many
claim, the more apt they might be to think of writing as a creative, even liberatory activity instead of a dreaded chore. There
ought to be a forum for faculty and students sympathetic with
this perspective. In this course students could write ongoing
diaries, daybooks, and journals, then move to short assignments
addressing stylistic concerns relevant to autobiographical prose:
constructing lively but believable description; discovering different ways of using first and third person narrative; techniques for
character development; strategies for incorporating dialogue into
a text, and so on. In essence, how to spin captivating nonfictional tales that are directly or indirectly related to the experience of
the writer. Just as "literary journalists" view reportage as a medium capable of blending professional objectivity with the subjective asides of the author, students can be shown that the
expository essay need not be a collection of raw data packaged
into the polished stuff of factual summary, but can also acquire
strength and aesthetic appeal through techniques used in story-
telling. The class might compare passages by Frederick Douglass,

Henry David Thoreau, Gertrude Stein, Virginia Woolf, Black Elk (John G. Neihardt), James Baldwin, Jim Carroll, Roland Barthes, Joan Didion, John McPhee, and Maxine Hong Kingston, for instance, exposing students to a breadth of rhetorical ideas and tricks they could try out within their own texts. From simple anecdotes and recollections to passionate arguments and manifestos, students could be encouraged to pursue a wide selection of themes and topics. Papers could be read in workshop formats, with peers providing considerable commentary on each other's texts. In essence, this would be something like many Expository Writing courses, only taught in a manner more closely related to the traditional notion of the creative writing course: that is, an emphasis on workshops, sharing of techniques and strategies, and attention to issues of description, characterization, plot, pacing, tone, setting, and so on.

Ethnorhetorical Investigations: Deeply aware that the academy's interest in "the humanities" has traditionally been marked by elitist and ethnocentrist biases, post–World War II scholars have gradually broadened our understanding of *world* humanities by creating new areas of inquiry like ethnomusicology and ethnopoetics. Rhetorical studies and composition theory are in need of such expansion in focus. Geneva Smitherman sums it up effectively:

> Despite the American ideal of equal opportunity for all, the oppressive "doctrine of correctness" still abounds. It is kept alive not only by popular misconceptions about "standard" English and "correct" speech, but also by persistent myths about languages in general. Perhaps one of the most prevalent myths is the notion that there are "primitive," "underdeveloped," or "inferior" languages. Another myth has to do with the belief that in any given country, some people are speaking "*the* language" while others are merely speaking "dialect" versions of "*the* language." Still another persistent myth is that the speech of certain persons in society is sloppy and unsystematic, while that of others is governed by rules and regulations. Through their study and knowledge of the various languages and cultures of the world, linguists have put the lie to all such myths, and have arrived at a

number of "linguistic universals" underlying all languages. [But] despite linguistic truths now well over a century old, this vitally needed scientific information has not filtered down to precisely the place where it could have the greatest impact—the public school. For . . . the public school is the main institution that continues to perpetuate myths and inaccuracies about language. (191)

That the study of classical rhetoric begins (and often ends) with the genius of Plato, Isocrates, Aristotle, Cicero, and Quintilian shows how culturally myopic we have been in investigating the various natures of critical discourse. To be sure, when one reads the writings of Martin Luther King, Jr., one will find the words of a man highly skilled in the tools of classical rhetoric. But listen to King's sermons, and you will hear (and see) an abundance of tropes and techniques never addressed in the *Rhetoric*. There is much in African American, Native American, Latino, and Asian discourse that falls outside the tenets of ancient European rhetoric or, for that matter, of recent revisionist theories of discourse offered by insightful scholars like Ann Berthoff, James Moffett, and George Dillon. Consequently, students of rhetoric and composition in contemporary American colleges rarely get a taste of how other cultures construct and compose their worlds.

One might begin by offering a course such as "Ethnorhetorical Investigations." (And though here I'm focusing exclusively on African American discourse, mainly because as of this writing I don't feel confident enough of my ability to talk extensively about Native American, Latino, or Asian modes of discourse at any length, a course like this would ideally either explore a cross-cultural range of differing cultural discourse forms—African, Indian, Chicano, Middle Eastern, etc.—or else divide them up into special topics courses that would be offered on a rotating basis.) First, one would be wise to start with what the students are most familiar with, and, since they could be required to have taken a course in academic discourse prior to this one, comparisons could be made between classical and academic notions of discourse and literacy and the rhetoric of African and African American performance. One could start by having students read a work like John Miller Chernoff's *African Rhythm and African Sensibility*, a lively and accessible piece of scholarship that gradually unravels, through anecdote and personal ethnographic investigation, the reasons behind the fundamental differences between Western and African musical (and thus discursive) sensibilities, bringing us closer to understanding the African's alternative sense of aesthetics and social action.[5] While reading this work (and perhaps simultaneously reading passages from, say, the *Poetics* of Aristotle for the sake of comparison), it would be necessary to have students listen to a great deal of African music, as well as watch and discuss films or videos highlighting various African and African-influenced performances.[6]

After this, the transition could be made from Africa to African American discourse, with texts like Amiri Baraka's (writing as LeRoi Jones) *Blues People* and Geneva Smitherman's *Talkin and Testifyin* occupying a central role within the class; Baraka because of his insightful history of black music in America, Smitherman because of her excellent historical overview of African American discursive tropes. In conjunction with the former, it would be imperative that students spend significant class time listening to a variety of blues, old and recent, moving up through a sampling of contemporary jazz and some R&B (hitting some of the more prominent names, perhaps—Leadbelly, Bessie Smith, Dinah Washington, Billie Holiday, Howlin' Wolf; Louis Armstrong, Duke Ellington, Count Basie, Charlie Parker, John Coltrane, Ornette Coleman, Cecil Taylor; and, certainly, James Brown), and showing how cross rhthyms, collaboration between audience and performer, call and response, coarseness of timbre, and extended repetition— all longstanding forms of African discourse—occupy a major role in blues and jazz (see Collier 10–11, 13–14). And while reading Smitherman's work (which is doubly effective because Smitherman not only outlines the African American tropes touched on in chapter three, but does so in a prose that bounces back and forth between "standard" English and Black English), students might make close readings of talks by Malcolm X, James Baldwin, Martin Luther King, Jr., the fragmented essays of Michelle Cliff, Ishmael Reed's Neo-HooDoo Manifestoes, the hybrid prose (sometimes academic, sometimes Black English) of June Jordan,[7] and the polyrhythmic dialects found in Zora Neale Hurston's short stories, analyzing the various strategies used in each text.

The course could then shift to the medium of rap, a logical extension of jazz. For as jazz is the "continuous . . . emancipation of the soloist from the accompanying rhythmic-harmonic framework" (Kofsky 14), so is rap a form where the M.C. (i.e., verbal poet-soloist) is emancipated from the instruments themselves, the music created through "sampling" riffs from old tapes and records, splicing them together out of context, and repeating them for long periods of time beneath the preaching and boasting (modern manifestations of "signifying" and "the dozens") of one or more rappers. In this way rap, at its best, is something of a verbal jazz having unexpected ties to past collagists like Picasso and Kurt Schwitters, who would construct new art from debris found in the streets. (Some of the rap artists I would examine might be Public Enemy, the Disposable Heroes of Hiphoprisy, and Digable Planets, while avoiding rappers who are blatantly misogynist and homophobic, of which there are quite a few. Like any commercially profitable medium, the artistry of "black culture" has its ugly side—Ice Cube's malt liquor ads, Ray Charles's odious Pepsi commercials—and rap certainly has its share of crap.)

As far as assignments go, the classroom could be envisioned as a highly performative, interdisciplinary exchange of dialects and art forms, an updated extension of the way Beatrice Landek has sought means of exposing elementary school children to African roots of discourse. Students might engage in class discussions and oral presentations while examining the debates between the English Only movement and proponents for bilingual education, for instance, weighing the pros and cons of arguments for the primacy of standard English—E. D. Hirsch's claim for a standardized national sense of literacy versus those suspicious of the concept of standard English (James Sledd's claim that standard American English is by nature a "class dialect, essentially an instrument of domination" [669], or George Dillon's feeling that "the notion that there is an independent body of rules called standard English that governs 'the careful speech of educated speakers' is . . . quite illusory" [38]). After this, students, regardless of their ethnicity, could become more conscious of the "nonstandard" dialects and rhythms embedded within their own speech by first reading the transcribed "spoken" essays of people like David Antin and Dennis Tedlock (see chapter two)[8] and then doing the same with

their own verbal texts: recording some spoken, impromptu monologue or conversation of theirs, and transcribing the results on
paper for rhetorical analysis.[9] Following this, students could give
oral presentations where the goal would be to incorporate several
new rhetorical strategies into their oral performance, or capitalize
on some of their innate communicative tendencies.

Note: offering a course like this *does not* mean granting students permission to get up in front of class and offer bad imitations of black dialect. Nor does it mean that the instructor would
have to "talk jive" while teaching the class. So long as the
instructor who is not a native speaker of African American discourse remembers that she's not an authority on her subject, but
rather an interested mediator of a communal investigation into
this particular arena, there is no need to require that only blacks
teach this kind of course (or that Native Americans have sole
rights to teach Indian discourse, feminist theory can only be
taught by women, only Marxists can teach Marxism, etc.). In
fact, in a course on African American discourse, I would not
require *anyone* to try their hand at performing "like an African
American," and I might easily dissuade certain students from taking this approach, as there is nothing more embarrassing than
white folks trying to talk black—or more insulting to black students within the class. Instead, students could single out specific
components of African American discourse and modify them
within their own innate writing and speech habits in new and
creative ways, just as jazz musicians have taken traditional
African forms and turned them into completely new hybrids.[10]
The value in such a course, ultimately, would be in helping students see—and hear, and hopefully feel—the rhythmic pulses
underlying African American systems of discourse: to help them
recognize the complexity and credibility of such discourse, to get
them to start comparing and contrasting this material to classical
Western assumptions about communication, and eventually to
start thinking more closely about the everyday rhetorical decisions, conscious or otherwise, inherent within their own speech
and performance.

Teachers, certainly, should be careful of teaching this kind
of class prior to familiarizing themselves with the cultural landscape under investigation, lest they present the material in an

overgeneralized and thus disrespectful fashion. (Recall James Baldwin, who wrote: "Well-meaning white liberals place themselves in great danger when they try to deal with Negroes as though they were missionaries. . . . A great price is demanded to liberate all those silent people so that they can breathe for the first time and *tell* you what they think of you" [330].) I fell into this trap when I first wrote about making the composition classroom more multicultural, specifically "Afrocentric" in design. In a paper presented at a Conference on College Composition and Communication several years ago, in my eagerness to discuss various African American rhetorical tropes I reductively confused "Afrocentric" with African American, treating the terms as interchangeable and thereby grossly misunderstanding the tenets of Afrocentric theory. Another embarrassing assumption I made was that the "academy" has an obligation to bring these alternative discourses into our curriculum, a notion flawed since that act of pulling *in* from the *outside* is itself a centrist argument. What I should have addressed instead was the need for academics and institutions unfamiliar with alternative cultural discourses to begin reaching out to other communities and colleges with large ethnic populations, and listen to them for advice and pedagogical input in an attempt to develop greater dialogue within our different institutions.[11] For those who are still quite new to these different cultural discourses (and I include myself here), we must continually remind ourselves that "teaching" material like this is not a matter of posing as authorities, but as guides organizing classroom atmospheres where everyone, including ourselves, explores the material at hand. Even more important is for departments to recruit faculty and guest lecturers who understand such discourse arenas from firsthand experience. I might know enough about African American tropes to introduce them to a class, but there's no way I can provide the genuine thing; anyone can tell right away that my knowledge about African American rhetoric has come from reading and listening, not creating this discourse (which is one of the reasons why I would emphasize so much *listening* within my version of this class). Yes, whites can teach African American discourse, just as males can teach courses on feminist theory. But from a student's perspective, chances are the course on African American discourse taught by the black Baptist preacher will get a larger enrollment than the same course taught by the white guy—and who can blame them; I know I'd rather spend a semester learning this material from Geneva Smitherman or Amiri Baraka than from myself. Consequently, administrations and departments have to realize that, if our college curricula are going to seriously diversify, new courses will have to be created in order to attract diverse and creative faculty, which in turn will attract diverse and creative student bodies. But neither can we wait to make these perspectives available; and those who have the interest will, through trial and error, have to seek ways of incorporating these cross-cultural discourses into the classroom.

Experimental, Avant-Garde, and "Feminine" Writing: If we are going to develop some sense, no matter how diluted it might be, of what "writing" can encompass, we need to try to put the compositional landscape into some degree of perspective. But if we have no sense of the extreme parameters of this landscape, its landmarks and boundaries, then orientation within that field becomes impossible: in order to put the landscape into some context we need to know the limits of that territory. If we hold that academic discourse, in all its manifestations, represents one extreme, what would constitute the opposite end of the spectrum? This course would begin exploring writing strategies that have been and often continue to be considered "cutting edge," radically experimental, and unapologetically multidisciplinary.

Consider: Hannah Weiner writes books where words are spliced together, torn apart, and overlap one another in narratives that pick up and leave off without warning. Armand Schwerner creates texts that derive their power in part from leaving much of the linguistic content absent, the empty spaces marked by asterisks and glyphs. In some of her essays Rachel Blau DuPlessis blackens out specific passages, only to leave the dark holes present in the final copy, reminding us of the frustration that comes with writing as a woman within a masculine grammar. Choosing to ignore conventional spelling, bill bissett wrote according to his own phonetic interpretations. David Melnick and P. Inman are two writers whose project has been to produce new languages, breeding conventional English with their own neologisms. Creating discursive spaces that are at once visual arrangements (paintings, models, architectures) and written texts, Madeline Gins and Arakawa explore the limitations of language and the metamorphoses of meaning with wonderfully mysterious and funny results. Mary Daly and Jane Caputi have constructed their own alternative feminist dictionary, an encyclopedic sourcebook of alternative antipatriarchal language usages. Ishmael Reed continues to write histories of himself and his culture that are mixtures of scholarly inquiry, surrealist fiction, contemporary mythology, and poetry, while for Michelle Cliff, articulation of her splintered cultural history is possible only from within an aesthetics of fragmentation, prose narratives perforated with gaps and silences.[12]

If we say that constructions like these are "just" the work of experimental writers and as such have little direct relevance to the business of composition theory, then we are saying that poiesis and experimentation have little if anything to do with composition studies. But if we admit that the explorations implicit in these texts are indeed relevant to the nature of composition and, consequently, to our discipline, then the assumptions upon which our field is built cry out for redefinition.

Therefore, a good way to start raising these questions and concerns might be to have students read Winston Weathers's landmark book, *An Alternate Style: Options in Composition*.[13] In this study Weathers differentiates between "Grammar A," or academic discourse, and "Grammar B," which would encompass a great deal of the writing covered here in previous chapters. Referring to the alternative rhetorics of writers such as Laurence Sterne, William Blake, Emily Dickinson, Walt Whitman, Charles Baudelaire, D. H. Lawrence, John Dos Passos, Tillie Olson, Gertrude Stein, John Barth, Donald Barthelme, Richard Brautigan, William Burroughs, and Thomas Pynchon, Weathers identifies a number of possibilities for an alternative style. Among them he lists the "crot" (an archaic term meaning "fragment"), the labyrinthine sentence, the sentence fragment, the list, double-voice (intended not in the African American sense, but rather as the presence of two or more dissimilar styles reverberating within the same text), repetitions (and repetends, or refrains), and language variation, or what Weathers describes as "orthographic schemes" (i.e., neologisms and customized vocabulary). With such forms at her disposal, the adventuresome student is granted a new bag of possibilities for composing, and Weathers offers a handful of ideas and models to help her fashion the rhetoric of "Grammar B" using such devices as montage, collage, pastiche, linguistic generation (wordplay), and supersaturation (intentional verbosity). There is, it should be noted, a conservative thread running through portions of Weathers's study that some readers might find problematic: his insistence on getting students to become "masters" of Grammar B (i.e., this need to perpetuate such loaded and authoritarian terminology), his rule that writers "must not switch" from one alternate form to another, and his need to distinguish his notion of alternate style, which is "mature" and "well-tested" as opposed to less rigorous experimental writing, examples of which are never really articulated. Still, these are small issues compared to the range of fresh ideas Weathers catalogues, all of which are made accessible to students.

After this the students could start exploring a hodgepodge of genre transgressions: the prose poetry of nineteenth-century French symbolists; the visual experiments of the Russian constructivists in the early twentieth century;[14] the "other" modernism, with its more exploratory compositions (Gertrude Stein's lectures, Mina Loy's manifestos, the notes of H. D., the historical musings of William Carlos Williams, and the cranky eclecticism of Ezra Pound's critical prose); the attention to chance operation in the texts of dadaists and surrealists, up through the work of John Cage and Jackson Mac Low; the prose of surfictionists and postmodern critics (Ihab Hassan, Raymond Federman, Campbell Tatham);[15] composers of sound poetry; zines and mailart circulating within the underground press; algorithmic writing and the Oulipian school; the experiments with syntax and grammar found in the writing of the Language poets and theorists. Students might be expected to compare and critique these various projects, and then create their own exploratory texts. Invention and variety would be the operative words as students sought ways of making essays, poetry, speeches, performances, and any multidisciplinary combination thereof, taking strategies and ideas from the texts read in class and applying them to their own works in progress.

This class would also introduce students to the possibility of a "feminine" discourse, the characteristics of which are closely related to experimentalist writing. The class could quickly be introduced to a handful of essays by feminist poets and literary theorists (Rachel Blau DuPlessis and Hélène Cixous, for example), leading to recent feminist analyses of language and considerations of its masculinist roots. The object would be to help students see that language—its logic, syntax, vocabulary, presentation, organization, tone—is not gender neutral but a social construct coded with the ideologies of those with the power to create, modify, and enforce discourse. Essays by various feminist experimental writers could be read (Madeline Gins, Susan Howe, Beverly Dahlen) as examples of various attempts to compose language systems representative of a desire to resist inflexible, masculinist authority. Students could practice writing both texts that for them epitomize blatantly masculinist and authoritarian discourse, and texts accentuating the presence of contradiction, silences, multidisciplinary tendencies, collaborative impulses, and other strategies that might be deemed indicative of a "feminine" resistance to *phallogocentrism*. Students could examine texts they have made in prior classes to analyze how their structure and arrangement were influenced by forces they were not aware of, and then rewrite those texts in alternative forms. Students might analyze and critique the prose styles of their textbooks and college catalogues (and even other "feminine" texts written in accordance with masculinist prose styles) through the lenses of feminist theorists and poets to determine to what extent these texts are the result of a male-dominated economy.

Aside from exposing students to new rhetorical horizons, a number of these alternative composing strategies could provide writers with new tools useful in the construction of more conventional texts. The student too preoccupied with bringing texts to some rigid sense of closure might find it beneficial to intentionally compose pieces that are "unclosed." Writer's block might be circumvented as one pursues alternative paths not normally permitted in the given discourse—the student writing an essay on Emily Dickinson might free herself by abandoning linear prose and breaking into poetry, assembling passages of impressionistic fragments that, depending upon the course and audience, could either be incorporated as is into the final text or reshaped to conform to a more linear code. Writers who find themselves stuck might imitate the stream of consciousness journals of Bernadette Mayer so as to stir up new perceptions in a more relaxed, nonacademic manner. After reading work by Beverly Dahlen students might come closer to understanding that journal writing is potentially a great deal more than a systematic record keeping of one's thoughts, can in fact be a valid and powerful art form in itself. Fashioning open texts in the tradition of Lyn Hejinian and Ron Silliman could be one way of helping students become cognizant of the perpetual flood of stimuli bombarding each of us at any given moment, all of it potential material for our compositions. In grade school it's not uncommon for students to gather photos and images from magazines which are then glued into a collage, the resulting assemblage then reflecting in some way the student's personality; in the same way one could assign students to make written collages, each sentence or paragraph a unique entity within itself addressing isolated and seemingly unrelated memories, emotions, and perceptions. After examining such collections of "new sentences" students might locate habits of perception or pinpoint interests that might otherwise have gone unrealized. One of the most common complaints heard by students is that they've nothing to write about—as if one could live eighteen years and not have an infinite storehouse of collected information to write from (no matter how much television one watches). Having students read open texts like those of Hejinian, then creating their own versions, might help them tap into those ongoing perceptions that rarely enter the realm of critical contemplation. After all, none of us really *receive* information, rather we *synthesize* it, either passively or constructively, which is ultimately an act of creation. Any means of weaning students off banking concepts of education that hide this fact are worthwhile fodder for the compositionist.

Computers and Composition: Though teaching composition with computers is nothing new, and while it helps students create texts with greater efficiency via word processing and electronic mail in addition to offering new opportunities for teacher-to-student communication and student-to-student collaboration, most computer-aided instruction probably goes toward getting students to create more academic discourse: linear-hierarchical texts informed by classical, Western discourse assumptions. By and large, courses using online writing have yet to capitalize on the possibilities available in hypertext. A writing course where students used computers to investigate the possibilities of hypertext, using various software to create their own hyperdocuments, would represent an entirely new direction in composition instruction: students could explore the atomization and dispersal of hypertext as alternatives to the obligatory linearity of academic discourse. Using hypermedia, multiple fields and sources of information could be brought together in unique constructions otherwise impossible with conventional prose. One exciting project for such a class could be the creation of essays, short stories, plays, poems, or a novel using collaborative software, where multiple students take different roles simultaneously writing a single, shared text (in a work of fiction, some students could write parts for different characters, while others develop setting and plot; in expository prose, some students could work on introductions and conclusions, others footnotes and citations; in a collective work of poetry, students could work alternately on metaphor, alliteration, end rhyme, image, scansion, etc.). By having students create their own collective works, chances are they might become more excited and involved during the editing and revising process of such a text than with many traditional assignments. At the end of the semester students could publish their work, using desktop publishing software.

Computer interaction provides the user with networks and communities of writers impossible to reach by any other means, thus allowing students the opportunity to work with others in different colleges, even different countries. Instead of writing isolated papers, students from widely different locations could collaborate on large projects: an economics major from New Mexico, a sociology major from Toronto, and a journalism major from New Zealand, each of them drawing upon their special areas, might generate information collectively, forming a unique document that all three could use for credit in their separate courses. While discussing, arguing, and compromising with each other online, students could gain insight into new disciplines (not to mention learn something about the fine art of compromise). A faculty mentor or guide could be assigned to work with various student groups to help facilitate discussion, offer advice, or serve as mediator in disagreements; a variety of professors from relevant disciplines could offer feedback on the work in progress, thereby giving students a range of comments from different professors in different fields.

Another benefit is that students from vastly different socioeconomic and cultural backgrounds could begin communicating with each other in ways unlikely or impossible in face-to-face encounters on campus. Though online communication tends to depersonalize the participants (body language, gender, voice, and ethnicity tend to remain buried beneath the sterility of the blinking screen), the ease and safety of online discourse renders interaction extremely accessible—one's words can be carefully weighed before sending them out, and the physical distance eliminates much of the tension typically accompanying visual communication.[16] As computers become more common in the classroom, there will be entire classes operating online, and not all of those enrolled in the course will necessarily be of the same college; in a sense, anyone could become a foreign exchange student without ever leaving her home campus, or her bedroom for that matter. It's not even difficult to imagine the time when colleges will no longer be self-contained and autonomous, but rather fragmented nodes connected to one another in large international academic networks.

With the changes computer technology brings to composition theory, new problems will have to be addressed. We've already seen how computer spelling checks can both improve and hurt student writing (fewer misspellings, but not necessarily new awareness of proper syntax, resulting in new types of errors). As programs that check one's spelling become more effective, the emphasis on the ability to spell correctly might fade (spelling bees, which once measured what was regarded as a valuable skill, might become little more than nostalgic reminders of a time when one had to rely on memory for accuracy, not on software). Ownership of text becomes another problematic issue, as online writers disregard copyright laws and disseminate entire articles and speeches without permission across electronic discussion lists. This will lead to our reexamining the nature of plagiarism, and ultimately redefining what will constitute textual theft, what will not, and even whether or not the issue warrants the same concern it has in the past, especially as texts become increasingly accessible to large audiences, each reader having the power to alter, edit, and embellish received information for her own purposes.[17] In fact, as we continue to explore hypertext, our notion of writing will probably continue to change in radically new ways. For example, where sentences and paragraphs were once the basic units of traditional rhetoric, hypertext makes *modularization* the primary unit: that is, a concern for how nodes of information will be divided, sized, and disseminated (Carlson 96). How much text fits on a screen at one time and how it can be arranged become new concerns. Even the idea of a single author becomes shaky, as computers encourage multiple audiences to work continuously on variations of the same extended text. One researcher has already discovered that many computer programmers aren't really "writers" in any conventional sense of the word, but more aptly characterized as systems designers and analysts who, in the process of using already existing programs, formulate ways other users can learn to access new software, much in the same way members of the Oulipo movement didn't write novels but discovered algorithms that others could use to read and write new texts (Zimmerman 281).

Though the technology necessary for widespread, cross-academic computer interaction is still absent in many colleges, as computers eventually become as cost-efficient and easy to use as telephones the opportunities for innovative electronic composition will become increasingly common. Preparation for the kinds of course offerings, pedagogical changes, and curricular modifications that will evolve with this new technology have already begun; those of us who haven't fully contemplated how computers are rapidly altering our understanding of composition have our work cut out for us. Pedagogies have already begun to evolve as a direct result of the new technology, represented in the words of Michael Joyce, hypertext author and teacher of writing, who sent these words to readers over a computer discussion list: "our purpose remains the same . . . : the violent overthrow of the state of the classroom by collaborative de-centering and hypertextual devolution of the hegemonic hierarchy of the printed text (whew!)."[18] In fact, computer technology might forever alter our understandings of literacy. Before too long people could be communicating not by typing texts into computers but speaking into microphones and conversing with one another over video; rhetorical prowess will then be measured not by anyone's ability to manipulate the alphabet, but by vocal and physical adroitness. Hypermedia and computer technology might eventually—and more speedily than we think—signal the death of literacy as we now know it, introducing us into a new age of high oral literacy.[19] Whether teachers of composition anticipate this drastic shift, a shift that could well be under way in several short decades, with excitement, dread, or a little of both, our educational environments are in for major changes. We can either begin imaginatively devising ways of using the forthcoming technology, or ignore the inevitable and allow others to determine for us how such technology will be used.

Comprehensive Developmental Assistance: It's important here to back up for a moment and address my concern for disadvantaged and developmental writers. Despite all my talk about incorporating more variety into the writing curricula, it's imperative that those students disadvantaged in a number of writing skills have the opportunity to work out some of those liabilities before taking any of the above courses. Without some vital preparatory work, developmental, disadvantaged, and certain nontraditional students could easily find the kind of curriculum I've outlined here terribly disorienting and chaotic. To promote a multirhetorical writing program without first meeting the concerns of those whose primary need is academic survival would constitute a pedagogical philosophy more exclusionary than that it seeks to replace. All of this hypothesizing and drawing up of new courses will amount to little more than colorful elitism unless we focus on the problems that accompany the English as a Second Language (ESL) student, English as a Foreign Language (EFL) student, and academically disadvantaged and/or nontraditional students requiring additional preliminary writing instruction.

As colleges and universities seek to diversify student enrollment—and this means not only bringing in more ethnic minority students but also nontraditional students from poor, working class, and neglected urban and rural communities, as well as other nontraditional students such as returning adults, commuters,

student athletes, and students with various physical and/or learning disabilities—the needs of these students will have to be met
from the moment they begin their first semester. This means
either making available a preliminary writing course for students
whose educational backgrounds have not sufficiently prepared
them for the expectations demanded by their professors, or at
least providing them with some form of ongoing one-on-one
tutorial assistance where they can spend significant time familiarizing themselves with processes of revision, as well as learn a few
techniques that might help them catch some of their more recurring errors. In addition it also means making sure that students
have access to a learning center, tutorial help in other subject
matters, committed mentors and advisors who take a proactive
role in gauging the progress and development of these students,
and counseling resources to help address problems both within
and outside the academic scope.

For nearly three years, while teaching part-time in an English
department, I worked full-time as a counselor in a Higher Education Opportunity Program at an upstate New York college, where
I spent a great deal of time with students who were both academically and economically disadvantaged. The vast majority of
these students had the potential to succeed at the college level,
despite their many obstacles, and succeed many of them did, as
every semester a significant number were rewarded with academic
honors. It was an interesting experience: watching students with
no money and less than impressive high school transcripts struggle through a strange environment (one where the campus community was often, unwittingly or intentionally, hostile to students
of color and low-income families), learning how to negotiate the
academic terrain, get involved in campus activities and organizations, and ultimately develop into students who got accepted into
graduate schools for programs like computer science, pre-law, and
secondary education. Basically, going from adolescents who were
taught that attaining a college degree was beyond their ability, to
students who worked hard and eventually claimed what so many
of their classmates took for granted.

The majority of these students grew up in environments where
they were encouraged to do extremely little reading and writing
on their own, and where reading and writing often held absolute-

ly no appeal nor obvious immediate benefit—either because such activities weren't creatively presented within their twelve years of schooling, or because there was little time or rationale for such intellectual activity within the home, or both. Most would never have made it in college had they not received some form of developmental assistance with their writing and study skills. Such developmental support is absolutely crucial to the welfare of such students when they first enter college, where they are made painfully aware that their writing skills are out of sync with the standards upheld by their professors. Nor is this a characteristic unique to student populations like those in the educational opportunity program I worked in; every semester at this same college I would encounter within my classes traditional, so-called mainstream students who had terrible writing skills, not because they were dumb but because they'd gotten lousy educations, and consequently needed a great deal of constant, individual tutorial assistance to, as many faculty put it, "bring them up to speed."

I am not equipped here to offer any substantive strategies for teaching this kind of course, aside from a few already well-documented techniques;[20] interested readers would do better to distill pedagogical strategies from the wealth of available material and modify that advice to suit their own individual courses, student populations, and teaching conditions. Suffice it to say that I firmly believe developmental writing courses, in addition to learning centers, abundant tutorial services, effective faculty advisors, and counseling centers, are vital to the academic welfare of many students, traditional and nontraditional alike—and that for colleges to accept students in need of such assistance, but fail to provide them with these services, is morally indefensible. Many students require assistance in developmental writing and reading skills. Many need effective, personable tutors who understand that tutoring is not a matter of lecturing to the student, but getting the student to discover ways of identifying her strengths and weaknesses so she may then use the tutor to help make sense out of what's not clear. Students need faculty members who can serve as intellectual role models, faculty who understand the specific deficiencies of their students and, without labeling or judging them, take an active role in monitoring their progress before they fail or withdraw. Students need advisors who take the time to understand a little of their students' educational histories, needs, and goals, so that they might prevent them from making mistakes early on in their academic careers that will haunt them until graduation. Finally, students need easy access to confidential counseling services so they can start tackling the slew of nonacademic situations that can easily prevent them from performing well academically. Teaching the developmental/disadvantaged student writer has as much to do with the counseling, tutoring, and advising going on *outside* of the classroom on a daily basis as it does with what takes place in it, a fact too often overlooked by teachers and administrators.

Nor do I think effective comprehensive introductions into academic, or ethnic, or feminist, or experimental discourses can occur unless the student can operate with at least a minimum degree of efficiency within the standard discourse her professors will expect from her. And I'm not talking about knowing how to write a thesis sentence and concluding statement, but rather about the student who can't hyphenate because she's not exactly sure what a syllable is, or who says she has never before heard of the terms "subject" and "predicate." Or the student whose attention span is so undeveloped that writing more than a few paragraphs or reading any text over ten pages proves terribly frustrating if not impossible. The student who can't distinguish between passive reading and critically engaged, active reading; the student who hasn't the slightest idea of how to begin managing her time. These are not isolated cases; I ran into these problems constantly. I had always suspected that many elementary and secondary schools did little to prepare students for the literacy demands required within the academy, but it wasn't until I began working closely with students as an academic counselor that I discovered just how ill-prepared many of them were.

And so, beyond teaching a mélange of courses in various styles of composition and rhetoric, we have to make sure that all of the incoming students are prepared for the demands such a variegated, conflicting curriculum would make on them. For those who are in need of some developmental assistance—whether with their writing, reading, or general study skills—we have to offer a bridge between high school and college, if for no other reason than because high schools generally do little to aid this transition. Of all the disadvantaged and academically unprepared students I have worked with, every one of them—whether white or minority, male or female—desired, on some level, to be able to improve their writing to the point that they could impress their professors. Certainly, students might come to disagree with the tenets and assumptions that inform the aesthetic preferences assumed by their professors when it comes to evaluating discourse—hence why offering courses in alternative, non-Western communicative strategies is essential. But they all, at least those I've worked with, urgently want to know how to criticize such assumptions within the language system(s) sanctioned by their institution. When the deficient educational histories of some students result in making them feel stupid around their professors and peers, they grow insecure, embarrassed, angry and, ultimately, apathetic. It's going to be difficult to teach such students much of anything, academic discourse or African American discourse, until the institution shows it's concerned enough to address some of their most basic deficiencies starting the moment they enter college, if not sooner.

2. Writing Across the Curriculum (WAC) programs will need to pay closer attention to theories of discourse falling outside those typically associated with the formalist/expressivist polarity. Much of the WAC movement is still fundamentally committed to helping students adapt to formalist or expressivist versions of academic discourse; as far as I'm aware no WAC programs are developing ways of teaching cross-cultural, feminist, or experimental discourses throughout the academy. As Daniel Mahala has pointed out, American WAC theory has either assumed the tenets of formalist writing instruction where students are conditioned to learn "supposedly normative ways of arguing and gathering evidence in disciplines," or adopted an expressivist approach that more often than not fails to cast a critical eye toward either the current-traditionalist assumptions it seeks to counteract or its own rhetorical biases (779). The result is that, in the former, "the pursuit of academic discourse as an end rather than a question [occurs], a foreclosure that suppresses dialogue about boundaries in the interests of schematizing knowledge" (782), while the expressivist angle risks envisioning a generic model of journal writing, without really addressing the wildly divergent range of student discourses that can drastically send the rhetoric of the journal into unexpected realms.

If the logic behind the pluralistic curriculum described above spilled over into the rest of the academy, we would see the same kind of rhetorical exploration in other departments. A history department, for example, might offer a course where majors and minors were introduced to several approaches to writing about history—from the formalism of the analytic research paper, to the "thick description" of the new historicism, to more experimental fusions between history and poetry (William Carlos Williams's essays on America, Paul Metcalf's historical "novels," Susan Howe's incorporation of historical research within her experimental poetics). Science departments could create spaces where students could practice writing not only the obligatory lab reports and journal reviews but more "readable" narratives about scientific phenomena, modeled perhaps after writers like Stephen Jay Gould, James Gleick, and Richard Rhodes. The women's studies department might offer its own course in *écriture feminine* and "feminine" rhetoric; an African American studies department could do the same with a course in African American discourse. The philosophy course addressing classical philosophy might require students to write their texts in accordance with Aristotelian rhetoric, while advanced and graduate students reading philosophers like Nietzsche, Barthes, Foucault, Derrida, and Deleuze might write in ways foregrounding a similar attention to playfulness, spontaneity, and intuition. Theater departments could feature a course in the discourse of performance; computer science departments might provide seminars exploring hypertext and hypermedia—and so on. As a college's writing curriculum undergoes major transformations, so too will its WAC program have to keep pace.

3. Tenured faculty who supervise Writing Centers, Writing Programs, and English departments will have to play a significant role in curricular reform. Tenured faculty involved in the creation and reform of the writing curricula—whether they are directors of programs, chairs of English departments, or monitor adjunct faculty who teach a number of entry-level writing courses—can use their influence to begin resisting the academy's monocultural preoccupation with Eurocentric standards of literacy. This would mark a genuine step toward actually "empowering" students, one that opens up for the student a range of viable means of making and interpreting her world and identifying herself within that world. Granted, unresponsive administrations can wreak havoc with faculty intentions of moving course offerings in more progressive, varied directions. But tenured faculty, if they can consolidate their collective concerns (admittedly, a very large "if"), do have an undeniable degree of influence to promote curricular change. If many of the changes discussed earlier in this chapter are to generate realities, consistent backing and support will have to come from tenured faculty, who have the luxury of not having to constantly worry about saying or doing the wrong thing out of fear for their job security. Untenured faculty and adjuncts, who comprise such an enormous part of English department faculty, will likewise need to develop an increased tolerance and respect for overlooked discourses, and seek ways of making their classrooms more pluralistic in scope. But unless they have the support and commitment of tenured colleagues, we can assume that any curricular change will occur in only the most local arenas—the private corners of one's own classroom—and remain invisible or superficial on a larger, departmental scale.[21]

4. The notion of "creative writing" as a rhetorical arena fundamentally distinct from "academic writing" will have to be rethought as conventional notions of genre and strictly defined writing communities give way to greater cross-disciplinary variation. With all this cross-fertilization among discourses and departments going on, the concept of the Creative Writing course begins to stand out as something of a dinosaur. Many of the above hypothetical courses would permit students the opportunity to work in such "creative" genres as poetry, fiction, and drama. One of the incentives beneath this revisionary mapping is to argue that "creative writing," as it generally refers to a collection of genres distinct from all other "normative" discourse, is a term that should finally be buried once and for all. One could argue that almost *all* writing, after all, ought on some level to be creative; otherwise, why bother? To distinguish between creative writing and the remainder is to keep alive a romantic dichotomy having little or no validity in the postmodern, cross-cultural, multidiscursive academy.[22] Certainly there could still be courses in poetry and fiction, but these would no longer be seen as fundamentally removed from any of the other courses focusing on specific discourse strategies. The student in the poetry course would not only experiment with a host of poetic forms, for example, but also write essays on her poetics, conduct research into the work of other poets and poetic movements, and maybe even pursue themes related to her major discipline, only presented within some poetic form. (It might be odd to imagine the accounting major building sestinas or one act plays based upon theories and terminologies learned from a Finance course, but this is exactly the kind of cross-disciplinary interaction that might be possible in composition; some of our most fascinating poets—Pound, Williams, Olson—were historians, philosophers, artists, physicians, and scholars who recognized that within a context of exploratory poetry, anything and everything was potential material.)

Currently most creative writing workshops exist because English departments feel obliged to offer a few poetry and fiction writing courses in halfhearted recognition that English majors should probably have a taste of what writing poetry and short stories might be like, even though these classes are regarded much less seriously than the advanced literature courses. But such classes are often little more than indoctrinations into the biases of a single instructor who, by virtue of her publication history, is endowed with the authority to tell students the secrets that differentiate good poetry from bad. While even the most selective professor of literature might feel the need in a survey course to teach authors or even periods that she despises, the Creative Writing professors aren't necessarily bound to cover a range of forms; instead their own preferences and processes are passed down and disguised as normative assumptions that any "creative" student writer ought to share. The fact that such biases are no more and no less than one privileged writer's personal taste is overshadowed as the English department seeks to present its token Creative Writing professor as something akin to a guru of linguistic creativity—a guru whose workshops can often discourage experimentation, serving instead as initiations into one published author's private aesthetics.

Consequently an important side effect of the multirhetorical curriculum is that the notion of creative writing would gradually dissolve, until we would be left with just multiple genres of discourse—sonnets, lab reports, journals, classical arguments, short stories, scripts for performance—forms within which the disciplines of the academy could be further explored. Faculty responsible for teaching poetry and fiction could no longer rely solely on the number of their publications, since such quantity indicates neither pedagogical creativity nor pluralistic tolerance for multiple rhetorics. Instead, other criteria would become more significant: the degree of inventiveness used to introduce students to a wide range of disparate styles, balanced with the ability to encourage students to write about a range of topics within such forms—that is, in addition to such potentially clichéd themes as love and nature, encouraging students to write about Reaganomics, chaos theory, ecofeminism (or whatever) within the creative writing course.

5. As a result of the growing awareness of legitimate alternative discursive forms, graduate students in composition and rhetoric now have a great deal of new terrain to explore. One of the most difficult problems graduate students seem to face is choosing a topic for their thesis or dissertation that constitutes relatively unexplored territory. Yet for those students interested in rhetoric, composition, and pedagogy, as well as feminist literary theory, cross-cultural literature, and experimental twentieth-century texts, the range of possible directions for further study is as exciting as it is broad. After all, in some ways this manuscript borders on the superficial—where I've devoted only a chapter each to African American, "feminine," and experimental discourse, others could easily write entire monographs. For instance:

• How might further investigation into the nuances of various cultural dialects and discourses offer practitioners new ideas for the contemporary classroom—from the elementary grades up through graduate school? What might an in-depth theory of discourse from a distinctly African American perspective look like? How might Western definitions of "critical thinking" contrast with African, Eastern, and Native American ways of experiencing the world? What importance does ethnopoetics have for the compositionist? In what ways does our definition of literacy require rethinking once we take into account the methods of social interaction that are alive and well in numerous world cultures? How could bringing music and performance into our realms of professional consideration change the very nature of our discipline, and get us thinking about the term "composition" in all its possible forms?

• While extraordinary amounts of scholarship concerning feminist poetics surface each year, the bulk of this is still solidly entrenched within the academic rhetorical tradition,[23] and so the critical possibilities for those receptive to composing from vantage points resistant to masculinist discourse are wide open. As such, how might a detailed examination of writings by academically ignored experimental women writers publishing in small presses lead to modified theories of reading and writing? How might a continued discussion of avant-garde writings by women writers alter the shape of feminist literary criticism? What if one were to engage in a study of gay and lesbian writers—would one find grammars informed by sexual preference? What might a "rhetoric of androgyny" be?[24] How might the discourse of our institutions—the way we write syllabi, mission statements, memos, contracts, and textbooks—gradually undergo changes as alternative composing styles informed by advancements in feminist composition become more widespread?

• What could we learn from interviewing experimental writers who teach college level composition—would their techniques inform their teaching practices? What might we learn from rereading modernist poets and critics like Mina Loy, H. D., Ezra Pound, Gertrude Stein, and the early William Carlos Williams as composition theorists—that is, writers intent on pushing the possibilities of written expression—and critically monitoring that process within their treatises and manifestos? What other ways might writers like Charles Olson, John Cage, Madeline Gins, Susan Howe, Amiri Baraka, Jerome Rothenberg, and Rachel Blau DuPlessis have relevance within the composition classroom? Taking our cue from Winston Weathers's discovery of "Grammar B," what additional grammars wait to be discovered?

• And finally, computer technology is changing our understanding of composition at lightning speed. What new breeds of collaborative texts can interactive computer software help us to create? As the writing classroom and the entire academic land-scape become one giant computer system with multiple users, how will this change the nature of writing—that is, will we reach a time when collaborative writing will be the primary mode of communication, and texts by individual authors seem romanti-cally quaint in comparison? How might virtual reality revolution-ize the nature of writing in ways many poststructuralists never imagined? What happens when our technology allows us to bypass keyboards altogether, and simply speak our messages into microphones attached to the computer, à la Star Trek—will this render print obsolete for most of us? (Remember—we already *have* this technology; what will result when these machines become as commonplace as our telephones?)

Actually, for the graduate student in search of new things to write about, the problem is no longer not being able to think up anything new, but rather how to grow accustomed to sensory and information overload. Today's compositionist almost has too much to think about.

6. Graduate faculty and chairs of dissertation committees ought to permit students the opportunity to construct alterna-tive forms of critical inquiry within their classes and projects. The freedom graduate students will have to explore alternative compositions will only be as flexible as their professors and disser-tation committees permit. Consequently, those who find them-selves chairing and advising graduate students at work on their dissertations might urge them to start probing these new philoso-phies of expression, and abandon the more stagnant, ponderous dialects of "dissertationese" in order to create a rhetorical space where information and theories are simultaneously (imagine it) fun, maybe even exciting, to read. Graduate students who write "creative dissertations"—i.e., volumes of poetry, fiction, or drama—generally have a tremendously difficult time having their work taken seriously once they pursue positions in academe; pro-fessors could help squelch the ridiculous oversimplification between "creative" and scholarly dissertations by allowing writers to jump various boundaries, fashioning texts that might utilize the strengths of essay, poetry, journal, scholarly prose, and addi-tional hybrids of multiple forms. Likewise, faculty could entertain alternative means of measuring graduate student proficiency—

that is, written and oral examinations might be supplemented with performance, readings, classroom activities, and so forth, depending on the various concerns and expertise of the degree candidate.

Of course, if graduate faculty do permit such experimentation, it would be absolutely necessary that they use everything in their professional power to make other colleagues and institutions aware that their candidates, who may have explored alternative forms of expression within their scholarly work, are no less serious or capable than those who have gone through more traditional graduate programs. Allowing graduate students the opportunity to explore and experiment is essential; but unless the department permitting such alternative scholastic work fails to use its influence in helping new candidates enter into professional life, a gross disservice has been performed.

7. Publishers and editors of professional journals and anthologies, as well as the selection committees for professional conferences, can actively solicit works from writers whose styles deviate from conventional standards of academic rhetoric. Those who serve on the editorial boards of academic journals and university presses could seek material that not only further investigates alternative and cross-cultural rhetorics, but indicates a willingness to take rhetorical risks. For example: issues, even entire journals devoted to highlighting an assortment of discourse styles; a monograph series where each volume explores overlooked cross-cultural theories of composition; anthologies where essays model themselves after some discourse or rhetoric largely ignored in academia. Panels could be organized at the Modern Language Association Conference and the Conference of College Composition and Communication where the differences within cultural, feminist, and experimental discourses are not only unraveled before an audience, but actively demonstrated and performed. Writers who work in experimental forms could read their work and afterward discuss its ramifications with the audience; roundtables could be offered where scholars of African American, Native American, Asian, and Latin American discourse theory could discuss the pedagogical possibilities for incorporating these dialects and composing habits into the curriculum; writers engaged in defining nonmasculinist writing tech-

niques could share their struggles via public performance and collaboration, discussing with the audience the theoretical motivations prompting such diversions.

At the very least those who organize the sessions and panels
for our professional organizations could begin using their imaginations to orchestrate these one- to two-hour gatherings into
open spaces for creative, exploratory interchange between colleagues. One of the mysteries of academe is that professors, who
commonly complain that their students are too quiet, too
reserved, and too unimaginative, will spend considerable time
and money traveling to hotels where the primary activity is sit-
ting in large rooms listening in silence to a panel of colleagues
read papers, many of which will be ponderously dull, written and
performed with little or no sense of how to pull an audience into
the performance. Everyone knows that the only time many of
these panels get interesting is when the readers are finished and
the audience is invited to ask questions (which, unfortunately,
too often means shooting down a panelist's argument so that
one's own ideological stance can be displayed). Since the most
invigorating part of these gettogethers is the postpanel verbal
sparring, more of them should capitalize on the audience's natural
desire to join in, be heard, and contribute to the discussion. This
would mean constructing a more participatory environment
where panelists don't recite academically sound expository essays
but instead toss out ideas, insights, concerns, and problems to an
audience, allowing more time for others in the room to probe,
question, and add to those ideas. In other words, organizing the
session around a selected series of topics and issues, any of which
might be explored and performed within a group dialogue. In
addition, those who orchestrate these panels could introduce as
much variety into the setting as possible, incorporating acts of
performance, group experiments, and visual or aural texts into
the event.

By now any reader will notice that I haven't addressed the mas-
sive resistance such proposals can expect from administrations
and conservative educators insisting on enforcing limited canons
of literacy. Or the overwhelming budgetary conflicts—how to pay
for all of these new courses, and the new faculty necessary to

teach them. Or the strong resistance many will give to my sugges-
tion that we all renounce our comfortable positions of authority
within our fields of expertise and dive into alien waters. These
are very real obstacles, especially within a field so seemingly
opposed to including the periphery (which, once considered, can
loom larger than the "centers" to which we clutch). And yet, if a
pluralistic education is indeed one or our primary goals, then
these suggestions, in some way, have to become realities. Either
we should proclaim at the outset which types of writings and literatures we value and which we comfortably ignore—or else do
our best to learn about the myriad of different forms and methods
of discourse operant in the world and, at the very least, give our
students a taste of these different systems. Our options are clear:
teach from a single rhetorical framework, and acquiesce to the
fact that our students will either have to adopt what we privilege
or be refused admittance into our conversation, or recognize the
need to seriously revamp our current curricula and begin teaching
a more global range of discourse alternatives, while in the process
unearthing the sociopolitical implications embedded within these
different forms: how issues of power, gender, culture, and class
affect, and are affected by, these conflicting writing and speech
practices. Resisting inherited conventions imposed by a lineage
of oppressive regimes is a courageous enterprise indicative of serious critical thought. To encourage our students to undertake similar positions may be one of the most effective messages we can
convey.

Besides, for all my talk of new and challenging composing
practices, the pedagogy I'm outlining hardly constitutes a radical
argument. Injecting diversity into the formula does not turn the
university into a pluralistic hotbed of multiple ideologies, all of
them equal to each other in influence. The most progressive of
institutions is still run by boards of trustees, presidents, provosts,
and vice-presidents, and these people do not privilege African
American tropes, Language poetics, or avant-garde feminist
reconstructions of language. None of us should hold our breath
while waiting to see any of these discourses represented in alumni
news bulletins, mission statements, or employee contracts. So
long as one's paycheck is given by the academy, one doesn't subvert the institution but perpetuates it. No matter how multicul-

tural, diverse, and motley the curricula, the university remains powered by a discourse that is sustained by a dominating batch of authorities, men and women shaped by their educational experiences with formalist modes of writing and speaking. And all of our universities are deeply, undeniably entrenched within a greater, all-encompassing capitalist infrastructure powered by profit, not liberal diversity; if pluralism is going to exist in the classroom, it will only be because those who regulate the academy permit it to exist; it will be, in a sense, *acceptable* pluralism.

And so my overriding objective is not to do away with academic discourse but fundamentally expand what academic discourse can eventually come to entail. My concern with enhanced diversity, cross-cultural interaction, and tolerance of the experimental is aimed not at turning academic discourse upside down (imagine the hypocrisy were I to use a university press in order to condemn the discourse of the university), but toward enhancing academic discourse within the limited power at our disposal: making it healthier, more reflective of its constituents, more relevant, more critically invigorating—more fun. The issue is not to eliminate academic ways of thinking and talking and writing, but to seek ways of curing academic convention of its debilitating restrictions, and make the term "academic" synonymous with "imaginative." Even if such a curative can't ever fully exist in our contemporary environment, we can at least seek the impossible, and in the process affirm our ability to remain active innovators and participants within our most immediate communities, be they the classroom, the family, or some corner of an English department. As Ron Silliman puts it, "I don't think anyone should propose, should imagine, should hallucinate, the idea that there is such a thing as either socialism or literacy in a single classroom, let alone in a single curricular strategy. What I do think there is is the possibility of linkage between the individuals within a faculty, between the individuals within different programs, between individuals across campuses" ("Canons and Institutions" 170). We can promote such linkage by making the interconnective paths within our reach as lively and inventive as we can, sculpting a fertile environment—an intensely *academic* environment of new dimensions—where any interested members are inspired to use the variety of thought at their disposal, and imaginatively seek to enrich that diversity with their own eccentric histories and motivations. The best way I can think of to make these connective links frequent and constructive, and thereby turn the university into a webwork of crisscrossing philosophies and energies, is by taking our own habits and tastes with a bit more humor and a lot more flexibility. Inelastic pedagogy, after all, signifies more than just a dramatic lack of imagination—it reveals a profound distrust for others involved in the educational process, and the changes that can result from that interaction with unlike individuals. It's in this spirit I offer these ideas, so that they might be reviewed, altered, stolen, and enhanced, depending upon the particular goals of any interested readers.

Coda

The question is always: what is the meaning of this language practice; what values does it propagate; to what degree does it encourage an understanding, a visibility, of its own values or to what degree does it repress that awareness? To what degree is it in dialogue with the reader and to what degree does it command or hypnotize the reader? Is its social function liberating or repressive? Such questions of course open up into much larger issues than ones of aesthetics, open the door by which aesthetics and ethics are unified. And so they pertain to not only the art situation but more generally the language of the job, of the state, of the family, and of the street.
—CHARLES BERNSTEIN

'What is art for?' Well perhaps art is for survival. The predominant function in art, the aesthetic, is concomitantly one of the functions of consciousness. Consciousness and aesthetics share the summary of their activity as patterns of connectedness, which are patterns necessary for life. They are patterns that provide the structures for ethical, moral, and social understanding and efficacy, and they change, can be changed. Loss of the renewing and changing capacity of this patterning . . . amounts to a loss of significant life.
—ALAN FISHER

THE problematics of empowerment (however one chooses to interpret that term), content, and critique have never been divorced from grammar. Mechanics, syntax, vocabulary, spatial arrangement on the page, font type, sentence and paragraph length, and the dynamics of vocal performance are not secondary issues: the grammar of a writing is always as much a part of its content as any thesis statement or concluding argument. This is true more than many of us realize, since grammatical decisions impose unconscious and therefore profoundly influential assumptions upon readers and listeners. While trained to remain preoccupied with the manifest subject matter of any given discourse (what is the author's primary idea? what is she trying to say?), we fail to recognize how much organizational design, inflection of speech, preference for hypotactic or paratactic structure, use of repetition, the presence (or absence) of silence, word choice, rhythmic patterning, and the punctuation or camouflaging of spontaneity all work subtle effects upon our habits of reception and communication. Form, as twentieth-century poets have been quick to remind us, has always been the extension of content; "philosophy has always turned on grammatical particles. With, near, next, like, from, toward, against, because, for, through, my" (James 24). Thus, new rhetorics evoke—and demand—new theories of composing.

But how much experimentation are we willing to allow? What new language literacies will we make room for within the academy, and which will remain outside? What are the boundaries of composition as we interpret them, as our profession interprets them? How will we justify our decisions to maintain conventional boundaries if this means rich cultures, perspectives, and opposing ideologies will continue to be shut outside the classroom, virtually erased in the minds of students and their instructors? Do cross-cultural, feminist, and experimental philosophies of composition really have a place in our field?

In *Criss-Cross: A Text Book of Modern Composition*, published in 1977, a playfully eclectic range of textual forms is presented to the reader: fictive narratives, lined poetry, typed passages complete with handwritten marginalia, blocks of text cut into geometric patterns (some of which can be cut out and folded into cubes), comic strips, newspaper collages, and alphabetic maps fashioned so as to reflect city landscapes. John Riddell, the author of these various compositions, briefly sums up his intentions in his preface:

during this century   traditional & avant garde literature have each virtually polarized around what I call   two
dogmas of literality

traditionalists will admit no textform other than
linear   into the arena   will consider experimentation to
be valid   only if conducted fundamentally   within this
frame of reference

the avant garde find the traditional approach to composition   too exclusive   will consider experimentation to be
valid   within any frame

a synthesis   may not be desired/is certainly not effected
by displacing both schools under the same roof   still
when brot together   the prospect of marriage does not
seem as remote   as may have been supposed

'criss-cross' is meant to entertain   offers a variety of
compositional techniques   hopefully will stimulate discussion   & furthur   explorations in the field   nor is it
difficult to foresee such explorations   extending into
novel areas ["a note on form," no page numbers]

Synthesis is *not* always desirable; certainly there are times when
learning forms of authoritative academic expository prose is infinitely more appropriate than catering to exploratory play, which
can be annoying and self-indulgent. But the reverse is also certainly true. The challenge is to acknowledge the legitimacy of
both extremes, the strengths and liabilities of each. William
James, in addressing the "curious antipathies" aroused in the
ongoing debate between rationalists and empiricists, exhibits a
tolerance worth remembering in our consideration of academic
versus nonacademic discourses. James wrote that for rationalists
to regard empiricists, and vice versa, as advocates of philosophies
wholly mistaken and untrue, is

sovereignly unjust, for all the parties are human beings with
the same essential interests, and no one of them is the wholly perverse demon which another of them imagines him to
be. Both are loyal to the world that bears them; neither

wishes to spoil it; neither wishes to regard it as an insane coherence; both want to keep it as a universe of some kind; and their differences are all secondary to this deep argument. They may be only propensities to emphasize differently. Or one man may care for finality and security more than the other. Or their tastes may like a universe that lends itself to lofty and exalted characterization. To another this may seem sentimental or rhetorical. One may wish for the right to use a clerical vocabulary, another a technical or professorial one. . . . But all such differences are minor matters which ought to be subordinated in view of the fact that, whether we be empiricists or rationalists, we are, ourselves, parts of the universe and share the same one deep concern in its destinies. We crave alike to feel more truly at home with it, and to contribute our mite to its amelioration. It would be pitiful if small aesthetic discourds were to keep honest men asunder. (127–28)

Not only would an inability to imagine alternative realities represent a pitiful absence of creative insight, but to quietly and firmly instill such biases in the minds of students, while keeping them in the dark about contradictory philosophies of composition and commuication, is indoctrination founded upon exclusion and deceit.

Stylistic innovations are never just aesthetic flavors; alternative preferences are nothing less than alternative social constructs. Our discourse is more than an extension of our personalities and our environments; our discourse *is* our personality, *is* our environment. In failing to recognize the relativism of discourse we situate our tastes at the center, forcing any resisting tendencies to circulate around us, cast like so many satellites into our silly ethnocentric notions of "the marginal." For the educator, who in some way always serves as a filter through which an unlimited number of students with equally unlimited histories, cultures, and desires learn new ways of interpreting their world, this is an impossible place to be. We cannot on one hand invite the students and colleagues of a linguistic community to think differently about a given philosophy or idea if at the same time we confine them to preselected, inflexible discourses hostile to changing ways of making knowledge with language. It's not a pejorative relativism we need to acknowledge, the dismissal of all ideology based on the fact that none are superior or inferior to one another, but a *constructive* relativism, one tolerant of shifts, conflicting traditions, and opposing imaginations. After all, diversity, pluralism, multiculturalism, all are in solidarity with the relativistic stance. What's required is a turn away from judgmental classification of unlike styles and a more conscious coping with the ever-present differences generated by unlike intellects. We won't be "all-purpose intellectuals," to use Richard Rorty's term, unless we cultivate more pluralistic thinking habits receptive to dissimilarities and contradiction. To be supreme generalists, open to new paradigms and vocabularies, is to be ultimately interactive and cross-disciplinary.

In 1963 James Baldwin, in his lecture "A Talk to Teachers," said the following:

> The purpose of education, finally, is to create in a person the ability to look at the world for himself, to make his own decisions, to say to himself this is black or this is white, to decide for himself whether there is a God in heaven or not. To ask questions of the universe, and then learn to live with those questions, is the way he achieves his own identity. But no society is really anxious to have that kind of person around. What societies really, ideally, want is a citizenry which will simply obey the rules of society. (326)

The challenge before teachers rests on how seriously we come to appreciate Baldwin's assessment, more valid now than ever before: how imaginatively we search for ways of spending time with our students that help us all rebel against the state's highly successful program of defining education as a process of rigid mechanization and self-effacement; how imaginatively we withstand the insidious, institutional drive to erase any and all creative ruptures as we advocate pedagogies of imaginative, constructive resistance.

Notes

CHAPTER ONE: Introduction / Surveying the Landscape

1. As readers of his book are probably aware, I owe my understanding of this terrain to fellow cartographer Stephen North, whose *The Making of Knowledge in Composition: Portrait of an Emerging Field* catalogues in detail the different inhabitants of these islands.

2. Blitz and Hurlbert have drawn some powerful conclusions while deconstructing this ever-present flotilla of institutional rhetoric (see their essay "To: You, From: Michael Blitz and C. Mark Hurlbert, Re: Literacy Demands and Institutional Autobiography"). Readers will notice that throughout the text I've used the phrase "literacy demands," a term that comes directly from their work.

3. For a similar "aerial snapshot" categorizing the current state of writing across the curriculum (WAC) programs, see Mahala 780.

4. Some might question my decision to limit overlooked discourse to these particular zones, consequently ignoring, say, the rhetoric of the "politically unhip": neo-Nazi skinhead organizations, the Moral Majority, Pentagon bureaucrats, the fraternity brother. But I find the defining linguistic characteristics of such discourse communities to be marked primarily by ideological tone and indigenous vocabulary more than by any comprehensive rhetoric unique to the politics of that community (plus, these lack the degree of historical complexity found in cross-cultural,

feminine, and experimental forms). Reactionary diatribes, whether from conservative or leftist or anarchist perspectives, can and do thrive within numerous contradictory stylistic frames. My interest here is not in whatever social and political ideas can be poured into any specific rhetoric, but rather in the submerged political motives that determine our preoccupation with a few rhetorical philosophies at the cost of others radically divergent in conception.

5. "Semantic philosophers are certainly correct in their emphasis on the final dictation of words over their users. But they often neglect to point out that, after all, it is the actual importance, *power*, of the words that remains so finally crucial. Words have users, but as well, users have words. And it is the users that establish the world's realities" (Baraka, "Home" 374).

6. One interesting study might be to examine any recurring rhetorical techniques used in many of the essays that have won College Composition and Communication's Richard Braddock Award since its inception in 1975. Such an examination might go far in helping us catalogue what our profession envisions as exemplary models of composition.

7. Whether poetry was ever alive within the academy is open to question; the teaching of poetry may have been an exercise in nostalgia much more than a call for creative praxis. "The impersonal lyric and the lyric epic—the sustaining forms of poetry in this century—are following the narrative poem and the verse drama into extinction. One doubts that either will survive into the next millennium. Of course, we let nothing die with dignity. Certain simulacra, supported by universities and government agencies, will continue to be produced, but no one, including their producers, will take much interest in them. I do not know that it was a matter of cause and effect, but the loss of vitality in poetry (and the other arts) coincided with the founding of the National Endowment for the Arts. Poetry thereafter became a kind of National Park, though of course it did not attract many visitors. There are no traffic jams around the Old Faithfuls of poetry" (Byrd 33).

8. Tucked away in a brief prefatory note in *The Web of Meaning*, Janet Emig offered an interesting comment: that she was going to soon take up the writing of poetry full-time ("I'm

interested in an audience for my poetry. And that's the only one I'm interested in"; 158). If Emig made good on her claim, she has been writing poetry for some time now; yet it would appear that her poetic endeavors have made little if any impact on the very people who made her a major figure in composition studies. One might think anyone capable of influencing so many with a land-mark work like *The Composing Processes of Twelfth Graders* would also attract the attention of readers with her poetry. The fact is that compositionists, though from time to time they might refer to poetics within their theoretical work, seem significantly unin-terested in spending much time reading, writing, and certainly publishing much poetry. For a discipline that claims to have an interesting in *writing*, it's obvious that it only intends specific forms of *prose* under such a heading.

9. "The problem with such slogans," writes James Seitz, "is that they institute a faulty opposition between texts of 'clarity,' from which the reader simply receives an unadorned message (or the-sis, as it is often called), and texts of ambiguity, from which the reader is unable to extract any absolute recognition of authorial intent. In such a scheme, one which leads teachers to evaluate student texts on the basis of their untroubled channeling of infor-mation, clarity will always be privileged over ambiguity; whose value cannot be recognized when the ideal reader is presumed to be a passive receptacle. But if we teachers of composition truly mean to take seriously the insights of contemporary reading theo-ry—which has long since abandoned the notion of reading as mere reception—we cannot continue to depend on such an obso-lete model of textual transmission" (816–17).

10. This book being no exception. It's a peculiar activity—to spend so much of your "free time" writing a manuscript that will be read by a small handful of people most of whom you won't ever know, and which will ultimately occupy so much space on various library shelves across the country.

CHAPTER TWO: Essaying Alternatives

1. Hall says we have the freedom to follow our thoughts wher-ever they may lead. But would thoughts like the following really have a chance of finding their way into an anthology like *The*

Contemporary Essay, whose readers are primarily professors and students?

In no case go to sleep on lies, on subsidies, on foundations of our truly contemptible universities, of pot-bellied toadying presidents of fat beaneries. In no case swallow fat greasy words which conceal three or four indefinite middles. . . .

In no case let one's sons spend money on "education" offered by cowards who dare not answer specific questions about their own subjects. In no case tolerate hired fools who take fifteen years to admit a truth because it is safer and more immediately profitable to them to go on teaching a falsehood. I mean, in this case, Professor X. Z., oh yes, and quite naturally.

The modern and typical prof holds his job because of his slickness in *avoiding* the thesis, because he crawls under the buggy rug of a moth-eaten curriculum in sheer craven terror of known fact and active discovery. That is what the half-louse is PAID for." (Pound, *Guide to Kulchur* 344–45)

2. For a discussion of the differences between prose, poetry, and prose poems, as well as some contemporary hybrids of all three forms, see "The New Sentence" in Ron Silliman's collection of essays of the same name (63–93).

3. This balance between the spontaneous composition and its realization has elsewhere been described by Antin as the performative relationship between the "scenarist-inventor" (i.e., composer, poet, artist, choreographer) and the "realizer" (musician, actor, dancer)—see "The Stranger at the Door" in Perloff 231. The logistics of this symbiotic relationship give way to a new means of interpreting the union between writer and reader: perceiving the author as inventor and the reader as realizer renders composition irreducibly dialogic, inherently communal.

4. See essays by Clark Coolidge, Bernadette Mayer, Fanny Howe, and Madeleine Burnside in *Code of Signals: Recent Writings in Poetics*, ed. Michael Palmer. See also essays by Robert Grenier, Chris Mason, Alan Davies, Ron Silliman, Bruce Andrews, Larry Eigner, Bernard Noel, Steve McCaffery, Lyn Hejinian, Christopher Dewdney, Abigail Child, Nick Piombino, Ted Greenwald, Kathleen Fraser, Beverly Dahlen, Ray DiPalma, and David

Bromige in such collections as *The L=A=N=G=U=A=G=E Book* (ed. Bruce Andrews and Charles Bernstein), *In the American Tree* (ed. Ron Silliman), and *O ONE/An Anthology* (ed. Leslie Scalapino). Also see Susan Howe's *My Emily Dickinson*, Anne Carson's *Eros the Bittersweet: An Essay*, Roland Barthes's *The Pleasure of the Text*, and such journals as *Acts*, *The Difficulties*, *HOW(ever)*, *M/E/A/N/I/N/G*, *Ottotole*, *Paper Air*, *Poetics Journal*, *The Raddle Moon*, *Sulfur*, and *Temblor* as sites for additional creative variations on the expository essay.

5. This passage shows how Cage, like many other twentieth-century writers (James Joyce, Raymond Queneau, Marcel Duchamp, Robert Grenier), anticipated the logic of hypertext years before it would become marketable software (see Bolter, *Writing Space* 131–46). Correlations between twentieth-century innovative compositionists and hypertext are explored below in chapter 5.

6. Statement made during the discussion following a talk presented with Kate Ronald and Hephzibah Roskelly, "Thinking in Threes: Beyond Opposition in Rhetoric and Composition," at the Conference of College Composition and Communication, Seattle, March 16, 1989.

CHAPTER THREE: Beyond Eurocentric Discourse

1. There are those, however, who would severely criticize the presumptions of academic discourse. Referring to much academic discourse as "dialects run amuck," Craig Werner writes: "The dialect of the dominant group (bourgeois Euro-American males) or a 'language' formed from the intersection of dominant groups (whites, males, lawyers, academics, businessmen) is elevated to universal. Members of the dominant group, typically unaware of the unstated premises of their own behavior, then, proceed as if by serving their own interests they are serving the ultimate good" (62). Plus this from Geneva Smitherman: "In the public schools, in the universities and in the popular mind, much of what passes for 'correct' English is nothing more than bombastic, convoluted, and jargon-filled language" (211).

2. The immediacy and spontaneity Brutus describes here echoes Carmen Tafolla's depiction of Chicano (and more specifi-

cally Chicana) literature that embodies "directness . . . [for there is] too much to be said to waste time on conventionalities, too much that is alien not only to the mainstream culture's literature but also to the literature and experience of men" (215).

3. Négritude is doubly intriguing when one marks similarities between Senghor's philosophy and experimental workings devised by contemporary feminist poets. As Paula Giddings writes, "Because both are motivated by similar economic, social, and psychological forces, it is only logical that those who sought to undermine Blacks were also the most virulent antifeminists" (6). Rachel Blau DuPlessis has called attention to parallels with négritude and feminine composition: "blacks excluded from a Western world of whiteness will affirm a connection to rhythms of earth, sensuality, intuition, subjectivity, and this will sound precisely as some women writers do" ("For the Etruscans" 285–86). Such similarities are reiterated by Charles Johnson: "Phenomenologically, the questions raised by feminists strike as deeply at the presuppositions of culture and esthetics as the radical critiques of Black Nationalists and surfictionists of an earlier era" (95).

4. For another perspective, see Wade W. Noble's *African Psychology*. Although seriously flawed in its blatantly homophobic and sexist agenda—a feature consistent with arguments launched by many other Afrocentric theorists (Molefi Kete Asante, Na'im Akbar, Haki Madhubuti; even Geneva Smitherman's early work seems not to be bothered by black poets who boast about gay bashing [142])—works like these nevertheless attest to the growing number of writers compelled to challenge racist biases that shape many of our assumptions about psychology, literacy, aesthetics, and philosophy. Incidentally, it should be noted that my argument for a pluralistic teaching of discourse, though drawing on insights and philosophies identifiable with Afrocentric theory, is itself fundamentally anti-Afrocentric. The Afrocentrist scholars I have read are not interested in a curriculum of diversity, but rather one centered in and around some (arguably romantic) notion of "African" thought—an Afrocentric university. While I understand how many African Americans, in order to survive intellectually and spiritually, need to sever themselves from intrinsically Eurocentric educational institutions, the peda-

gogical framework I'm proposing is one where teachers interact with a continually fluctuating blend of students and colleagues of multiple backgrounds and cultures. Ideally, in such an atmosphere students would have opportunity to investigate Afrocentric thought, but this would be presented in conjunction with a range of conflicting cultural philosophies. The goal is to give students the critical tools with which they might eventually decide for themselves which discourses, paradigms, and value systems they want to pursue; not to decide for them what they should adopt and discard. Such pluralism is in direct opposition to Afrocentric and other cultural systems of belief that resent the intrusion of alien philosophies.

5. The congregation, at times, is by no means averse to critiquing the preacher during the actual sermon. A black preacher once told my father (a lay minister himself) that there was an elderly woman who always sat up front in his church and would unabashedly pipe up, whenever the preacher took too long to make his point, with comments like, "C'mon now, bring it home," and "Hep him, Jesus, hep him."

6. In a talk delivered to a predominantly white, Irish Catholic audience during the spring of 1990 at Siena College, New York, musician and historian Bernice Johnson Reagon effectively demonstrated the African American method of call and response, with mixed results. Beginning her lecture with song, Reagon urged the audience "not to be good slaves" and to sing along with her, considering this "an exercise in not being invisible." The operative for her rhetoric, she explained, was that the more one stands out, the better one appears. Despite her charismatic attempts to get the large audience to interact within her participatory dynamic, after an hour and a half it was still visibly painful for most students and faculty (myself included) to raise their voices above an audible murmur, so deep was the drive to remain silently respectful of the authority behind the podium. This compulsory inexpression seems wholly antithetical to much of African American rhetoric.

7. On the other hand ex-slaves, pressured by abolitionists interested in setting blacks, but not their discourse, free, consciously adopted writing styles affectedly subdued and objective, lest any outbursts of emotion, anger, rage, or spontaneity be used by ene-

mies as "proof" of the African American's inability to converse according to educated, Eurocentric rhetorical standards. This explains why so many slave narratives are told in a calm, reserved, almost neutral tone—which, ironically, often compounds the horror of their tales (see Jahn 126ff. and Bayliss 77–90).

8. John Miller Chernoff describes this difference in a comparison between listening to a concerto performance by the Russian cellist Mstislav Rostropovich, and to Koyaté Djimo play the *kora* (a twenty-one-stringed gourd-harp) with the National Dance Company of Senegal. "Both these artists, each a disciple of a great musical tradition, brought their aesthetic command to effective display, but the meaning of their virtuosity was in each case different. Rostropovich's aesthetic effect was implicitly moral, an inspiration to be appreciated and internalized; Koyaté's aesthetic effect was explicitly moral, a display to evoke participation and respect. In Africa the practice of art is an explicitly moral activity because African art functions dynamically to create a context of values where criticism is translated into social action. The meaning of the music is externalized through an event in which participation parallels the musician's artistic purpose: an artist's coolness lends security to intimacy, and the rhythms of an ensemble become the movement of an event when people dance" (143).

9. "The rhythm is more important than the meaning of the words. Our gods respond to rhythm above all else. When the rhythm changes, their behavior shifts accordingly." (A Macumba priestess in Brazil, quoted in Bramly 47.)

10. In other words, an arabesque will show up in all kinds of ballets, regardless of the "message" or the rhythm of the music, just as kids in clubs (white kids especially) can be seen dancing the same insufferably dull steps all night long, no matter what the DJ plays. Conversely, African dance is intricately tethered to, and "informed by" the immediate ritual at hand. One European parallel, though, to the African's way of becoming "possessed" by deities via the music is described in Federico Garcia Lorca's "Play and Theory of the Duende," where the duende is a force accompanying intense artistic, musical, and poetic activity, "a mysterious power which everyone senses and no philosopher explains. . . . [It] is a power, not a work; it is a struggle, not a

thought. I have heard an old maestro of the guitar say, 'The duende is not in the throat; the duende climbs up inside you, from the soles of the feet.' Meaning this: it is not a question of ability, but of true, living style, of blood, of the most ancient culture, of spontaneous creation" (43). Lorca continues, "The duende works on the body of the dancer as the wind works on sand. With magical power he [the duende] changes a girl into a lunar paralytic, or fills with adolescent blushes the broken old man begging in the wineshop, or makes a woman's hair smell like a nocturnal port, and he works continuously on the arms with expressions that are the mothers of the dances of every age. But he can never repeat himself. This is interesting to emphasize: the duende does not repeat himself, any more than do the forms of the sea during a squall" (51).

11. See D. Emily Hicks's "Deterritorialization and Border Writing."

CHAPTER FOUR: When Male Means Marginal

1. Ann Rosalind Jones levels similar objections against French feminists who have characterized *féminité* and *jouissance* as universal female characteristics, thereby homogenizing the complex diversity of African, Middle Eastern, and Third World women whose definition of womanhood stems from psychosocial backgrounds significantly removed from the middle-class, academic perspectives associated with the psychoanalytic readings of Hélène Cixous, Luce Irigaray, and Monique Wittig. "All in all, at this point in history, most of us perceive our bodies through a jumpy, contradictory mesh of hoary sexual symbolization and political counterresponse. . . . The French feminists make of the female body too unproblematically pleasurable and totalized an entity" (368).

2. Although I agree with the sentiments expressed in this quote, one has to wonder whether the writers of this volume have examined the problematics of criticizing the "standards of capitalistic structure" within a book published by Basic Books, Inc., a subsidiary of Harper & Row Publishers. Like many large publishing corporations, Harper & Row does little to foster the types of radically nonconformist voices the authors want to privi-

lege. (Indeed, the monopolistic power of huge publishing companies like Harper & Row is a major obstacle to the livelihood of alternative, marginal publishers and writers.) Also, though the writers consider themselves "radicals," their premises might have been more forceful had their writing styles and rhetorical methodologies reflected the innovative, subversive claims they promote . . . but of course had they done this, the book wouldn't have been published through Harper & Row—hence the difficult double bind of making "radical" arguments through decidedly conventional avenues. This also holds for our most respected academic journals: consider how *College English,* while publishing articles advocating feminist perspectives, has also printed insultingly sexist advertisements—the ad in a 1980 issue, for instance, which, in order to help sell two new books on progressive writing pedagogy, catches the reader's eye with the prominent come-on "STIMULATE PASSIONATE WRITING IN YOUR STUDENTS . . . ," accompanied with a drawing of a curvaceous, drowsy-eyed woman dressed in a skimpy, frilly negligee, with the ellipsis aimed across the woman's well-exposed thigh and toward the area between her legs (see the very first page of the February 1980 *College English,* 41.6). The point being that the content of the prose we publish will always indirectly promote any marketing strategies used by our publishers, and vice versa.

3. Though Elbow, like so many process-oriented theorists, hesitates to outline definitively what "proper order" actually is, one might assume that his own prose is offered as a window into such successful ordering of linguistic elements. The irony of this is that one of the most common characteristics of Elbow's prose style is constant reiteration of his primary points; one might think, from his advice on cut-throat editing, that his texts would be as pithy as a Hemingway tale. An interesting idea for a future study would be a close examination of Elbow's rhetoric, and how it may or may not be the most appropriate reflection of the kind of texts he advocates. (For me, what makes Elbow's texts interesting is that his love of writing about process clashes with his desire to pare the text down into its most succinct form.)

4. In addition, the only models Coles offers throughout his book are works by canonical writers, all of them male: Spenser, Henry Miller, Beckett, Golding, and Milton. To be fair, this is

hardly a trait belonging solely to Coles—the assumption that successful rhetoric ought to parallel writing strategies devised by Euro-American white males is one of the most common errors made in our profession. My point is that, as teachers and writers interested in the possibilities for composition, we need to examine the correlations between the texts we read and how those works surface, consciously or otherwise, within our pedagogical assumptions of what constitutes "good" and "bad" writing. It would be enlightening, for example, if someone conducted a study in which composition theorists were examined and interviewed in order to discern their favorite authors. Once we could pinpoint the specific essays, novels, and poetry praised by teachers of writing, along with some they deemed aesthetically deficient, we'd come closer to determining what kinds of rhetorical methodologies would most likely be stressed in their pedagogy, and which would be devalued.

5. In a paper presented at the 1990 MLA ("Composition Theory and the Myth of the Self-Made Man: Authentic Voice and the Rhetoric of Masculinity"), James Catano drew attention to some of these same passages (as well as others in works by Elbow), the pedagogies of which he argued show a deeply rooted and unquestioned preference for what he labels "masculine authenticity."

6. Page Smith tells a similar tale of how, when he submitted his doctoral dissertation to a typist, she contacted him shortly thereafter to express her fear that the piece would not be accepted, since she was finding it enjoyable reading. (For more on Smith's lively and bitter attack on the academy's "Cult of Dullness," see *Killing the Spirit: Higher Education in America*.)

7. Ann Rosalind Jones: "If men are responsible for the reigning binary system of meaning—identity/other, man/nature, reason/chaos, man/woman—women, relegated to the negative and passive pole of this hierarchy, are not implicated in the creation of its myths" (366). Also, see Moi on Kristeva in *Sexual/Textual Politics* 166.

8. Winston Weathers makes a similar plea for a rhetoric of contradiction, although motivated by stylistic rather than social and political concerns: "The 'contrary' or 'alternate' completes a picture, saves us from the absoluteness of one single style, pro-

vides us with the stimulating, illuminating, and refreshing oppo-site that makes the traditional grammar of style even more mean-ingful and useful: as the alternate grammar of style more and more takes on strong and viable identity, so the traditional style is lifted from the lethargy/monotony of its solitude" (11–12).

9. Mary Belenky, however, one of the four authors of *Women's Ways of Knowing*, has some conservative views regarding collabo-ration. In an interview she commented that, for her, collabora-tion had to have limits, that it could not overstep the bounds where the various writers' voices merged into new hybrids. Basi-cally, her notion of collaboration is a gathering of autonomous voices, working in tandem but maintaining their sovereignty—hence her reservations about people sharing computer disks and changing each other's texts: "If you send your disk around and people start changing it, your words and theirs get merged too fast; you need some sort of balance. Writing collaboratively gets very confusing because, when you're really working together, when the dialogue really starts, ideas grow and change and no one has real ownership. Yet you have to keep, or you ought to keep, your own voice" (Ashton-Jones and Thomas 32). But there is another possibility for collaboration, one that has barely been tapped and holds great potential for composition: the writing of texts by multiple authors using computer technology where the various voices, through countless editings and revisions, merge entirely, to a point where the finished text resembles none of the individual styles of its authors but shows evidence of their involvement.

10. Taken to its most extreme degree, one can "write" texts that consist entirely of the words of other people. "Inlaws/Out-laws: The Language of Women," an "essay" by Virginia Tiger and Gina Luria (in Butturff and Epstein), is one such example, a text comprised entirely of quotes by other women artists, writers, poets, and literary figures. Here authors acquire the mannerism of a subtle choreographer, whose signature is reflected only in her "absence" and in the patterns implicit within the collage (paral-lels here with the readymades of Marcel Duchamp, the collages of Kurt Schwitters, the found object sculptures of Joan Miró, and other similar twentieth-century constructions).

11. Women, of course, aren't the only ones denied access to

these hierarchies of power, for this female aesthetic moves beyond gender; these are potential models of composition for anyone interested in resisting oppressive standards of discourse. In this respect "feminine" discourse might be seen as "a specialized name for any practices available to those groups—nations, genders, sexualities, races, classes—all social practices which wish to criticize, to differentiate from, to overturn the dominant forms of knowing and understanding with which they are saturated" (DuPlessis, "For the Etruscans" 285).

12. A passage from Cixous's novel *Angst* taken at random: "My love, my fiancé, while I was resting, our first night, you couldn't stop yourself, speak, speak, there's still time, even now, I've still got time to lose for you, blood to shed for you, do I have to bleed again? Didn't I promise you? Give you everything? In advance? To the last drop? He was calling me: join me! Isn't that my one desire? But where? How? Hadn't he told you clearly? Right here? In the room? How come you can't do it? Every second thrust you further away. Didn't you want anything to do with us? His heatless voice. But his voice. And it is speaking to you. Offering the greatest joy. Don't you want to come close? Every sentence called to me, pushed me away. Oh I do want, I did want, I want so much, I begged, I cried out. So you don't want to talk to me? Why don't you say so then?" (207) After reading passages like this, it's not hard to understand why Julia Kristeva felt compelled to call *écriture féminine* "naive whining" and "marketplace romanticism" (482), "a reiteration of a more or less euphoric or depressed romanticism and always an explosion of an ego lacking narcissistic gratification" (478).

13. From "The Laugh of the Medusa:" "Men say that there are two unrepresentable things: death and the feminine sex. That's because they need femininity to be associated with death; it's the jitters that gives them a hard-on! for themselves!" (255)

CHAPTER FIVE: Contemporary Innovations

1. Small Press Distribution, Inc.: 1814 San Pablo Avenue, Berkeley, CA 94702. *Factsheet Five*: Box 170099, San Francisco, CA 94117-0099. See also the Segue Foundation's catalog: 303 East 8th Street, New York, NY 10009.

2. See Gregory L. Ulmer's "Textshop for Post(e)pedagogy," and Geoffrey H. Hartman's "Understanding Criticism" (150).

3. If it hasn't already been done, it would be interesting to undertake a study of the syllabi used by composition and literature instructors in order to discern the rhetorical assumptions lurking in such texts. Just as one could learn much of a composition teacher's pedagogy by analyzing the kinds of authors she likes and dislikes, it could be telling to deconstruct the habits by which writing teachers exhibit themselves and their craft in their syllabi. On a larger scale it would be valuable to analyze syllabi taken from multiple disciplines, from a cross section of American colleges, to see how the rhetoric of academic institutions is defined by these documents. My guess is that we'd discover our collective academic rhetoric to be more disciplinarian and intimidating than many of us would like to admit, since syllabi, as much as anything, are warnings and mappings of potential punishments and rewards as they tell students what they should and should not do. That these mandates are the first order of business for most college classrooms, whether traditional or progressive, could very well have an impressive cumulative effect on students.

4. Also noteworthy here is Richard Palmer's division of temporal awareness according to three distinct historical realms: modern, where "Time is the medium of personal being, experienced in relation to the cycle of seasons and death (time experienced relationally)"; premodern, in which "Time is a linear continuum in which processes of change can be abstractly measured and symbolized (time seen in spatial terms)"; and postmodern, where "Time may not be abstract and linear but round and whole—an essential dimension of being. It may even be free of space and multiperspectival. Intensive rather than extensive, it may hold both past and future in a unity that adds depth to a now that always is" (24; 27).

5. Ihab Hassan, in *Paracriticisms*: "It is not unreasonable to ask that criticism evolve a method which takes deeper cognizance of the evolving character of life as of literature. The point is almost too obvious: contemporary letters can be judged as little by the standards of pure formalism as, let us say, Romantic poetry can be evaluated by the strict conventions of neo-Classicism" (21).

6. "What I've been taught to construct is: the well-made box. I

have been taught to put 'what I have to say' into a container that is always remarkably the same, that—in spite of varying decorations—keeps to a basically conventional form: a solid bottom, four upright sides, a fine-fitting lid. Indeed, I may be free to put 'what I have to say' in the plain box or in the ornate box, in the large box or the small box, in the fragile box or in the sturdy box. But always *the box*—squarish or rectangular. And I begin to wonder if there isn't somewhere a round box or oval box or tubular box . . . " (Weathers 1–2). (Or, one might add, a porous box, a collapsible box, a magician's box with hidden compartments . . .)

7. I want to be careful, though, in applying this particular philosopher's views to composition theory. Not only do the pedagogical concerns surrounding the teaching of writing seem to hold little interest for Rorty, but his brand of relativism is compromised by his attraction to the conservative philosophy of E. D. Hirsch. See the interview between Rorty and Gary Olson in *(Inter)views: Cross-Disciplinary Perspectives on Rhetoric and Literacy*, 233.

8. For further examples of the analytic lyric see *O ONE/An Anthology*, edited by Leslie Scalapino.

9. Drawing from the early work of William Carlos Williams (*Kora in Hell* and *Spring and All*), as well as the constructions of Gertrude Stein, *Tender Buttons* in particular, a growing body of writers have experimented with nonlinear composition and open texts, among them Carla Harryman, Bob Perelman, Barbara Einzig, Barrett Watten, Clark Coolidge, Bruce Andrews, Charles Bernstein, Stephen Rodefer, Steve Benson, Kit Robinson, Jackson Mac Low, Rosmarie Waldrop, Larry Price, Alan Davies, Diane Ward, James Sherry, John Cage, Christopher Dewdney, John Mason, Robert Grenier, Jed Rasula, David Bromige, and Peter Seaton.

10. For one writing project Stephen Benson used fifty blue examination books as the site for his compositional improvisations: "Within a field supposedly without horizons, and quite in the dark as to what functions my investigative motives might engage, I wanted to project a don't-look-back spotlight of attention, let it rush headlong, hesitate, veer, double back, without presuming any option of revision." See *Blue Book*.

11. The 1980 edition of the book is 37 sections long, matching the author's age at the time. The second edition of the book, pub-

lished seven years later, contains all material from the first while adding eight new prose sections, in addition to eight new sentences to each of the former sections in order that it continue to reflect the author's current age. The book remains continually open, there being no definitive copy since Hejinian keeps on writing her life (or living her writing). In this way *My Life*'s ongoing evolution makes it one of the most apropos of autobiographies.

12. Mayer, from *Studying Hunger*: "I wanted to try to record, like a diary, in writing, states of consciousness, my states of consciousness, as fully as I could, every day, for one month. . . . I had an idea before this that if a human, a writer, could come up with a workable code, or shorthand, for the transcription of every event, every motion, every transition of his or her own mind, & could perform this process of translation on himself, using the code, for a 24-hour period, he or we or someone could come up with a great piece of language/information" (7).

13. In his essay Slatin reminds us that Ezra Pound, whose Cantos anticipated the aggregate nature of hypertext, referred to humans as *nodes* through which ideas continually flowed, anticipating the hypertextual means of conveying information via multiple, cross-referencing electronic *nodes*.

14. In 1981 Charles Bernstein, though not directly writing about hypertext per se, clearly anticipated its multidiscursive flexibility: "One vision of a constructive writing practice I have, and it can be approached in both poetry and philosophy, is of a multidiscourse text, a work that would involve many different types and styles and modes of language in the same 'hyperspace'. Such a textual practice would have a dialogic or polylogic rather than monologic method" (*Content's Dream* 227).

15. See Linda Dalrymple Henderson's extended discussions of "hyperspace philosophy" in *The Fourth Dimension and Non-Euclidean Geometry in Modern Art*.

16. Quoted from the hypertext version of *Writing Space*; no page number.

17. Ed Sanders went so far as to write a small ode praising the tangential aside, titled "The Art of the Elegant Footnote": "The art of the elegant / footnote is ever to / be practised . . . A footnote is a dangling data-cluster / much like a shaped piece of metal in / a Calder mobile" (162).

18. Quoted from the hypertext version of *Writing Space*; no page number.

19. Storyspace and Readingspace are trademarks of Eastgate Systems, Inc. (PO Box 1307, Cambridge, MA 02238), copyright 1984–89 by Jay David Bolter, Michael Joyce, and John B. Smith.

20. The Center for Narrative and Technology at Jackson Community College has gained particular attention as one of the more innovative sites investigating the possibilities of the new technology.

CHAPTER SIX: Implications for Practice

1. Grading is, of course, the most hateful part of our jobs, and far more subjective than most of us are willing to admit. What I usually do is give students a grade based on a spread of different criteria: how much time and effort they put into revising their work, how diligently they work at turning in writing that is as error-free as they can make it (i.e., have they proofread their papers, did they take the time to run it through a spelling check), whether or not they've come to see me with any problems when necessary, how active they are in their participation, whether or not they turn their work in on time, how well they support their opinions in their responses to assigned readings, and how much work they put into commenting on the writings of their peers which they read during workshops. If, after taking all this into consideration, I think the student is doing what I consider average work, she gets around a C; if it's better than average, she gets something in the B range; if it's superlative work, or if the student is making a tremendous effort and showing great improvement, I give her an A. Anything else is D or failing. If students are unhappy with a grade, I allow them a week after each portfolio review within which they can revise any of their papers. The advantage to this system is that I have plenty of criteria from which to evaluate their overall performance; the bad part is it takes up a lot of my time.

2. Some composition theorists might wince at what must seem such mundane and anticlimactic advice. But the more I teach, the more I become convinced that students, at least those I've worked with, are most appreciative if you give them

what you believe to be succinct, simple, honest, and direct advice.

3. Selections from the *Selected Essays of Edward P. J. Corbett* would be ideal for this.

4. Students might read passages from *Essays on Classical Rhetoric and Modern Discourse*, for example (ed. Robert J. Connors, Lisa S. Ede, Andrea Lunsford), versus selections from *Rhetorical Traditions and the Teaching of Writing* by C. H. Knoblauch and Lil Brannon.

5. One of the reasons Chernoff's book is worth reading is because it was written from the viewpoint not of an anthropologist trying to feign clinical objectivity, but of someone who traveled to Africa first and foremost to learn the art of drumming. ("Probably because I enjoyed music more than scholarship, I was interested in finding a place for myself within a musical context rather than finding a place for my involvement with music within a scholarly context" [170].)

6. Since there are so many recorded forms of African music, and since I am by no means an authority on the subject, the best thing for the interested teacher would be to spend some time digging through library collections, record stores with good international selections, and any music catalogues belonging to the college's music, anthropology, film, and audiovisual departments, and simply select a broad range of samples to bring in to class— particularly those exemplifying forms of call and response, extended repetition, talking drums, and so forth. As far as visual sources go, one video I would definitely use in such a course would be Maya Deren's stunning 1947 account of Haitian Voudon rituals, *Divine Horsemen: The Living Gods of Haiti.* (Available through Mystic Fire Video, PO Box 9323, Dept. C5, S. Burlington, VT 05407.)

7. See the essays "Nobody Mean More to Me Than You And the Future Life of Willie Jordan," and "White Tuesday: November, 1984" in Jordan's collection *On Call: Political Essays.*

8. Or, students might take a look at *The Blues Line*, an anthology of blues lyrics collected by Eric Sackheim, who visually arranged the texts on the page in an attempt to evoke some semblance of the blues rhythm within each song.

9. The advantage to having students focus on the characteris-

tics of their oral rhetoric is that they can view their discourse in a new light, heightening the awareness of their everyday spoken texts; students might become aware of their favorite vocabularies and rhetorical techniques, to which they could then add additional strategies. Transcribed in this way, students might come to view their own verbal discourse as if it were the equivalent of a relief map: as voices are frozen on the page, the speaker/writer is provided with yet another angle from which to view herself as a maker of discourse. Perhaps the most significant reward from an investigation like this is that the means by which students present themselves orally would be examined with a scrutiny similar to that aimed at their written papers, thereby helping them become more aware of their speaking habits and how their their spoken style might be modified for various audiences.

10. Though the blues and jazz are distinctly black musical forms, we need to remember that appreciation of this music is dependent on one's aesthetic perspective, not one's ethnicity. Currently the majority of audiences who attend blues concerts are white, and rap artists continue to grow in popularity among non-black audiences. My hesitation about encouraging students, and this includes even certain black students, from naively *mimicking* African American rhetorical strategies within the classroom is that they might be too naive to understand how such imitative performances can be deemed offensive and racist to others. That's why my approach is to encourage students, regardless of their ethnicity, to select certain elements of African African discourse and create their own personalized forms out of this new material. Just as the goal in a composition class that privileges classical rhetoric isn't to talk like Socrates, neither is the goal of the course on African American discourse to make everyone speak like Richard Pryor. Essentially, I want to abandon "race" entirely as a mode of classification and substitute in its place an ongoing consideration of diverse, unlike *cultures*. (More and more I've come to believe that the very concept of "race" can be fundamentally pejorative, if not downright evil—hence why it's important for me to disassociate myself from "Afrocentric" schools of thought, which do emphasize race as a necessary mode of separation and distinction.)

11. It was Henry Evans who politely and patiently pointed out to me that in my talk of cultural tolerance I had assumed, in typi-

cal Eurocentric, racist fashion, that all colleges were predominantly white, ignoring the wealth of predominantly black (not to mention Native American) institutions where African American dialects have long been taken seriously in the classroom.

12. Hannah Weiner: *Spoke* and *The Clairvoyant Journal*; Armand Schwerner: "The Tablets I–XXIV;" Rachel Blau DuPlessis: *The Pink Guitar*; bill bissett: *Beyond Even Faithful Legends*; David Melnick: *Men in Aida: Book One*; P. Inman: *Ocker* and *Red Shift*; Arakawa and Madeline Gins: *The Mechanism of Meaning*; Madeline Gins: *What the President Will Say and Do!!*; Mary Daly and Jane Caputi: *Webster's First New Intergalactic Wickedary of the English Language*; Ishmael Reed: *Mumbo-Jumbo* and "Neo-HooDoo Manifesto/The Neo-HooDoo Aesthetic;" Michelle Cliff: "If I Could Write This in Fire I Would Write This in Fire." Regarding the latter, Cliff writes, "We [Jamaicans] are a fragmented people. My experience as a writer coming from a culture of colonialism, a culture of Black people riven from each other, my struggle to get wholeness from fragmentation while working within fragmentation, producing work which may find its strength in its depiction of fragmentation, through form as well as content, is similar to the experience of other writers whose origins are in countries defined by colonialism" ("A Journey into Speech" 60).

13. It wasn't until late in the writing of this book that I got around to investigating the work of Winston Weathers—a good thing, because had I read Weathers's investigations into "Grammar B" early on, the tendency to overcite many of his insights would've been hard to resist. For in *An Alternate Style*, Weathers spells out with particular clarity a number of the same points I have labored to make here. What's interesting is that, since graduate school and my involvement with professional conferences, I've yet to hear anyone speak at length on Weathers's alternative style.

14. A book that could be used here is Gerald Janecek's *The Look of Russian Literature: Avant-Garde Visual Experiments, 1900–1930*.

15. One might have students skim through essays like Campbell Tatham's "Mythotherapy and Postmodern Fictions: Magic Is Afoot," or Federman's "Federman: Voices within Voices" (both in Benamou and Caramello's *Performance in Postmodern Culture*),

intriguing pieces complete with cutouts, different fonts, multiple columns, fragmented passages, lists, poems, and other unexpected forms.

16. To be sure, online communication does lend itself to a great deal of "flaming"—the act of firing a message that severely criticizes or attacks another user or her argument. This is due in large part to the speed of the medium: someone publicly makes a statement to which someone else takes offense, thus triggering a domino effect of people hopping into the fray, eager to get their two cents in before the argument is left behind in the fast pace of the electronic discussion. But while flaming like this is popular, I've noticed that the flames are often extinguished as quickly as they are fanned—mainly because, with all of the information accumulating on the network, it's hard to focus solely on one line of contention for a long period of time. In fact, it's common that people will continue an argument to the point where it's hard to remember the gist of the original entries that started the whole thing. Part of the appeal of electronic communication is that there's no room for sticks and stones, but only rhetorical debate. Plus, if someone gets really upset, a typical reaction is to simply sign off—exiting the fight, since the only other option is to continue writing. And, all things considered, it might be more beneficial at times to have students "flame it out" from isolated sites rather than resort to physical harassment and intimidation.

17. The practice of lifting material from other sources and using it within one's own work is certainly no new concept: from Marcel Duchamp's readymades, to the writings of Paul Metcalf, many of which are comprised entirely of passages taken from historical documents and quoted verbatim, to Ray Federman's concept of "pla(y)giarization" (161), the concept of textual "ownership" has become a very sticky issue.

18. Permission to quote granted by author.

19. I was first made aware of this profound and revolutionary possibility during a discussion with Don Byrd.

20. Mina Shaughnessy opened my eyes, like many writing teachers', by showing that student errors were not arbitrary and random but followed their own alternative logic, and that the challenge was how to give students the means by which they could identify and alter their most recurrent errors (*Errors and*

Expectations: A Guide for the Teacher of Basic Writing). Personally, I found it most successful to read several drafts by a student, circle all the errors I could find but without explaining why I thought they were mistakes, then give the student back the drafts, whereupon she would identify which errors were merely typos or the result of careless (or nonexistent) proofreading, while highlighting all others that she either couldn't fix or couldn't identify as errors. (Since only some students would bother to do this extra work, this alone allowed me to distinguish between those more eager to work and those less motivated, thus allowing me to spend more time with the former—an important distinction, especially when one has only a short amount of time each week to address the needs of numerous students.) After this I would review the errors the student wasn't able to correct, and from that make a list of recurring glitches (problems with possessives; a tendency to make run-ons; misunderstanding between the proper usages of "their," "there," and "they're," etc.), and then meet with the student in brief conferences where we would address no more than a few of her most frequent errors. I would have the student begin compiling a list of these, which she was to refer to when she revised her writings (I would have her use this in conjunction with a spelling check, for example). In addition, I tried to teach students various time management skills, so they could then organize their schedules to make room for repeated revisions. I also did whatever I could to get students to use the writing center frequently, and to meet with their professors about upcoming papers. None of these are revolutionary ideas, but they show how I spent the bulk of my time while working individually with academically disadvantaged writers.

21. Since it will take some time before the kind of proposals presented here take root, faculty can at least begin by introducing greater thematic variety into their writing curriculum. The Expository Writing Program at Harvard University, for example, tries to make its writing courses appealing and relevant to freshmen by offering a wide range of entry-level writing courses under such categories as: Literature, History, Social and Ethical Issues, the Essay, and the Writer's Craft. Within each of these a handful of special topics courses are offered, where students might investigate issues pertaining to detective fiction, disease, slavery, cultur-

al studies, the history of science, love stories, and so forth. Not only does the variety inherent in an arrangement like this have the potential to make students happier, it also allows faculty the freedom to develop courses where they can capitlaize on their specialties and particular interests.

22. "If the distinction between theory and practice is identified as illusory, the institutional role within the academy of the creative writing program is called into question. If the original rationale behind these programs was to keep one side of that equation, theory, from organizationally overwhelming the other, practice, it has achieved this only by lobotomizing one sphere of poetic activity, isolating it from the other." Ron Silliman, "Canons and Institutions: New Hope for the Disappeared," in Bernstein, *The Politics of Poetic Form* 167.

23. Even recent critics (Gould, *Writing in the Feminine*, and Wolff, *Feminine Sentences*, for example) interested in investigating women writers struggling to create their own individual rhetorics choose to do so from within the safety of conventional scholarly prose.

24. See Gregory Hewett's dissertation, "A Rhetoric of Androgyny: The Composition, Teaching, and Ethics of Gender."

Works Cited

Abrahams, Roger D. *Deep Down in the Jungle…: Negro Narrative Folklore from the Streets of Philadelphia*. Chicago: Aldine, 1970.
——. *Talking Black*. Rowley, MA: Newbury House, 1976.

Adams, Hazard, and Leroy Searle, eds. *Critical Theory since 1965*. Tallahassee: Florida State UP, 1986.

Allen, Donald, and Warren Tallman. *The Poetics of the New American Poetry*. New York: Grove P, 1973.

Allen, Paula Gunn. *The Sacred Hoop: Recovering the Feminine in American Indian Traditions*. Boston: Beacon Press, 1986.

Amato, Joe. "A Re/View of Bolter's *Writing Space*." *EJournal* 2.1 (May 1991).

Andrews, Bruce, and Charles Bernstein, eds. *The L=A=N=G=U=A=G=E Book*. Carbondale: Southern Illinois UP, 1984.

Anozie, Sunday O. *Structural Models and African Poetics: Towards a Pragmatic Theory of Literature*. Boston: Routledge and Kegan Paul, 1981.

Antin, David. "The Stranger at the Door." Perloff 229–47.
——. *talking at the boundaries*. New York: New Directions, 1965.

Anzaldúa, Gloria. "Tlilli, Tlapalli: The Path of the Red and Black Ink." Simonson and Walker 29–40.

Arakawa, and Madeline Gins. *The Mechanism of Meaning*. New York: Abbeville P, 1988

Armantrout, Rae. "Mainstream Marginality." *Poetics Journal* 6 (1986): 141–44.

————. "Poetic Silence." Perelman, *Writing/Talks* 31–47.

Asante, Molefi Kete. *The Afrocentric Idea*. Philadelphia: Temple UP, 1987.

————. *Afrocentricity*. Trenton: Africa World Press, 1988.

Ashton-Jones, Evelyn, and Dene Kay Thomas. "Composition, Collaboration, and Women's Ways of Knowing: A Conversation with Mary Belenky." Olson and Gale, 1991.

Atkins, G. Douglas, and Michael L. Johnson, eds. *Writing and Reading Differently: Deconstruction and the Teaching of Composition and Literature*. Lawrence: UP of Kansas, 1985.

Baker, Jr., Houston A. *Blues, Ideology, and Afro-American Literature: A Vernacular Theory*. Chicago: U of Chicago P, 1984.

————. *The Journey Back*. Chicago: U of Chicago P, 1980.

Baldwin, James. "A Talk to Teachers." *The Price of the Ticket: Collected Nonfiction 1948–1985*. New York: St. Martin's P, 1985. 325–32.

Baraka, Amiri. *Daggers and Javelins: Essays, 1974–1979*. New York: William Morrow, 1984.

————. *Home: Social Essays*. New York: Morrow, 1966.

Barrett, Edward, ed. *Text, ConText, and HyperText: Writing with and for the Computer*. Cambridge: MIT P, 1988.

Barthes, Roland. *The Pleasure of the Text*. New York: Noonday P, 1975.

Bartholomae, David, and Anthony Petrosky. *Facts, Artifacts, and Counterfacts: Theory and Method for a Reading and Writing Course*. Montclair: Boynton, 1986.

Bayliss, John F., ed. *Black Slave Narratives*. London: Collier Books, 1970.

Belenky, Mary Field, Blythe McVicker Clinchy, Nancy Rule Goldberger, and Jill Mattuck Tarule. *Women's Ways of Knowing: The Development of Self, Voice, and Mind*. New York: Basic Books, 1986.

Benamou, Michel, and Charles Caramello, eds. *Performance in Postmodern Culture*. U of Wisconsin-Milwaukee, Madison: Coda Press, 1977.

Benson, Stephen. *Blue Book*. Great Barrington, MA: The Figures; New York: Roof, 1988.

Benston, Kimberly W. "Amiri Baraka: An Interview." *boundary* 2 (Winter 1978): 303–16.

————. "Ellison, Baraka, and the Faces of Tradition." *boundary* 2 (Winter 1978): 333–54.

————. "I Yam What I Am: The Topos of Un(naming) in Afro-American Literature." Gates, *Black Literature* 151–72.

Bernal, Martin. *Black Athena: The Afroasiatic Roots of Classical Civilization. Vol. 1*. London: Free Association Books, 1987.

Bernstein, Charles, ed. "Comedy and the Poetics of Political Form." Bernstein, *The Politics of Poetic Form* 235–44.

————. *Content's Dream*. Los Angeles: Sun & Moon Press, 1986.

————. *The Politics of Poetic Form: Poetry and Public Policy*. New York: Roof Books, 1990.

Bey, Hakim. *Chaos: The Broadsheets of Ontological Anarchism*. Grim Reaper Books: Anti-copyright 1985.[1]

Bissett, Bill. *Beyond Even Faithful Legends*. Talonbooks, 1980.

Blitz, Michael, and C. Mark Hurlbert. "To: You, From: Michael Blitz and C. Mark Hurlbert, Re: Literacy Demands and Institutional Autobiography." *Works and Days: Essays in the Socio-historical Dimension of Literature and the Arts* 13 7.1 (1989): 7–33.

Bolter, Jay David. *Writing Space: The Computer, Hypertext, and the History of Writing*. Hillsdale: Lawrence Erlbaum Associates, 1991.

————. *Writing Space: The Computer, Hypertext, and the History of Writing*. Hypertext diskette. Jackson, MS: Riverrun, 1991.

Bramly, Serge. *Macumba: The Teachings of Maria-José, Mother of the Gods*. New York: St. Martin's P, 1977.

Britton, James. *Prospect and Retrospect: Selected Essays of James Britton*. Montclair: Boynton, 1982.

---

[1] One of the most glaring ironies of books claiming some radical perspective, whether written by feminists, Marxists, poststructuralists, or avant-garde poets, is that any radicalism they posit is severely undermined by their being published within a capitalist economy, adhering as they do to all copyright laws and regulations. The work of Hakim Bey is a refreshing exception, and as such perhaps the most (only?) genuinely radical work in this entire bibliography: on the last page of this particular edition one finds the message: "No copyright 1985. May be freely pirated and quoted—the author & publisher, however, would like to be informed at . . . ," etc.; then, at the bottom of the page: "Also, no ISBN number, no Library of Congress catalog number, no Imprimatur, no Nihil Obstat. Manufactured in Hyperborea."

Brossard, Nicole. "Poetic Politics." Bernstein, *The Politics of Poetic Form* 73–86.

Brummet, Barry. "Relativism and Rhetoric." *Rhetoric and Philosophy*. Ed. Richard A. Cherwitz. Hillsdale: Lawrence Erlbaum Associates, 1990. 79–103.

Brutus, Dennis. "English and the Dynamics of South African Creative Writing." Fiedler and Baker 1–14.

Burke, Carolyn. "Without Commas: Gertrude Stein and Mina Loy." *Poetics Journal* 4 (1984): 43–52.

Butturff, Douglas, and Edmund L. Epstein, eds. *Women's Language and Style*. Akron: L & S Books, Department of English, U of Akron, 1978.

Byrd, Don. "How Does One Articulate the Symbolic Content of Burning the Flag?" *Tyuonyi* 6/7 (1990): 33–4.

Cage, John. *A Year from Monday*. Middletown, CT: Wesleyan UP, 1969.

Calvino, Italo. "Prose and Anticombinatorics." Motte 143–52.

Capek, Milic. *The Philosophical Impact of Contemporary Physics*. Princeton: D. Van Nostrand, 1961.

Carlson, Patricia Ann. "Hypertext: A Way of Incorporating User Feedback into Online Documentation." Barrett 93–110.

Carson, Anne. *Eros the Bittersweet: An Essay*. Princeton: Princeton UP, 1986.

Catano, James. "Composition Theory and the Myth of the Self-Made Man: Authentic Voice and the Rhetoric of Masculinity." MLA Convention. Chicago, December 1990.

Chennault, Stephen D. "Black Dialect: A Culture Shock." *Minority Language and Literature: Retrospective and Perspective*. Ed. Dexter Fisher. New York: MLA, 1977. 71–79.

Chernoff, John Miller. *African Rhythm and African Sensibility: Aesthetics and Social Action in African Musical Idioms*. Chicago: U of Chicago P, 1979.

Cixous, Hélène. *Angst*. Trans. Jo Levy. New York: Riverrun P, 1985.

———. "The Laugh of the Medusa." Trans. Keith and Paula Cohen. Marks and de Courtivron 245–64.

———, and Catherine Clément. *The Newly Born Woman*. Trans. Betsy Wing. Minneapolis: U of Minnesota P, 1986.

Cliff, Michelle. "If I Could Write This in Fire, I Would Write This in Fire." Simonson and Walker 63–81.

————. "A Journey into Speech." Simonson and Walker 57–62.

Coles, Jr., William E. *The Plural I: The Teaching of Writing.* New York: Holt, Rinehart, and Winston, 1978.

Collier, James Lincoln. *The Making of Jazz: A Comprehensive History.* New York: Delta, 1978.

Connors, Robert J., Lisa S. Ede, and Andrea A. Lunsford, eds. *Essays on Classical Rhetoric and Modern Discourse.* Carbondale: Southern Illinois UP, 1984.

Corbett, Edward P. J. *Selected Essays of Edward P. J. Corbett.* Ed. Robert J. Connors. Dallas: Southern Methodist UP, 1989.

Cornell, Sarah. "Conversations." Sellers 141–54.

Cortés, Carlos E. "The Mass Media Curriculum on Race and Ethnicity: Implications for Higher Education." Paper presented at the American Association for Higher Education. Washington, DC, March 1991.

Dahlen, Beverly. *A Reading 1–7.* San Francisco: Momo's P, 1985.

————. From "The Tradition of Marginality." *Poetics Journal* 6 (1986): 72–73.

Daly, Mary, and Jane Caputi. *Webster's First New Intergalactic Wickedary of the English Language.* Boston: Beacon P, 1987.

Davidson, Michael. "Palimtexts: Postmodern Poetry and the Material Text." Perloff 75–95.

Davies, Alan. "*31* Assertions, Slowly." *L=A=N=G=U=A=G=E* 1.4 (August 1978): 3–4.

Delany, Paul, and George P. Landow, eds. *Hypermedia and Literary Studies.* Cambridge: MIT P, 1991.

Deleuze, Gilles, and Félix Guattari. *A Thousand Plateaus: Capitalism and Schizophrenia.* Minneapolis: U of Minnesota P, 1987.

Dewdney, Christopher. *Spring Trances in the Control Emerald Night & The Cenozoic Asylum.* Berkeley: The Figures, 1982.

Dillon, George L. *Constructing Texts: Elements of a Theory of Composition and Style.* Bloomington, IN: Indiana UP, 1981.

Divine Horsemen: The Living Gods of Haiti. Video. Dir. Maya Deren. Ed. Teiji and Cherel Ito. Mystic Fire Video, 60 min.

Dundes, Alan. *Mother Wit from the Laughing Barrel.* Englewood Cliffs: Prentice-Hall, 1973.

DuPlesis, Rachel Blau. "For the Etruscans." Showalter 271–91.

————. "Otherhow." *Sulfur* 14 (1985): 27–38.

————. *The Pink Guitar.* New York: Routledge, 1990.

————. *Tabula Rosa*. Elmwood, CT: Potes and Poets P, 1987.

Eagleton, Mary, ed. *Feminist Literary Theory: A Reader*. Oxford: Basil Blackwell, 1986.

Elbow, Peter. *Writing without Teachers*. New York: Oxford UP, 1973.

Emig, Janet. *The Web of Meaning: Essays on Writing, Teaching, Learning, and Thinking*. Upper Montclair: Boynton, 1983.

Federman, Raymond. "Federman: Voices within Voices." Benamou and Caramello 159–98.

Fiedler, Leslie A. "Literature as an Institution: The View from 1980." Fiedler and Baker 73–91.

————, and Houston A. Baker, Jr. *English Literature: Opening Up the Canon*. Baltimore: Johns Hopkins UP, 1981.

Fisher, Allen. "Postmodernism as Package." *Poetics Journal* 7 (1987): 100–05.

Fournel, Paul. "Computer and Writer: The Centre Pompidou Experiment." Motte 140–42.

Frank, Francine Wattman. "Women's Language in America: Myth and Reality." Butturff and Epstein 47–61.

Frey, Olivia. "Beyond Literary Darwinism: Women's Voices and Critical Discourse." *College English* 52 (September 1990): 507–26.

Frobenius, Leo. "Paideuma." Rothenberg and Rothenberg 36–40.

Gates, Jr., Henry Louis. *Black Literature and Literary Theory*. New York: Methuen, 1984.

————. *The Signifying Monkey: A Theory of Afro-American Literary Criticism*. New York: Oxford UP, 1988.

Gayle, Jr., Addison, ed. *The Black Aesthetic*. Garden City: Anchor Books, 1972.

Geertz, Clifford. "Blurred Genres: The Refiguration of Social Thought." Adams and Searle 514–23.

————. *The Interpretation of Cultures*. New York: Basic Books, 1973.

Giddings, Paula. *When and Where I Enter: The Impact of Black Women on Race and Sex in America*. New York: Bantam, 1984.

Gins, Madeline. *What the President Will Say and Do!!* Barrytown: Station Hill P, 1984.

Gould, Karen. *Writing in the Feminine: Feminism and Experimental Writing in Quebec*. Carbondale: Southern Illinois UP, 1990.

Graves, Donald H. *Writing: Teachers and Children at Work*. Portsmouth, NH: Heinemann Educational Books, 1983.

H. D. *Notes on Thought and Vision & The Wise Sappho*. San Francisco: City Lights Books, 1982.

Hall, Donald. *The Contemporary Essay*. 2nd ed. New York: St. Martin's P, 1989.

Hartman, Geoffrey H. "Understanding Criticism." Atkins and Johnson 149–68.

Hassan, Ihab. *Paracriticisms: Seven Speculations of the Times*. Chicago: U of Illinois P, 1975.

Hazlitt, William. *Selected Writings of William Hazlitt*. Ed. Christopher Salvesen. New York: Signet, 1972.

Hejinian, Lyn. *My Life*. Los Angeles: Sun & Moon Press, 1987.

———. "The Rejection of Closure." Perelman, *Writing/Talks* 270–91.

Henderson, Linda Dalrymple. *The Fourth Dimension and Non-Euclidean Geometry in Modern Art*. Princeton: Princeton UP, 1983.

Hewett, Gregory. "A Rhetoric of Androgyny: The Composition, Teaching, and Ethics of Gender." Diss. State U of New York at Albany, 1989.

Hicks, D. Emily. "Deterritorialization and Border Writing." *Ethics/Aesthetics: Post-Modern Positions*. Ed. Robert Merrill. Washington, DC: Maisonneuve Press, 1988. 47–58.

Hinds, John. "Contrastive Rhetoric: Japanese and English." *Text* 3 (1983): 183–95.

Hirsch, E. D. *The Philosophy of Composition*. Chicago: U of Chicago P, 1977.

Hogan, Patrick Colm. *The Politics of Interpretation: Ideology, Professionalism, and the Study of Literature*. New York: Oxford UP, 1990.

Hogue, W. Lawrence. *Discourse and the Other: The Production of the Afro-American Text*. Durham: Duke UP, 1986.

———. "Literary Production: A Silence in Afro-American Critical Practice." *Belief vs. Theory in Black American Literary Criticism*. Ed. Joe Weixlmann and Chester J. Fontenot. Greenwood: Penkevill, 1986. 31–45.

Howard, Richard. "A Note on the Text." Barthes vii.

Howe, Susan. "Encloser." Bernstein, *The Politics of Poetic Form* 175–96.

———. My *Emily Dickinson*. Berkeley: North Atlantic Books, 1985.

Hutcheon, Linda. " 'The Pastime of Past Time': Fiction, History, Historiographic Metafiction." Perloff 54–74.

Inman, P. *Ocker*. Berkeley: Tuumba, 1982.

———. "One to One." Bernstein, *The Politics of Poetic Form* 221–25.

———. *Red Shift*. New York: Roof, 1988.

Irigaray, Luce. "This Sex Which Is Not One." Trans. Claudia Reeder. Marks and de Courtivron 99–106.

Jaffer, Frances. Quoted in DuPlessis, "For the Etruscans" 278.

Jahn, Janheinz. *Neo-African Literature: A History of Black Writing*. Trans. Oliver Coburn and Ursula Lehrburger. New York: Grove P, 1968.

James, William. *Essays in Radical Empiricism and A Pluralistic Universe*. Ed. Ralph Barton Perry. New York: Dutton, 1971.

Janecek, Gerald. *The Look of Russian Literature: Avant-Garde Visual Experiments, 1900–1930*. Princeton: Princeton UP, 1984.

Jaynes, Joseph T. "Limited Freedom: Linear Reflections on Non-linear Texts." *The Society of Text: Hypertext, Hypermedia, and the Social Construction of Information*. Ed. Edward Barrett. Cambridge: MIT P, 1989, 148–61.

Johnson, Charles. *Being & Race: Black Writing Since 1970*. Bloomington: Indiana UP, 1988.

Johnstone Koch, Barbara. "Presentation as Proof: The Language of Arabic Rhetoric." *Anthropological Linguistics* 25 (1983): 47–60.

Jones, Ann Rosalind. "Writing the Body: Toward an Understanding of l'Écriture féminine." Showalter 361–77.

Jones, LeRoi (Amiri Baraka). *Blues People*. New York: William Morrow, 1963.

Jordan, June. *On Call: Political Essays*. Boston: South End P, 1985.

Joyce, Michael. Quoted from a message sent via electronic mail to readers of the "Megabyte University (Computers & Writing)" BITNET discussion list, May 10, 1991.

Knoblauch, C. H., and Lil Brannon. *Rhetorical Traditions and the Teaching of Writing*. Upper Montclair: Boynton, 1984.

Kofsky, Frank. "Revolution, Coltrane, and the Avant-garde." *The Black Giants*. Ed. Pauline Rivelli and Robert Levin. New York: World Publishing, 1970.

Kolenda, Konstantin. *Rorty's Humanistic Pragmatism: Philosophy Democratized*. Tampa: U of South Florida P, 1990.

Kristeva, Julia. "Women's Time." Adams and Searle 471–84.

Lakoff, Robin Tolmach. "Women's Language." Butturff and Epstein 139–58.

Landek, Beatrice. *Learn to Read/Read to Learn: Poetry and Prose from Afro-Rooted Sources*. New York: David McKay, 1975.

Le Lionnais, François. "Lipo: First Manifesto." Motte 26–28.

———. "Second Manifesto." Motte 29–31.

Lescure, Jean. "Brief History of the Oulipo." Motte 32–39.

Levi Straus, David. *ACTS* 7 (1987): frontispiece.

Lorca, Federico Garcia. *Deep Song and Other Prose*. Ed. and trans. Christopher Maurer. New York: New Directions, 1975.

Loy, Mina. *The Last Lunar Baedeker*. Ed. Roger L. Conover. The Jargon Society, 1982.

Mackey, Nathaniel. "Sound and Sentiment, Sound and Symbol." Bernstein, *The Politics of Poetic Form* 87–118.

Madhubuti, Haki R. *From Plan to Planet: Life-Studies: The Need for Afrikan Minds and Institutions*. Chicago: Third World Press, 1987.

Mahala, Daniel. "Writing Utopias: Writing across the Curriculum and the Promise of Reform." *College English* 53.7 (November 1991): 773–89.

Major, Clarence, ed. *The New Black Poetry*. New York: International Publishers, 1969.

Malotki, Ekkehart. *Hopi Time: A Linguistic Analysis of the Temporal Concepts in the Hopi Language*. New York: Mouton Publishers, 1983.

Marius, Richard. "On Academic Discourse." *Profession 90*. New York: MLA, 1990. 28–31.

Marks, Elaine, and Isabelle de Courtivron, eds. *New French Feminisms*. New York: Schocken Books, 1981.

Martin, Stephen-Paul. *Open Form and the Feminine Imagination (The Politics of Reading in Twentieth-Century Innovative Writing)*. Washington, DC: Maisonneuve Press, 1988.

Mayer, Bernadette. *Memory*. Berkeley: North Atlantic Books, 1975.

————. *Studying Hunger*. Berkeley: Big Sky, 1975.

McClure, Michael. "Phi Upsilon Kappa." Allen and Tallman 416–29.

Melnick, David. *Men in Aida: Book One*. Berkeley: Tuumba, 1983.

Mitchell-Kernan, Claudia. "Signifying." Dundes 310–28.

Moffett, James. *Teaching the Universe of Discourse*. Boston: Houghton Mifflin, 1968.

Moi, Toril. *Sexual/Textual Politics: Feminist Literary Theory*. New York: Methuen, 1985.

Morris, Adalaide. Quoted in *HOW(ever)* 4 (1987): 16.

Motte, Jr., Warren F., ed. *Oulipo: A Primer of Potential Literature*. Lincoln: U of Nebraska P, 1986.

Moulthrop, Stuart. "Reading from the Map: Metonymy and Metaphor in the Fiction of Forking Paths." Delany and Landow 119–32.

Mura, David. "Strangers in the Village." Simonson and Walker 135–53.

Murray, Donald. *Learning by Teaching: Selected Articles on Writing and Teaching*. Montclair: Boynton, 1982.

Nobles, Wade W. *African Psychology: Toward Its Reclamation, Reascension, & Revitalization*. Oakland: A Black Family Institute Publication, 1986.

North, Stephen M. *The Making of Knowledge in Composition: Portrait of an Emerging Field*. Upper Montclair: Boynton, 1987.

O'brien, John. *Interviews with Black Writers*. New York: Liveright, 1973.

Olsen, Tillie. *Silences*. New York: Laurel/Seymour Lawrence, 1978.

Olson, Charles. *Call Me Ishmael*. San Francisco: City Lights Books, 1947.

————. *Selected Writings of Charles Olson*. Ed. Robert Creely. New York: New Directions, 1966.

Olson, Gary A., and Irene Gale, eds. *(Inter)views: Cross-Disciplinary Perpsectives on Rhetoric and Literacy*. Carbondale & Edwardsville: Southern Illinois UP, 1991.

Palmer, Michael. *Code of Signals*. Berkeley: North Atlantic, 1983.

Palmer, Richard. "Toward a Postmodern Hermeneutics of Performance." Benamou and Caramello 19–32.

Perelman, Bob. "Plotless Prose." *Poetics Journal* 1 (1982): 25–34.

———, ed. *Writing/Talks*. Carbondale, IL: Southern Illinois UP, 1985.

Perloff, Marjorie, ed. *Postmodern Genres*. Oklahoma: U of Oklahoma P, 1989.

Pound, Ezra. *Guide to Kulchur*. New York: New Directions, 1970.

Purves, Alan C., ed. *Writing across Languages and Cultures: Issues in Contrastive Rhetoric*. New York: SAGE Publications, 1988.

Queneau, Raymond. *Exercises in Style*. Trans. Barbara Wright. London: Gaberbacchus Press Ltd., 1958.

———. "A Story As You Like It." Motte 156–58.

Rasula, Jed. "Notes on Genre." Andrews and Bernstein 102–03.

———. "What Does This Do with You Reading?" *Poetics Journal* 1 (1982): 66–67.

Reed, Ishmael. *Mumbo-Jumbo*. New York: Bantam, 1972.

———. "Neo-HooDoo Manifesto/The Neo-HooDoo Aesthetic." Rothenberg and Rothenberg 417–21.

Rich, Adrienne. "Toward a Woman-Centered University." *On Lies, Secrets, and Silence: Selected Prose 1966–1978*. New York: Norton, 1979.

Rico, Gabrielle Lusser. *Writing the Natural Way: Using Right-Brain Techniques to Release Your Expressive Power*. Los Angeles: J. P. Tarcher, 1983.

Riddell, John. *Criss-Cross: A Text Book of Modern Composition*. Toronto: Coach House Press, 1977.

Rosenblatt, Louise M. *The Reader The Text The Poem: The Transactional Theory of the Literary Work*. Carbondale: Southern Illinois UP, 1978.

Rothenberg, Jerome. "New Models, New Visions: Some Notes Toward a Poetics of Performance." Benamou and Caramello 11–17.

Rothenberg, Jerome, and Diane Rothenberg. *Symposium of the Whole: A Range of Discourse Toward an Ethnopoetics*. Berkeley: U of California P, 1983.

Roubaud, Jacques. "Mathematics in the Method of Raymond Queneau." Motte 79–96.

Sackheim, Eric, ed. *The Blues Line: A Collection of Blues Lyrics*. New York: Schirmer Books, 1969.

Sanders, Ed. *Thirsting for Peace in a Raging Century: Selected Poems 1961–1985*. Minneapolis: Coffee House P, 1987.

Scalapino, Leslie, ed. *O ONE/An Anthology*. Oakland: O Books, 1988.

Scholes, Robert. *Textual Power*. New Haven: Yale UP, 1985.

Schwerner, Armand. *sounds of the river Naranjana & The Tablets I–XXIV*. Barrytown: Station Hill, 1983.

Scollon, Ron, and Suzanne B. K. Scollon. *Narrative, Literacy and Face in Interethnic Communication*. Norwood: ABLEX Publishing Corp, 1981.

Scott, Kesho, Cherry Muhanji, and Egyirba High. *Tight Spaces*. San Francisco: Spinsters/Aunt Lute, 1987.

Seitz, James. "Roland Barthes, Reading, and Roleplay: Composition's Misguided Rejection of Fragmentary Texts." *College English* 53.7 (1991): 815–25.

Sellers, Susan, ed. *Writing Differences: Readings from the Seminar of Hélène Cixous*. Milton Keynes: Open UP, 1988.

Senghor, Léopold Sédar. *Prose and Poetry*. London: Heinemann, 1976.

Shaughnessy, Mina P. *Errors and Expectations: A Guide for the Teacher of Basic Writing*. New York: Oxford UP, 1977.

Showalter, Elaine, ed. *The New Feminist Criticism: Essays on Women, Literature and Theory*. New York: Pantheon, 1985.

Silko, Leslie Marmon. "Language and Literature from a Pueblo Indian Perspective." Fiedler and Baker 54–72.

Silliman, Ron. "Canons and Institutions: New Hope for the Disappeared." Bernstein, *The Politics of Poetic Form* 149–74.

———, ed. *In the American Tree*. U of Maine at Orono: National Poetry Foundation, 1986.

———. *Ketjak*. San Francisco: This, 1978.

———. *The New Sentence*. New York: Roof, 1987.

———. *Tjanting*. Berkeley: The Figures, 1981.

Simonson, Rick, and Scott Walker. *Multicultural Literacy: Opening the American Mind*. St. Paul: Graywolf Press, 1988.

Slatin, John M. "Hypertext and the Teaching of Writing." Barrett 111–29.

Sledd, James. "In Defense of the *Students' Right*." *College English* 45 (November 1983): 667–75.

Smart-Grosvenor, Verta Mae. "The Kitchen Crisis." *The Black Woman: An Anthology*. Ed. Toni Cade [Bambara]. Chicago: Signet, 1970, 119–23.

Smith, Page. *Killing the Spirit: Higher Education in America*. New York: Viking, 1990.

Smitherman, Geneva. *Talkin and Testifyin: The Language of Black America*. Boston: Houghton Mifflin, 1977.

Spellmeyer, Kurt. "A Common Ground: The Essay in the Academy." *College English* 51 (March 1989): 262–76.

Stein, Charles, ed. *Being = Space x Action: Searches for Freedom of Mind through Mathematics, Art, and Mysticism*. Berkeley: North Atlantic Books, 1988. 8–21.

Stein, Gertrude. "Composition as Explanation." *Selected Writings of Gertrude Stein*. Ed. Carl Van Vechten. New York: Modern Library, 1962.

Summerfield, Judith, and Geoffrey Summerfield. *Texts and Contexts: A Contribution to the Theory and Practice of Teaching Composition*. New York: Random House, 1986.

Tafolla, Carmen. "Chicano Literature: Beyond Beginings." *A Gift of Tongues: Critical Challenges in Contemporary American Poetry*. Ed. Marie Harris and Kathleen Aguero. Athens: U of Georgia P, 1987. 206–25.

Tatham, Campbell. "Mythotherapy and Postmodern Fictions: Magic Is Afoot." Benamou and Caramello 137–57.

Tedlock, Dennis, trans. *Finding the Center: Narrative Poetry of the Zuni Indians*. New York: Dial Press, 1972.

———. "Tell It Like It's Right in Front of You." Rothenberg and Rothenberg 375–76.

Tembo, Mwizenge S. "The Concept of African Personality: Sociological Implications." *African Culture: The Rhythms of Unity*. Ed. Molefi Kete Asante and Kariamu Welsh Asante. Westport, CT: Greenwood P, 1985.

Ulmer, Gregory L. "Textshop for Post(e)pedagogy." Atkins and Johnson 38–64.

wa Thiong'o, Ngugi. *Decolonising the Mind: The Politics of Language in African Literature*. Portsmouth, NH: Heinemann, 1986.

Wagner, Roy. *Symbols That Stand for Themselves*. Chicago: U of Chicago P, 1986.

Waldrop, Rosmarie. "Alarms & Excursions." Bernstein, *The Politics of Poetic Form* 45–72.

Weathers, Winston. *An Alternate Style: Options in Composition.* Rochelle Park, NJ: Hayden Book Co., 1980.

Weiner, Hannah. *The Clairvoyant Journal.* New York: Angel Hair, 1978.

———. *Spoke.* Washington, DC: Sun & Moon Press, 1984.

Werner, Craig. "New Democratic Vistas: Toward a Pluralistic Genealogy." *Studies in Black American Literature Vol. II: Belief vs. Theory in Black American Literary Criticism.* Ed. Joe Weixlmann and Chester J. Fontenot. Greenwood, FL: The Penkevill Publishing Co., 1986. 47–83.

Whorf, Benjamin Lee. "An American Indian Model of the Universe." *Language, Thought, and Reality: Selected Writings of Benjamin Lee Whorf.* Ed. John B. Carroll. Cambridge: MIT P, 1964.

Williams, Martin. Liner notes. Ornette Coleman. *Free Jazz: A Collective Improvisation by the Ornette Coleman Double Quartet.* Rec. 21 December 1960. Atlantic, 1364–2, 1961.

Williams, William Carlos. *In the American Grain.* New York: New Directions, 1956.

Wolff, Janet. *Feminine Sentences: Essays on Women and Culture.* Berkeley: U of California P, 1990.

Zimmerman, Muriel. "Are Writers Obsolete in the Computer Industry?" Barrett 279–88.

Index

Teresa Hewitt

About the Author

Derek Owens teaches expository writing
at Harvard University. He lives in
Medford, Massachusetts, with his wife,
Teresa, and their newly born son, Ryan.